BEST MUSIC WRITING
2011

PREVIOUS EDITIONS OF *BEST MUSIC WRITING*:

BEST MUSIC WRITING 2010
ANN POWERS, GUEST EDITOR
DAPHNE CARR, SERIES EDITOR

BEST MUSIC WRITING 2009
GREIL MARCUS, GUEST EDITOR
DAPHNE CARR, SERIES EDITOR

BEST MUSIC WRITING 2008
NELSON GEORGE, GUEST EDITOR
DAPHNE CARR, SERIES EDITOR

BEST MUSIC WRITING 2007
ROBERT CHRISTGAU, GUEST EDITOR
DAPHNE CARR, SERIES EDITOR

DA CAPO BEST MUSIC WRITING 2006
MARY GAITSKILL, GUEST EDITOR
DAPHNE CARR, SERIES EDITOR

DA CAPO BEST MUSIC WRITING 2005
JT LEROY, GUEST EDITOR
PAUL BRESNICK, SERIES EDITOR

DA CAPO BEST MUSIC WRITING 2004
MICKEY HART, GUEST EDITOR
PAUL BRESNICK, SERIES EDITOR

DA CAPO BEST MUSIC WRITING 2003
MATT GROENING, GUEST EDITOR
PAUL BRESNICK, SERIES EDITOR

DA CAPO BEST MUSIC WRITING 2002
JONATHAN LETHEM, GUEST EDITOR
PAUL BRESNICK, SERIES EDITOR

DA CAPO BEST MUSIC WRITING 2001
NICK HORNBY, GUEST EDITOR
BEN SCHAFER, SERIES EDITOR

DA CAPO BEST MUSIC WRITING 2000
PETER GURALNICK, GUEST EDITOR
DOUGLAS WOLK, SERIES EDITOR

BEST MUSIC WRITING

2011

Alex Ross, *Guest Editor*

Daphne Carr, *Series Editor*

DA CAPO PRESS

A MEMBER OF THE PERSEUS BOOKS GROUP

Set in 10 point Warnock Pro by The Perseus Books Group

Library of Congress Cataloging-in-Publication Data
  Best music writing 2011 / Alex Ross, guest editor ; Daphne Carr, series
editor.—1st Da Capo Press ed.
    p. cm.
  ISBN 978-0-306-81963-6 (paperback : alk. paper)—ISBN 978-0-306-
82057-1 (e-book) 1. Musical criticism—United States. I. Ross, Alex,
1968– II. Carr, Daphne. III. Title.
  ML3785.B47 2011
  780.9—dc23

                                        2011032064

First Da Capo Press edition 2011
Published by Da Capo Press
A Member of the Perseus Books Group
www.dacapopress.com

Da Capo Press books are available at special discounts for bulk
purchases in the U.S. by corporations, institutions, and other
organizations. For more information, please contact the Special
Markets Department at the Perseus Books Group, 2300 Chestnut
Street, Suite 200, Philadelphia, PA 19103, or call (800) 810-4145, ext.
5000, or e-mail special.markets@perseusbooks.com.

10 9 8 7 6 5 4 3 2

CONTENTS

INTRODUCTION

Alex Ross

On February 13, 2011, the jazz bassist, singer, and composer Esperanza Spalding received a Grammy for Best New Artist, besting the teenaged pop sensation Justin Bieber. Seconds after the award was announced, a lively discussion broke out on Twitter. Here are some selections from the first few hours of commentary, with the inevitable racial slurs omitted:

> WTF!! Who the hell is Esperanza Spalding??!!? She did NOT deserve new artist of the year!! This is gaayy!

> "Knock knock." "Who's there?" "Esperanza Spalding." "Esperanza Spalding who?" "EXACTLY."

> okay seriously esperanza spaulding isnt even verified on twitter as a real celeb @justinbieber i love you your always the best in my mind :)

> Gonna have to go home and download some songs by Esperanza Spalding . . . really feeling her music.

> I've never heard of Esperanza Fever.

Congrats to Esperanza Spalding. Apparently jazz music is more relevant than billboard chart toppers like *@justin-bieber* and *@drakkarnoir*.

While I had no clue who Esperanza Spalding was before today (I thought she invented the basketball), anyone who pisses off Bieber fans WINS.

#justin bIeber was ROBBED! Who is esperanza? What impact has she had on pop music or culture? Bieber is truly talented. [Bonnie Fuller, editor]

i dread nothing more when the bland non taste of mainstream america's radar discovers my secret. ESPERANZA SPALDING is too smart for ya. [Questlove, drummer and DJ]

As for the awards . . . of course I wanted to win. Its been & still is a dream to win a grammy. Was I upset . . . yes. But I was happy for her also [Bieber himself]

Like most folks on Twitter that night, I thought of Arthur Schopenhauer. The sage of Frankfurt had many good points to make about the blind striving of the will and the joy of self-obliteration, but he missed the mark when he stated that music is "in the highest degree a universal language." On certain sunny days, music does make the people come together, but nearly as often it seems to tear them apart. The most popular artists can also be the most lustily hated. In some ways, this is as it should be. Just as we would not want to live in a world that adhered to one language, one political system, or one mode of religious belief, we would not want to live in a world that imposed a single musical taste. Totalitarian regimes have in common an urge to foist such concepts on the population.

Almost twenty years ago, the ethnomusicologist Mark Slobin published a brilliant short book titled *Subcultural Sounds: Micromusics of the West.* In it, he proposed the existence of a "superculture"—a ubiquitous but nebulous zone that he associated with "the usual, the accepted, the statistically lopsided, the commercially successful, the statutory, the regulated, the most visible." He then set about studying how myriad subcultures jockey for position, rise to popularity, define themselves in opposition, or fuse with other forms. Slobin's analysis is even more pertinent in the fractured, late-digital age than it was in the early nineties, which now look vaguely Amish in retrospect. With the rise of the Internet and the decline of the record business, the superculture has lost some of its mojo. In the summer of 2010, the blogger Proper Discord noticed that the top-selling album in America that week—Katy Perry's *Teenage Dream*—had been purchased by only one in sixteen hundred U.S. consumers. A certain number of miscreants may have obtained the music by other means, but the aggregate of listeners fell far short of a majority. All music is subcultural; no music is everywhere beloved.

The withering of the mainstream seems a recent development, something that's come to pass since the Internet arrived. For the writer Nancy Griffin, whose haunting portrait of Michael Jackson appears in this collection, the release of the "Thriller" video, in December 1983, feels like "the last time that everyone on the planet got excited at the same time by the same thing." Well, almost everyone—I was ignoring pop, and getting excited about the prospect of seeing Leonard Bernstein conduct Mahler's "Resurrection" Symphony. Admittedly, I was a peculiar case, but the superculture has never enjoyed total domination, and it has existed only as long as electronic media have enabled a mass public for music to exist. It began, effectively, when Caruso sold a million copies of "*Una furtiva lagrima*" in the first years of the twentieth century. Before then, it was physically impossible for everyone on the planet to get excited about the same thing. Now, digital culture is atomizing the market once again.

So how do you map a micromusical landscape? Is there a universal language of criticism that can be spoken across the borders of genre? Those questions kept coming up as I worked with Daphne Carr to assemble the articles in this book. We hoped to bring in as many different worlds as possible—more than we were finally able to accommodate. Yet we wished to avoid producing a Tower-of-Babel experience in which stalwarts in various fields shouted trivia at each other without engaging the casual listener. What excited us were pieces that led the reader into an unfamiliar realm or marked new paths on well-trod ground—pieces that assumed no prior knowledge, only a spark of curiosity. Obviously, much excellent music writing fails to fit that description: reviews written for fellow fans, analyses composed for fellow experts, all-out blog wars deploying armies of straw men. But, for the most part, such work doesn't appear here. You'll have to go elsewhere for your Vampire Weekend smackdowns or your pro- and anti-Marsalis screeds. We didn't look for articles by and for insiders; we wanted writerly seductions.

As one who dwells in the classical shadowlands, I face the challenge of hooking the distracted reader every time I unsleep my computer, and, needless to say, I fail more often than I succeed. From time to time, I find myself sitting on the subway next to a commuter who's flipping through *The New Yorker*, seeking something to occupy his attention between Columbus Circle and Penn Station. He happens upon one of my articles and looks at the headline. "Oh jeez, not a piece about *classical music*," I hear him thinking. He flips ahead to Anthony Lane, who promptly works his charms. But every once in a long while I succeed in grabbing an innocent bystander's attention. True, I've never seen it happen right in front of me on the 1 train, but instances have been reported, and nothing makes me happier. Before I was a critic, I was an enthusiast, foisting my Alban Berg records on college roommates and anxiously scanning their faces for flickers of interest. When a connection is made, it can feel momentous, especially when you have managed to break through a resistance born of stereotypes and received ideas. A subculture is escaping from its ghetto and finding new life through unexpected affinities. Slobin, back in the early nineties, sensed the growing buzz of such one-on-one transmissions, and the Internet now allows them to happen on a global scale, with no need to trap a friend in front of the record-player. The micro can go macro in a viral instant.

Music is not now and never has been a universal language, but it can reach across the human universe with astonishing ease, whether it's a mass of Philippino prisoners mastering the steps of "Thriller" or thousands of Japanese amateur choristers singing along to Beethoven's Ninth. (In a typical micro/macro paradox, classical music appears to be more marginal than ever, yet its global audience is exponentially larger than it was a hundred years ago.) Despite the disputes that flare up endlessly across the fences of taste, music always seems to remember back to a lost bond of common feeling. Long-form articles are crucial because they permit that longing to speak. They go far beyond the bland announcement of like or dislike—all the entrenched sniping that filled Twitter on the night Esperanza Spalding won Best New Artist. The long read remains, in my experience, the most potent means of musical persuasion.

The book begins, naturally, with Beethoven. Justin Davidson revisits the premiere of the "Eroica" Symphony, a work that marked the onset of what might be called Beethoven's supercultural phase. It's the first great rebel yell in musical history, the birth of the individualist artist hero. Yet it also heralds the glorification of the Great Classical Composer, which, by the end of the nineteenth century, had begun to overshadow living artists and inhibit the expressive freedom of performers. Every genre since has felt that uneasy slippage from the revolutionary moment to the cult of the past.

Several more classical items follow, but none is the work of a full-time classical critic. With apologies to Anthony Tommasini, Anne Midgette, Steve Smith, and many other esteemed colleagues, I was eager to bring in some alternative voices—articulate insiders, sympathetic outsiders. The masterly pianist Jeremy Denk, proprietor of the blog Think Denk, gets fed up with smugly tedious program notes. Ann Powers, a dominant force in pop criticism, reveals her love of

Wagner and studies the Los Angeles Opera production of the *Ring* through a pop-culture lens. The critic, novelist, and editor Wendy Lesser ventures into a very dark corner of the contemporary European avant-garde. And the exuberant winners of Marcia Adair's Twitter #operaplot competition summarize maximally convoluted librettos in minimum space.

Jazz, too, has made the unnerving journey from superculture to subculture, from center to apparent margin. Geoffrey O'Brien, in this collection, gives a photographically evocative picture of Duke Ellington, who spelled out more powerfully than any early jazz figure the high aspirations of African-American culture, even as he maintained a careful distance from highbrow jargon. No contemporary jazz musician, not even Wynton Marsalis, cuts such a profile today. Yet jazz fans, like their classical counterparts, perhaps dwell too much on what is putatively lost when their heroes no longer get the cover of *Time*. The likes of Jason Moran, Esperanza Spalding, Ethan Iverson, and Fred Hersch—the last portrayed here by David Hajdu— demonstrate how modern jazz is free to be "genre-blind," in Hajdu's phrase, open to every imaginable current sound.

Country music is a commercial titan, not least because its audience is still willing to pay for music up front. The veteran journalist Chet Flippo, who writes a column for the Country Music Television website, pointedly asks whether that corporate clout—now fully ratified by *American Idol*—has hollowed out the "heart and soul" of the music. He probably speaks for critics in many other genres when he writes: "Country music is a wildly erratic radar screen these days. Random, unexpected blips are popping up all over the place and with no consistent patterns. May as well study tornado paths." By contrast, Franklin Bruno's mini-biography of the country songwriting team of Felice and Boudleaux Bryant takes us back to the musical equivalent of the old Hollywood studio system, when tight commercial control didn't prohibit the exercise of meticulous craft.

Metal—heavy, black, death, or otherwise—has also strengthened its grip on the marketplace, but its doomy soul seems intact: the scene is friendlier to antisocial eruptions of dissonance and noise than almost any musical sphere outside the state-funded European new-music circuit. (The first black-metal band to master fully the methods of spectralism may cause unprecedented mayhem.) The blogger Mike Turbé, as Atanamar Sunyata, makes his way to a cozy little club called The Acheron, in Brooklyn, and gives us an earful of Wormrot, Defeatist, Mutant Supremacy, Psychic Limb, and Curandera. The outer edges of the DJ scene are also hospitable to suspect harmonies. Philip Sherburne, in his piece on Pantha du Prince, relates him both to the experimental tradition and to the older yearnings of the German Romantics.

As for the pop mainstream, however you might define it, it's captured here from a few widely spaced vantage points. Jonathan Bogart, in a gleefully exhaustive five-thousand-word blog essay, goes all-out formalist on Ke$ha's *Animal* EP, microscopically inspecting details that only a few pedants in the studio could have been aware of. Vanessa Grigoriadis takes a panoramic shot of Lady Gaga, emphasizing the old-school bohemian philosophy that informs an amazing pop-culture artifice. Chris Norris, in a clear-eyed, not always merciful profile of Will.i.am, diagrams an interchange of music and commerce so effortless that after a while you can't tell them apart.

The self-affirmations of American pop have a very different resonance in places where youth populations are yearning for freedom, or, even worse, have had their freedom rescinded. Nothing in this collection is quite as charged as Morad Mansouri's piece on the underground music scene in Tehran: there, up-to-date hip-hop beats and ancient Persian texts are being mashed together in a way that seems considerably more pointed than what you hear on the average public-radio world-music hour. You get the sense that if the gates were lifted Iran might produce a counterpart to M.I.A., whose combustible brand of anti-imperialist pop drew a heavy backlash this past year. Jessica Hopper, in the *Chicago Reader*, has a cannily even-handed take on the mercurial agitator.

I've always admired the fearlessness with which pop critics address prickly issues of politics, class, race, and sexuality. (We classical critics are always too ready to flee into the art-for-art's-sake refuge.)

Nitsuh Abebe sorts through his conflicted feelings about racial signals in the music of CocoRosie. Amy Klein, speaking from the point of view of a working female musician, lets us know how she felt when, flipping through an issue of *Rolling Stone*, she saw only four women who were fully clothed. Caryn Ganz, writing for *OUT* magazine, probes the touchy topic of sexuality in hip-hop, eliciting playful and elusive answers from Nicki Minaj. Drew Daniel, of Matmos and Johns Hopkins University, recounts a gay listener's complicated relationship with Morrissey, talking about how The Smiths provided a soundtrack to coming out (some editorial identification here) and how their music has more recently spoken to him with unexpected rawness.

Three stories in the collection—all of them, coincidentally, published by the *Washington Post*—show how music is woven into the fabric of cities and neighborhoods. Lauren Wilcox Puchowski follows a wedding singer named Kenney Holmes, who argues for his profession in the face of couples who want to play songs off their iPods. Jason Cherkis hangs out with Ian Nagoski, a fanatical Baltimore record collector who, while working at the True Vine store, came into possession of 78-RPM records by the Greek singer Marika Papagika and almost single-handedly spearheaded a revival of interest in her. And, in a piece that quickly became legendary among pop scribes, Chris Richards goes in search of the Mothership, the spectacular Parliament-Funkadelic stage prop, which was last seen in a junkyard behind a gas station in Prince George's County, Maryland.

Perhaps the trickiest kind of music writing, and potentially the most exhilarating, is the kind that threads multiple genres together. Jace Clayton looks into slowed-down music—screw, witch house, drag, and so on—and draws links between hip-hop, synth pop, the noise scene, and classical experimentalism. Dave Tompkins, in an excerpt from his staggering Vocoder history *How to Wreck a Nice Beach*, traces geneaologies from Afrika Bambaataa back to wartime army projects and stalwarts of the postwar avant-garde. There are yet more surprising connections to be made: Kelefa Sanneh compares Jay-Z's lyrics with those of Stephen Sondheim; Nate Chinen ponders what it means that Neil Young and Miles Davis shared a bill in 1970; and James Wood finds uncharted common ground between the aesthetic realms of Glenn Gould and Keith Moon. It always makes me happy when a writer drops in a reference that opens up a larger perspective, as when Sasha Frere-Jones, listening soulfully to Sade, calls her "an ambient version of country music."

Grouped toward the end of the book are several pieces that bring us intimately close to a particular artist, often baring the scars of celebrity in the process. Sasha's appreciation of Sade is one of these; Griffin's memoir of Michael Jackson at the zenith of his "Thriller" fame is another. Evelyn McDonnell writes a heartbreaking profile of Sandy West, the drummer for the Runaways, whose voyage into substance-abuse hell did not end in a Hollywood-ready scene of redemption. And Joe Hagan, in a harrowing portrait of Nina Simone, transcribes diary entries that we feel we shouldn't be reading but that we can't forget when we return to the music.

Having begun with a Germanic titan, this edition of *Best Music Writing* gives the last word to a contemporary Austrian, Georg Friedrich Haas, who inhabits a subcultural space and makes it seem infinite. Haas's Third String Quartet is played in total darkness. Wendy Lesser describes what it is like to hear music with one sense deprived. She concludes that it makes you listen as never before, as if your life depends on it. That kind of listening is what we all strive for.

Beethoven's Kapow

Justin Davidson

If I could crash any cultural event in history, it would be the night in April 1805 when a short man with a Kirk Douglas chin and a wrestler's build stomped onto the stage of the Theater an der Wien in Vienna. Ludwig van Beethoven, 34 years old and already well along the way to deafness, swiveled to face a group of tense musicians and whipped them into playing a pair of fist-on-the-table E-flat major chords (*blam! . . . blam!*), followed by a quietly rocking cello melody. If I listen hard enough, I can almost transport myself into that stuffy, stuccoed room. I inhale the smells of damp wool and kerosene and feel the first, transformative shock of Beethoven's Third Symphony, the "Eroica," as it exploded into the world.

Before it was a work of genius, the "Eroica" was a provocation, and I sometimes wonder how I would have reacted if I had been in the crowd on that night in 1805. I might have concurred with the critic who felt "crushed by a mass of unconnected and overloaded ideas and continuing tumult by all the instruments." The performance probably flirted with chaos. Beethoven himself conducted, and he was a volatile man who could barely hear. The band of musicians had never grappled with a score so mountainous and rugged, and the audience hadn't either. Someone yelled, "I'll give another kreutzer if the thing will only stop!" It's easy to dismiss that wag as a philistine, but the first performance, unlike most of the thousands upon thousands that followed, didn't take admiration for granted.

This week, Lincoln Center hosts the conductor Iván Fischer leading two ensembles—one period, the other modern—in a comparative festival of Beethoven's symphonies. The Orchestra of the Age of Enlightenment plays the "Eroica," plus Symphonies Nos. 1, 2, 5, and 8, just as they purportedly sounded 200 years ago. The Budapest Festival Orchestra performs the remaining symphonies in their plusher, louder, and more modern incarnation. The difference between those styles is usually framed as a distinction between music's authentic past and its dynamic present, between scholarship and technology, the latest framing of a 40-year movement that goes by various cumbersome and misleading titles: Original Instruments, Early Music, Authentic Performance Practice. But in truth both paths pursue the same illusion: that a certified masterpiece has just come blaring out of the composer's brain.

Why do we reenact these rituals of revolution, when revolution is no longer at stake? How can an act of artistic radicalism retain the power to disturb after two centuries? What's left when surprise has been neutralized and influence absorbed? Beethoven toyed with expectations we do not have and dismantled conventions that no longer guide us. As a result, the "Eroica," which emerged with such blinding energy that some of its first listeners thought its composer must be insane, sounds like settled wisdom to us. His contemporaries had never experienced such wild, loud, assaultive sounds outside of combat. Our ears are attuned to a rougher sonic landscape: The construction site that edges Lincoln Center is far more raucous than whatever goes on in the hall.

If the composer flailed against the constraints of his world, today's Beethoven performers battle the legacy he bequeathed: the whole stultifying tradition of greatness. Conductors have various strategies for making even connoisseurs forget the scriptural familiarity of those notes. They can exaggerate idiosyncrasies or whisk up an irritatingly manic sense of excitement. They can buff the playing to a technocratic gleam and engineer an interpretation so faithful to the written score that it becomes fanatically neutral. Or they might emulate the corporate approach of Herbert von Karajan, who drew from his orchestras a rich, emulsified sound and treated Beethoven's symphonies as monuments to be gilded with fresh applications of elegance.

The most thrilling versions of the "Eroica" I've heard have felt like quests, crackling with desperate urgency. In the mid-nineties, John Eliot Gardiner led his private band, the Orchestre Révolutionnaire et Romantique, in a complete cycle of Beethoven symphonies that enshrined their violent defiance. He achieved that effect through scrupulous historicism and tolerance for the technical imperfections inherent in period instruments. Natural horns occasionally bobbled a difficult passage. Gut-string violins struggled to balance wooden flutes that wandered out of tune. Even with a full-arm wallop, the timpanist could only eke a muffled thud from his early-nineteenth-century Viennese kettledrums. But those challenges added to the revolutionary élan, and to the exhilarating suspicion that at any moment the whole apparatus might fall apart.

Beethoven craved that sense of imminent collapse. As a pianist, he pummeled the keyboard and tried to force it into playing lower, higher, louder, and softer than it could. The "Eroica" rattled the Theater an der Wien, a grand and modern space by 1805 standards, but an ornate little shoebox when compared with, say, Carnegie Hall. There's a moment in the middle of the first movement, when the symphony shudders as if it were coming unglued. The pulse grinds down and the burbling theme stops short, overpowered by a chain of dissonant blasts that, in the first performance, must have ricocheted off the graceful walls and buzzed through the audience's bones. In the early nineteenth century, listening to orchestral music was a full-body experience.

But the epic scale of Beethoven's symphonies created a new, supersized infrastructure that gradually swallowed his music. Larger audiences and bigger orchestras required more spacious venues, where music reaches the ears only after picking up resonance and losing its edge. The most authentic, and exciting, way to hear

Beethoven's symphonies would be in cramped rooms rather than in great, flattering halls. (The Lincoln Center concerts take place in the relatively cozy Alice Tully Hall.)

We can't unravel a history of listening, and the work can't easily slough off its encrustations of meaning. Beethoven's music comes to us at once impoverished by time and marinated in meanings: Wagner's analytic raptures, Schroeder's obsession in *Peanuts*, the Morse code V-for-victory of the Fifth during the Battle of Britain, *A Clockwork Orange*, Bernstein's substitution of *Freiheit* (freedom) for *Freude* (joy) in the Ninth at the collapsing Berlin Wall, and so on. We also can't recapture the heat with which the nineteenth century debated the meaning of that cryptic subtitle. Is the hero Napoleon, the composer himself, or perhaps a more archetypal figure? A moral but unconventional loner? A vessel of humanity's most intense feelings? An artist-genius? It hardly matters now, when the whole notion of a hero-worshipping symphony seems impossibly hoary. What sort of figure would we enrobe in music of such complexity, fury, and moral struggle? Tiger Woods? David Petraeus?

For much of today's public, even the most thoroughly tilled symphonic turf has become unexplored terrain. The orchestral Establishment treats that widespread musical illiteracy as a disaster, but it's also a chance to give works of "Eroica"-like stature an infinite number of premieres. The fact that many audience members have never heard the piece should be a bracing thought for the players on the stage: To dispense revelation is a daunting responsibility.

Classical-music neophytes often worry that they don't have enough background to appreciate a performance, but the opposite is often true: They're the ones who listen without preconceptions and who are primed for danger and unpredictability. The "Eroica" was the first symphonic psychodrama, a chronicle of a character's interior battles. Already in the opening seconds, the restless theme spins away from its expected course to go skating through patches of harmonic uncertainty, disruptive syncopations, and asymmetrical phrases. Moods change with mercurial quickness. Beethoven knits his structure out of conflict and unease, turning unpleasant states of mind into artistic virtues.

If the first movement romanticizes anxiety, the second makes misery seem celestial. It is a funeral march, but the orchestration suggests it is an imagined event, a procession unfolding in the protagonist's mind. The sounds are softer, rounder, than a street parade. We hear no brass. Cellos and basses play the role of muffled drums. An oboe takes the place of a mournful bugle. The march coaxes intimate emotions into the public realm. If Beethoven's music still speaks to us now, it's because, like that roomful of startled Viennese two centuries ago, we want to hear suffering transfigured, too. Pain is ugly and joy fleeting, but each performance of the "Eroica" offers to shape everyday disorder of the mind into something luminous and sublime.

Whether the upcoming Beethoven festival does justice to Beethoven will not depend on the vintage of instruments or the historical purity of technique. Modern orchestras and period ensembles can both pluck excitement out of the past. What matters instead is whether Iván Fischer and his two groups are faithful to the intertwining of nuances and extremes. If the performers etch the contrasts between a lonesome horn and a full orchestral roar, if they savor the abyssal terror of a silence, snap off an accented chord before it becomes pillowy and fat, bring out the pleasurable sourness of dissonance, dispel complacency, and banish habit, then they just might summon the prickle and panic of that first night.

Keep Tickin and Tockin
Work It All Around the Clock

Jonathan Bogart

We are in the second week of the third month of 2010, and if the pop charts are any kind of measure, then the most important woman in the pop year to date is Kesha Rose Sebert, a twenty-three year old singer born in the San Fernando Valley and mostly raised in Nashville, who calls herself Ke$ha and pronounces the first syllable of her name to rhyme with bleah, or meh.

The reaction to her slow-bursting fame has been predictably varied. Her debut single, "TiK ToK," hit the top of the *Billboard* Hot 100 just as the new year turned, which seems like it should be significant, the way all random synchronicity does, and various voices have been raised suggesting that a) she represents the bottoming-out of popular culture, a new low beyond which we cannot go, b) her witless, party-all-the-time persona is yet another cruel blow to the self-respect and potential self-determination of a generation of young women, c) she's a dumb whore and should be punished for it (and incidentally for inflicting knowledge of her existence on us), and d) hey shut up her music is fun to dance to and you're the stupid one you big jerkface.

All of these (even c) have their place, and indeed are integral to what for lack of a better phrase I'll call the Ke$ha Project. But this isn't a reportorial piece: I'm not interested here in what the Ke$ha Project's intentional goals are (I assume they don't go much further than making Ke$ha a star and her producers, songwriters, managers, and record label a lot of money, and to the extent there's more involved it's standard-issue self-delusion), but what its cultural, aesthetic, and ideological implications are.

Buckle in. This is gonna get long.

ERRBODY GETTIN CRUNK CRUNK

Let's start with "TiK ToK," because that's where she first came to most of our notice. I heard it in the early fall just after it was released, because I was downloading and listening to everything the Singles Jukebox covered, but I heard it a few days after reading about it and had forgotten which one she was, and the first time I listened to it I thought she might be British and/or black. (I wasn't listening to the vocals so much as I was responding to the thick, twisty blurt of the music under her; I could hear it coming from the land of Aphex Twin and Dizzee Rascal.) When, around Christmastime, I heard it on the radio, I got a little excited: wow, this weird underground pop song I'd mentally filed away as "not horrible" was making inroads into the mainstream.

And then of course I looked her up and saw that she had never been as underground as I'd thought, that she'd sung the hook for Flo Rida's "Right Round" and was produced by Max Martin and Dr. Luke, and I made a seamless transition from being mildly interested in her weird bitchy noises to totally fucking rocking out in the car whenever this stupid awesome fizzy-candy song came on the radio. (My relationship with pop radio can basically be summed up as that of a thirteen-year-old boy to superhero comics: I don't care how unlikely any of it is as long as I get that fix of eye-bleeding color, abstract sexuality, and stylized violence.)

"TiK ToK" is Ke$ha's original statement of purpose, so fully and completely representative of her aesthetic that it ends up sounding a little washed-out and pointless on *Animal*, the subsequent full-length, because it only reinforces the entire message of the album and takes no developing turns into psychotic balladry or maudlin self-pity or aspirational indie rock. Its jocking beats and buzzing, squelchy synths back up a vocal that goes out of its way to annoy anyone with a more settled pair of ears than the thirteen-year-old to which it is pitched, to sound bratty and clumsy and full of entitlement. It hovers just on the edge of being characterless, and its most thrilling trills and melismas are entirely the product of electronic manipulation.

(Which, if I may go big-picture for a bit, is actually rescuing pop vocals from the contentless affectations of the "soul" diva still much imitated on *American Idol*, which is always several years behind: those electronic melismas, precisely because they're unachievable by the human voice, divorce the undeniable thrill of the sound from the ability of the performer, leaving the singer free to focus on the emotion at the heart of the song rather than showboating for showboating's sake. Yes, I'm about to make a claim that Ke$ha's affectless snottiness gets to the emotion at the heart of her songs.)

But Ke$ha's affectless snottiness, the quality in her vocal delivery which irritates even practiced pop listeners unaccustomed to think of themselves as irritable, has a purpose beyond merely dog-whistling *this is music which your parents and teachers will HATE.* She is playing a character here, and the degree to which the character matches up with the details of her biography is essentially unimportant: what matters is the fidelity of the portrait. The reason it's easy to hate Ke$ha is that it's easy to hate the girl she's playing, the entitled white skank with dead eyes and an aggressive, bottomless need for attention, the feminine equivalent of what in the modern taxonomy of youth culture is commonly called the Douchebag. (A point only underscored by the fact that 3OH!3, the avant-garde heroes of Douchebag Pop, guest on her second single.)

But let's back up and take a closer look at two words I used to describe the character she plays in "TiK ToK." "White skank" would probably be a pretty uncontroversial description of that character, at least among people for whom the word "skank" is a stable descriptor of something that exists in the world (as opposed to a statement about the state of mind of the person who says it). But we'll get to that. First let's unpack "white."

Since Ke$ha has been in the public eye she's very much played up her whiteness, cultivating a shaggy blonde mane and choosing publicity photos that accent the pale freckles across her face; but her first (anonymous) introduction to most ears came as the singer of a hook on a hip-hop song, and in the "Right Round" video her presence is only suggested by a black model. She doesn't sound particularly black; but neither does she sound particularly white, at least when singing hooks. (The party-girl half-talk-half-rap delivery of verses, however . . . see below.)

Which is nothing new; if you've been paying attention to pop music at all over the last ten years, you know that it's impossible to demarcate where pop ends and hip-hop begins, especially in terms of production technique. Ke$ha is only the latest instance of the slow merge of black and white, from Eminem + Dre to Timbalake to the rainbow Pussycat Dolls—in fact several observers would probably mock me for even bringing up the old-fashioned idea that there's any distinction in 2010 between "white music" and "black music." And certainly Ke$ha's use of bog-standard hip-hop tropes like phones blowing up, getting crunk, having swagger, etc. isn't terribly remarkable; except I keep looking at her and thinking it is.

(Theory for later development: is the reemergence of country as a powerhouse pop form e.g. Taylor Swift a way for white people uncomfortable with all this blackness to rope off a pop preserve unindebted to hip-hop norms, Darius Rucker being the token redshirt so we can claim non-racism?)

Of course, race is always complicated by class in America. Hip-hop or not, Ke$ha's music is intentionally, gloriously *vulgar*, full of hard, jacking beats, shiny synths and excessive, tacky AutoTune—which it shares with the emerging up-from-the-depths agenda of (pop) hip-hop as set by Soulja Boy, Kid Cudi and Lil Wayne. The elegant excess of Beyoncé and the highbrow madness of Lady Gaga are equally beyond her reach; Ke$ha is without their poise and so decides that her clumsy obviousness isn't a bug, but a feature.

Which brings us to "skank," a word that connotes as much a class slur as a gender one. Skanks are not only easy, they're cheap—anyone from any social stratum can be a whore or a bitch or a slut, but a skank is judged not only for her promiscuity but for her low intelligence, offensive person and poor taste. To call Ke$ha (or, properly, her persona) a skank is to imply that she has no value on any level, a brainless aggregate of bad impulses void of self-respect who therefore (for some reason) deserves none from us. "Us" being the implicated listener, we who are called to sit in judgment on this woman for being a skank.

There are more misogynist, classist, racist, and nihilist implications in the common use of the word than can easily (or briefly) be teased out here; enough to say that the Ke$ha Project, without ever using the word or as far as I know caring one way or the other about its use, reclaims skankiness as a positive attribute in much the same way that 90s feminists did with words like bitch, by turning the concept from one of other-focused moral judgment to one of self-focused strength.

Yes, the lyrics to "TiK ToK" are ridiculous; no one with functioning taste buds brushes their teeth with a bottle of Jack, no one with a sense of self-preservation declares so blithely that when they leave for the night they're not coming back. And nobody born after 1960 thinks Mick Jagger is any ideal of hotness. That's not the point; the point is that by naming these things as possible *in the world of the song* (all songs create sub-universes in which they are true, just like stories; didn't you know?), she basically turns herself into a superhero, a woman whose appetite for alcohol, sex and dance is so strong that she's basically indestructible. (Can you think of an image more terrifying to what feminism with such enviable economy calls the patriarchy?) The only moment of vulnerability, appropriately enough for a story told in song, is when the DJ addressed in the second person plays music, when she's out the dancefloor that is the object of her heroine's quest, where she raises her hands in the classic image of surrender, and at the end of the bridge, has what I can only describe as an electronic orgasm.

Followed by "Now the party don't start till I walk in," which is simply a statement of fact. This song is Ke$ha's world, bought and paid for; *nothing* in it has existence without her.

FIGHT TILL WE DO IT RIGHT

That was a long way to go just to talk about one song. The lady has thirteen more to her name so far; but not all of them are created equally.

As I've said, "TiK ToK" lays out Ke$ha's party-past-the-point-of-fun agenda. What happens past that point depends on the song, or even on the moment in the song; ecstasy, regret, psychosis, depression, and a mystic oneness with the universe (and more) are all on offer on *Animal*. This is an unusual pop-star album for a couple of reasons: first, despite being entirely produced under the supervision of the Max Martin/Dr. Luke factory, it's oddly schizophrenic in its sound. Aside from Ke$ha's own wasted drawl (when she's not submitting to the Zen discipline of AutoTune), there's nothing to tie the songs together sonically, unless Frank Kogan's formulation of Kat Stevens' "bosh" is it. (Those massive, brain-numbing Eurodance beats, basically.) The other reason it's odd is that it's incredibly coherent lyrically. Ke$ha is listed as the principal songwriter on every track in the album, which helps—but she repeats herself, slipping the same themes and even the same phrases into song after song.

Perhaps the least-analyzed (that I've seen) line in the chorus of "TiK ToK" is "Imma fight till we see the sunlight," in itself an admirably concise distillation of the party-as-ritual (and not necessarily an enjoyable one) ethos of the album. Bodies wear out, brains fry, but Ke$ha promises not to give up on the party; she will push past her own exhaustion, boredom, whatever, to achieve its transcendence. But "fight" has other meanings too, of course.

The chorus of "Party At A Rich Dude's House" contains the line "We're gonna fight till we do it right" (in the middle of a very "Kids In America" mass singalong; note that for later). Again the implication is that partying is a discipline which must be practiced to be perfected; but the verses bring out the destructive, violent connotations of the phrase. It's in this song that she promises to piss in the Dom Perignon, throw up in the closet, and in short act like the worst nightmare of the rich dude in question.

Which brings up class again: Ke$ha identifies herself as "young and broke" in the bridge, and it's easy to see her trashing of the place as a pathetic attempt to take revenge on the inequities of the social structure. Which I'm all for, don't get me wrong! but she *encourages* this view by giving us no information at all about the rich dude. He's rich, and that's enough of a reason. (Apparently at least some of these lyrics are based on incidents at Paris Hilton's place. Which matters more for Hilton's symbolic status as the culture-wide whipping girl for unearned privilege than for the truthfulness of the anecdote.)

But class solidarity is never stable in America, and Ke$ha's destructive glee turns just as easily on her young and broke peers as on the rich dudes and dudettes of Hollywood. "Backstabber" is a snotty kiss-off to gossiping friends (she inconsistently—but it's perfectly consistent with the character!—accuses her friends of making her private life public when she does nothing else over the course of the album). It's a solid little Lily Allenesque character piece with a punchy phased horn sample and a lyric that repeats words so many times that they become a recursive echo. In fact the echo is laid so heavily on the song that I can't help wondering whether it's all taking place in her head. My cue was that she rambles towards the end into the line "you're looking like a lunatic"—but hold that thought too.

After rich dudes and so-called friends, who's left to fight with? Boyfriends, of course, which she manages in two different ways (well, three, but the last one's a special case; see below). "Kiss & Tell" suffers from an over-obvious chorus, but is otherwise satisfyingly nasty, making fine distinctions between "baller" and "tool," calling the cheating bastard "a chick" and ending a verse dismissively "I hope you cry." That's bad feminism, of course, using gendered referents to imply weakness and pitifulness; but who expected feminism from the Ke$ha Project? Anyway the real feminist point is that Ke$ha, far from being a victim of the entrenched double standard in which guys play the field while girls are either virgins or sluts, is the one enforcing her own standards. Again she's a superhero, a larger-than-life fantasy figure dishing out revenge on behalf of the girls branded sluts everywhere. In the crude terminology of dick-measuring contests, hers is bigger than his.

The same is true of the other boyfriend kiss-off on the album, "Blind." This time it takes something out of her: she admits to feeling low, but even more so the music is darkly dramatic, a sobbing emotional backdrop suitable for a post-Brown Rihanna ballad. But in Ke$ha's hands the darkness turns again to revenge: she's not going to cry, he's the one who'll miss her till the day he dies. Death and blindness are the overriding images of the chorus, but they don't apply to her. This is the destructive impulses of "Party At A Rich Dude's House" taken to operatic extremes; she's snuffing out a life for cheating on her.

If "TiK ToK" gave us the best-case scenario for the Party—dancefloor ecstasy—these other fighting songs give us other options: class warfare, girlfights, emasculation, death. None of these are the party done right; but they're also not particularly original topics for pop. Ke$ha can go weirder.

EVIL GIRLY GAMES

Two phrases that she employs with some regularity throughout the album are "hot mess" (surely non-coincidentally the title of a recent Cobra Starship album) and "sick obsession." The first is a tidy encapsulation of the persona she's putting forward; the second hints at darker, or at least less usual, themes.

Partying past fun can land in ecstasy, or in the banality of Jerry Springer relationships. But it can also end in weirder places. Of course Ke$ha is very far from being the first pop star to claim to be a freak; in fact her most blatant "I'm a freaky girl watch out" song, "Take It Off," is one of the least inspired on the album, a conventional riff on the "there's a place I know" theme not helped by borrowing the hook off "The Streets Of Cairo" (better known on playgrounds, or it was in my day, as "All The Girls In France"). There's more destruction and violence in the verses, but for the most part it tells rather than shows. This doesn't apply, by the way, to the buzzy, gothy music behind her rote choruses—there's a dark sparkle to the production that almost convinces that Ke$ha's partying has a more sinister edge than the booze-sex-dance trivium we've seen. But ultimately the pathology of "Take It Off" is theatrical, played rather for campy kicks than as anything serious.

"Your Love Is My Drug" goes more or less the same route, a bunch of winking references to drug use and addiction covering up one of the shallower love songs in recent memory (not only is it a poor introduction to the album, it's not even as good as the Puffy AmiYumi song of the same name, let alone Roxy Music's epic cathedral). But as the standard bosh of the chorus winds down, Ke$ha's personality peeps through, singing short phrases at irregular intervals (probably to give Dr. Luke AutoTune fodder), cracking up at herself, and then ending in a mocking gurgle, "I like your beard."

The pathology of drug addiction was just a pretense for a love song; but that muttered phrase points to other possibilities. She sounds like a teenager trying to get a rise out of an authority figure, phrasing her mockery in the form of a compliment in order to say "whut I said I *liked* it" and cackle with her friends when he goes predictably off. The fake freakiness of "Take It Off" isn't Ke$ha (or even her character)—but the infuriatingly charming brat who picks and pecks, finds an annoyance and rides it, is.

And then there's the real freakiness.

"Stephen" has become my favorite song on *Animal*, and I hate it. Well, that's not quite fair. I would probably have hated it, or even been afraid of it, when I was younger; but the tempered judgment that comes with age appreciates its craft and the elegance of its misdirection. I can't listen to it often, though, or not without being seriously creeped out, because far more than "Every Breath You Take" or "Can't Get You Out Of My Head" or "You Belong With Me," this is a perfect encapsulation of stalkerdom as actually practiced by young, insane women who think they're cute.

The production is far lighter than on the rest of the album, giving her an almost Caribbean setting for her voice, which she deploys within a narrow range high in her register. Throughout the rest of the album when she hits the chorus she goes all out in a foghorn blast, pushing the needle into the red and the dynamic range past the edge of coherence, but on "Stephen" she uses a voice synthesizer and drags her phrases out into curlicues and simpers, throwing every silly affectation she can think of into the performance. If you're the kind of guy whose nerves grate when girls play up the ultrafeminine eyelash-batting cute squeak (I am), this is already kind of off-putting. But then the lyrics start twisting.

It starts out ordinarily enough: she likes this guy's ass, she thinks his girlfriend's a bitch, and wants him for herself. So far so Ke$ha. Then she calls him her sick obsession. She's feeling pathetic, she can't take rejection. This isn't the Ke$ha who stomped a guy's balls for being a slut—and then the bridge comes in. She's doing the little-girl thing on purpose: "I've got guys waiting in a line / For me to play my evil girly games with all their minds / Just watch me, got it down to a simple art / Just bat my eyes like this and there's a broken heart." (To cap it off she pronounces "eyes" with the New York accent of Helen Kane, whose voice Betty Boop was originally a parody of.) Delusional, confident; this is more like our Ke$ha. Then "I'm thinking that maybe you think I'm crazy." Well, there's crazy and then there's crazy. "Don't you think I'm . . . pretty," she simpers, and alarm bells go off. (Really, it's a masterpiece of pronunciation.)

"Cause you're my object of affection, my drug of choice," she sings again, "my sick obsession / I want to keep you as my pet to play with and hide under my bed / Forever." Okay; this is Kathy Bates with a sledgehammer stuff, and once I realized that I got chills every time I heard that line, as well as the subsequent "I'll knit you a sweater [WHAT not Ke$ha], I want to wrap you up in my love forever / I will never let you go."

Maybe I'm a commitment-phobe. Maybe I've heard one too many comedy sketches where Casey Wilson plays a psychotic obsessive ex-girlfriend. But if Stephen isn't running his legs off to get away from this girl, he's a doomed man.

Which is of course awesome. This is the song that most thoroughly breaks with the party ethic of the album, and it's interesting to speculate on why. Is this the girl Ke$ha would be if she didn't have the release of partying? (Since she admits to being wasted in the first verse, unlikely.) Is it another in our maze of choose-your-own-adventure endings to the party, ending in psychosis and whimpering, dehumanizing need? Is it (more frighteningly) a real song to a real person?

And then I thought about it and I can't name a single other song written by a woman to a man that uses the man's name like this one does. Men, of course, sing women's names all the time: Alison, Amie, Angie, Billie Jean, Caroline, Cecilia, Gloria, and on and on. But outside of conscious gender-benders like Tori Amos, there aren't too many songs of direct address sung by young females. Which fits with the conventional gender roles reinforced by pop, of course: men are direct and confrontational and specific, women are indirect and deflective and general. Except Ke$ha's in ur gender roles redrawin the lines.

I'M ABOUT TO BARF SERIOUSLY

I brought up Casey Wilson not just because I'm a comedy nerd and happened to hear her recently on the Comedy Death-Ray podcast, but because one of the unremarked engines of the Ke$ha Project is comedy.

Not comedy in the organized, semi-official industry sense—there are no jokes in her music, no setups and punchlines, and it would be shitty if there were, we don't need a distaff Weird Al—but in the sense that her approach to her music contains the anarchic sensibilities that are also present in a great deal of modern comedy. The "I like your beard" interjection (and the decision to retain it), the over-the-top delivery of so many lines on the album from "oh my god I think I'm still drunk" to "I can find someone way hotter, with a bigger . . . well" are meant to provoke laughter—or at least they do provoke laughter in the sample group of one which is my only research instrument.

Of course the most comic song on the album, and therefore the most deliriously awesome, is "D.I.N.O.S.A.U.R.," which has drawn comparisons with Daphne & Celeste, L'Trimm, and Northern State (and I'd throw Fannypack, Toni Basil, and Aqua into the mix). It's a one-joke song, bagging on the old guy who thinks he's still cool enough to hang out with Ke$ha's (character's) young-and-broke crowd, and while none of the actual put-downs are terribly amusing in themselves, there's an infectious energy to the chant—plus a stroke of loopy production genius, a sample of a giggle that pans all over the stereo space while shifting up and down in pitch—and one line that always makes me laugh, which is in bold at the top of this section. (It's the delivery.)

Speaking of barfing, I haven't done an exhaustive study or anything but I have to imagine this album has one of the highest ratios of vomit to love song in pop history. This is of course another comic trope—a particularly juvenile one, but as Dave Holmes pointed out Ke$ha's persona is a thirteen-year-old's idea of an adult, when vomit is still funny as well as gross instead of just an indicator of having made poor choices.

Bagging on old people and authority figures: also popular with middle schoolers. The only two people I've ever heard sing a Ke$ha song in public came out of the women's restroom giggling hysterically and were collectively not old enough to drink.

WITH EVERY MOVE I DIE

But of course Ke$ha is not thirteen; she's twenty-three, and there are still a couple of options unexplored in the maze.

"Hung Over" and "Dancing With Tears In My Eyes" are, inasmuch as I can determine a consensus, the least-liked songs on *Animal*, ballads (even power ballads) where she turns a) regretful and b) suicidal, respectively. As character pieces, they suffer from being standard-issue and maudlin; if I liked emo better or had more of a tolerance for self-pity in any form, I might have more to say about them. I'll only say that they're entirely consistent with her character: if "TiK ToK" is about the preparation for the party and the excelsis during it, "Dancing With Tears In My Eyes" is the maudlin aftermath—or *a* maudlin aftermath. There are always more options, which is why the record doesn't end there.

"Animal" is the last song on *Animal*, and it's a complete gear shift. (At least until the chorus kicks in; there's the bosh.) Ke$ha sings the verses in an exaggerated indie croon, which people have compared to Feist and Kate Bush, but I mostly hear as Dolores O'Riordan. Regardless, it's right out of the Arcade Fire wing of inspirational indie: world ending, last chance to connect, truly be alive, in love with everything. She does it well—at least whenever the jackhammer disco thumps leave her alone—and I'm caught between thinking she's devaluing the rest of her album by comparing it to this Real Serious Music, and believing that she's elevating the tropes of inspirational indie by incorporating them into her own weird, pulsing, trashily *alive* hot mess.

BABY SHUT UP HEARD ENOUGH

Well, that, as far as I can work it out, is the Ke$ha Project. I don't think it's entirely successful, but it's a first album and the Martin/Luke factory isn't really known for its quality control. I wanted to spend the rest of my wordcount talking about what else I heard in the record, what I jotted down as "influences and reminiscences." Influences you'd have to read interviews and do some biographical work to find out about; but of whom do I find her reminiscent? I thought you'd never ask.

It struck me as I was marveling at the weird mind games of "Stephen" for the fourth or fifth time this week that Ke$ha may be the first pop star to grow up with two Courtney Loves as a role model, both the angry, sarcastic feminist of *Live Through This*, and the desperate party-hound of the past decade. In fact her publicity shots are sometimes startlingly like the cover image of *Live Through This*. I have no idea, obviously, how feminist (or not) Ke$ha herself is; but the worlds she builds in her songs don't map very well onto the standard patriarchal narratives, especially the ones about sluts and skanks.

One of the benefits of the half-talk-half-rap delivery she uses for many of her verses is that it's infinitely plastic; she can adopt any tone, apply any level of sarcasm or referentiality. At various times throughout the album I thought I heard Kim Gordon, Moon Unit Zappa, Johnnette Napolitano, Debora Iyall (Romeo Void), Deborah Evans-Stickland (Flying Lizards), Kathleen Hanna, and Laurie Anderson. Which if you're trying to make a list of feminist forebears is about as good as you can hope for, and I hope I'm not just hallucinating the similarities. (Definitely not with Laurie Anderson.)

There are two songs I haven't covered. "Blah Blah Blah" is the current single, featuring 3OH!3 in a marvelous Skank & Douchebag Power! gesture of solidarity—perhaps the only way the Ke$ha character could find satisfaction with a guy is if he's just as much an invulnerable, selfish dick as she is—and "Boots & Boys" is resisting my efforts to nail it down. Something about the rubbery synth makes me want to pull in comparisons with mid-'90s Blur, and there's something about how the tightly wound crescendo in the middle eight mirrors the vocal orgasm in "TiK ToK," but it's not coming together and it's already far too late.

I'm not going to post this immediately, but if I read it over and decide to let it go, then this is what you're stuck with. I'm not writing more than 5,000(!) words on Ke$ha. Until she puts out another record, this is my definitive take.

The Grandest Duke

Geoffrey O'Brien

On more than one occasion Duke Ellington described his childhood in Washington, D.C., as a sort of paradise, at least for him and those around him in the family circle. In the song "My Mother, My Father" (written for his 1963 musical show *My People*) he wrote:

> *My mother—the greatest—and the prettiest*
> *My father—just handsome—but the wittiest . . .*
> *I was raised in the palm of the hand*
> *By the very best people in this land*
> *From sun to sun*
> *Their hearts beat as one*
> *My mother—my father—and love*

Born Edward Kennedy Ellington in 1899, he was a child of African-American privilege as understood in the early twentieth century. His father James, whose schooling stopped at the eighth grade, was a sometime butler and caterer (he worked on some parties at the Warren G. Harding White House) who later drew blueprints for the Navy; an omnivorous reader fond of operatic music, he "always," according to Ellington, "acted as though he had money, whether he had it or not. . . . He raised his family as though he were a millionaire."

Ellington's mother Daisy was a high school graduate of strong religious convictions who played piano and insisted on piano lessons for Edward (with the unforgettably named Marietta Clinkscales). Daisy ran her household along lines of Victorian propriety, considered lipstick unacceptable, and disapproved of the blues. She was the object of Ellington's lifelong devotion. It was in a period of depression following her death in 1935 that he wrote his breakthrough composition "Reminiscing in Tempo." She had imparted to him the sense of a special destiny, often repeating, as recounted in his autobiography *Music Is My Mistress*: "Edward, you are blessed. You don't have anything to worry about. Edward, you are blessed!"

In the social world in which he grew up he was made aware of fine gradations:

> I don't know how many castes of Negroes there were in the
> City at the time, but I do know that if you decided to mix
> carelessly with another you would be told that one just did
> not do that sort of thing.

At his segregated school, his eighth-grade teacher taught that "as representatives of the Negro race we were to command respect for our people. . . . Negro history was crammed into the curriculum, so that we would know our people all the way back." As a teenager he saw and was much impressed by W.E.B. Du Bois's 1915 pageant of black history *The Star of Ethiopia*. This was at just the moment when Woodrow Wilson was lavishing praise on *The Birth of a Nation* and enforcing segregation at all levels of his administration. In 1919, during the so-called "Red Summer" in which white-on-black violence escalated across America, a five-day riot erupted in Washington. At the dedication of the Lincoln Memorial in 1922, black spectators were restricted to a roped-off area, and the only black speaker was not permitted to sit on the dais.

Music was not a predestined career choice for Ellington. He liked to draw and attended a commercial art school, and in his teens ran a sign-painting business. But by age fifteen he had discovered the profits and pleasures of music, acquiring the musical knowledge he

needed not systematically—he had abandoned Mrs. Clinkscales's lessons early on—but by absorbing what he could from every musician
he encountered, whether formally trained or not, plunging into the
heart of an emerging musical culture of vital exchanges: "The ear
cats loved what the schooled cats did," he wrote, "and the schooled
guys, with fascination, would try what the ear cats were doing." By
the time he was twenty he was living on his own and leading a local
band at society parties where they played (in drummer Sonny Greer's
words) "anything and everything—pop songs, jazz songs, dirty songs,
torch songs, Jewish songs."

In 1923 Ellington relocated to New York to get to the center of
the music business, and the city remained his ostensible home—although his life for the next fifty years really was to be lived on the
road, in a thousand hotel rooms. His nightly radio programs from
the Cotton Club made him nationally famous; the New York *Daily
Mirror* described his band in 1930 as "the most prominent Negro
broadcasters on the air . . . as heartily admired by the white as the
colored people." By the early 1940s he figured simultaneously as a
supremely popular entertainer; as an uncompromising experimenter
who presented challenging compositions at Carnegie Hall; and, as
Harvey Cohen documents in great detail, as the African-American
artist who had succeeded on an unprecedentedly wide scale in over-
coming racial barriers and stereotypes. Whatever the medium or the
location, he found ways to present himself on his own terms, creating
his own definition of reality, a definition that the world around him—
and eventually that included more or less the entire world—was
charmed rather than forced into accepting.

Harvey G. Cohen's *Duke Ellington's America* sets about explaining
how exactly he managed that feat of persuasion. The book joins an
already vast literature on Ellington. Neither an intimate biography
nor a comprehensive study of his music, it seeks to map out Ellington's

total enterprise, detailing the obstacles he faced early and late, and at what cost and through what relentless personal effort that enterprise was sustained. Drawing extensively on the Ellington archive at the Smithsonian Institution, Cohen surveys in particular Ellington's external dealings—his relations with managers, agents, publicists, record producers, journalists, and all the other intermediaries whom he had a knack for keeping at just the right distance. Cohen also, in his most crucial pages, quotes at length from Ellington's unpublished poetic outline for the never quite finished suite *Black, Brown and Beige*—material in which Ellington reveals a great deal that he never otherwise acknowledged about his artistic intentions. Bringing together many different voices and sources, Cohen conveys the genuinely epic quality of this career.

Reading Cohen's book we begin in one nation and end in quite a different one, and as we track Ellington's musical revolution, we find ourselves at the heart of the changes that brought about that transformation. Cohen's subject is both the America that shaped Ellington and the other America that—through both his music and his projected self-image—he played a part in creating. The process of sorting out Ellington's music and his life and parsing what they meant for the life of the past century has hardly begun. There is simply so much there, and its import goes so far beyond matters of musical style. His music is inextricably of a piece with the way he lived and thought.

Of many artists it can be said that deep cultural currents can be read through their work; much rarer are those who, like Ellington, worked so powerfully and subtly on those currents as to transform them. As a personality Ellington had many of the traits one associates more readily with the founders of religious orders or political movements than with lone artists absorbed in self-expression. In a close reading of the details that Cohen amasses, Ellington emerges as a prophetic figure imposing himself almost by stealth, using all the skills of an entertainer and a consummate diplomat.

He lived at the highest energy level every day, and despite his dread of being the subject of a biography (a life written down could only be a life approaching its end) left such abundant traces of himself that Cohen's six hundred pages can be little more than an abbreviated résumé. Consider his activities in a single unremarkable week in May 1966, when he was sixty-seven: sleeping three hours a night, he scored the Frank Sinatra film *Assault on a Queen*, performed concerts in Wichita, Little Rock, and San Francisco, recorded the Sinatra score in Los Angeles while playing a three-night gig at Disneyland, then left the morning after the last show for a two-week tour of Japan, all the while carrying on an incandescent social life.

Yet some of those closest to him described him as essentially solitary. His granddaughter said that for all his devotion to family and friends, "I really do think he felt more at home in a hotel room with his piano." "I'm a hotel man," he once said. "I like being alone, you know. I don't know why." The first of his Sacred Concerts, the trilogy of religious works that were a central focus of his later years, was prefaced with the statement: "Everyone is so alone—the basic, essential state of mankind." Foremost among the many and profound paradoxes that Ellington embodies is this duality of the man alone in the hotel room and the man so thoroughly enmeshed with his orchestra and with a world of listeners.

He was, after all, the composer of "Solitude," and of so many other works ("In a Sentimental Mood," "Dusk," "The Single Petal of a Rose") that feed into a quintessence of aloneness, however little the most expansive reaches of his music—the fusion of multiple and sometimes abrasive textures and styles, the constant reaching across racial and social and national boundaries—seem to speak of isolation. Quite the contrary: his music is unimaginable without the voices of which it is made. "Ellington" is of necessity shorthand for Billy Strayhorn and Johnny Hodges and Cootie Williams and Bubber Miley, Paul Gonsalves and Ivie Anderson and Harry Carney and Ray Nance and a hundred others. These most extravagant individualities were somehow fused in an unmistakable, utterly personal sound.

His music attains self-expression through the expression of selves. Voices contest, cajole, regret, argue, instruct, protest, entreat, give praise: not programmatic description but actual speech, captured in the moment. In every ensemble one hears the separate voices, and at the same time senses the enormous ear tuned in to all of them. Hodges and Carney and the rest are not simply the people who play Ellington's music; they are the music, as in one way or another he reiterated countless times, usually in some variation of the formula "My band is my instrument."* Billy Strayhorn, who as pianist, arranger, and composer had been deeply involved in Ellington's music since 1939, gave this notion definitive articulation: "Each member of his band is to him a distinctive tone color and set of emotions, which he mixes with others equally distinctive to produce a third thing, which I like to call the Ellington Effect."†

Although I have been listening to Ellington's music for almost as many years as he spent recording it, I feel far from grasping its totality. He was responsible for thousands of compositions (many, from the late 1930s to the late 1960s, in collaboration with Strayhorn), and constantly reworked and rearranged many of those compositions. It is easy to become engaged with one or another period (the late 1930s, say, or the early 1960s) and temporarily forget the others, from the Cotton Club in the mid-1920s to the final works of the early 1970s.

---

* There was of course another side to this collaborative process, and more than one Ellington band member would express regret at not sharing in the profits from this or that motif that Ellington had so artfully incorporated into his copyrighted compositions. On the other hand, the fusing and completing force in the process was always Ellington's, and it is hard to imagine the works as we know them arising in any other way. Even Strayhorn—who had his own issues about the degree to which he was credited for his work with Ellington, in one of the most intricately intermeshed artistic collaborations of the twentieth century—acknowledged as much: "The proof is that these people don't go somewhere else and write beautiful music. You don't hear anything else from them. You do from Ellington."

† *Down Beat*, November 5, 1952; reprinted in *The Duke Ellington Reader*, edited by Mark Tucker (Oxford University Press, 1993), p. 270. Tucker's anthology is an indispensable and endlessly entertaining sourcebook.

If he weathered many different fashions, it was not by following them but by becoming more himself. To go from "Reminiscing in Tempo"— the extended lyrical piece, released on four 78s, that in 1935 pushed radically against marketplace limits on the length and form of jazz recordings—to *The River*, his 1970 ballet suite (not released until 1989), is to register a continuity of creative impulse seizing every opportunity to expand and experiment.

Even the mid-1950s period that Cohen describes as his commercial and aesthetic "nadir"—happy, it must be said, is the artist whose low point is of such short duration—generated some remarkable music and was followed by a renewal cut short only by his death in 1974. Albums like *Afro-Bossa* (1962), *The Far East Suite* (1966), . . . *And His Mother Called Him Bill* (1967), *New Orleans Suite* (1971), and *The Afro-Eurasian Eclipse* (1971, released 1975) exemplify the riches of this last period without exhausting them.

One of the many valuable aspects of *Duke Ellington's America* is the ample space it gives to these later decades, correcting a long-standing tendency to focus more on the work of the 1930s and (especially) the 1940s. A generation of listeners understandably overwhelmed by the 1940–1942 recordings (featuring Jimmy Blanton on bass and Ben Webster on tenor sax, and marking the emergence of Billy Strayhorn as Ellington's intimate collaborator) made them a yardstick by which his subsequent work was sometimes found wanting.* It is hard to argue with the perfection of "Concerto for Cootie," "Harlem Airshaft," "Pitter Panther Patter," and so many others from a moment when Ellington's popularity and artistic innovation were both at a peak; but there is no need to reduce the rest of his career to an afterthought.

---

* The complete master takes of the Blanton-Webster band have been reissued on *Never No Lament: The Blanton-Webster Band, 1940–1942* (RCA Victor, 2003). Beyond these, the line recordings collected in *The Duke Box* offer an expanded sampling of Ellington's 1940s work.

His accomplishment—everything it had taken to shape the sound of his orchestra and market that sound as both art and popular music—becomes all the more extraordinary when one traces, with Cohen, the extreme deliberateness with which Ellington managed his career. Nothing seems fortuitous. Even apparent compromises or trade-offs can be read as artful accommodations leading to eventual triumphs. The book makes nuanced sense of the hard choices at every turn, in years when it often fell to Ellington to pioneer new audiences and new venues, and to insist on a level of dignity rarely accorded to African-American artists.

The nuance is especially valuable in the account of Ellington's long and enigmatic relationship with Irving Mills, his manager, publisher, and business partner from 1926 to 1939, a man who, in Cohen's words, "with Ellington's knowledge and tacit approval . . . made millions of dollars during ensuing decades by putting his name to dozens of Ellington's compositions of the 1920s and 1930s that he almost certainly did not help write." Despite Mills's hogging of credits and disproportionate profit share, Ellington (even after breaking up the partnership in 1939) never publicly criticized Mills, and later wrote:

> In spite of how much he made on me, I respected the way
> he had operated. He had preserved the dignity of my name.
> Duke Ellington has an unblemished image, and that is the
> most anybody can do for anybody.

For Cohen, Mills played the crucial role in defining the public's perception of Duke Ellington: as an artist of singular genius and global significance, distinct from the vulgar and racially stereotyped associations of "jazz music." Ellington's Cotton Club "jungle music" had made his reputation, and as late as 1931 he was being quoted in a Mills Music handbook on the subject of the "weird, queer effects of primitive Negro melodies." But Mills's publicity gradually moved away from that approach, emphasizing not so much the primitive and exotic as the complex and modern:

> Only the important things in art and life merit serious discussion and create critical controversy. . . . Whatever your musical opinion of this latest work in the modern idiom created by Duke Ellington—trailblazer in the newest music—it will not be indifferent!

Mills's positioning of Ellington as serious artist was amplified when a hugely successful tour of England in 1933 elicited critical comparisons ranging from Liszt and English madrigals to Ravel and Schoenberg. This foreign praise began to filter back into American newspapers, until before long the *Memphis Scimitar*, for instance, was writing of the "unorthodox, frenzied jazz" of "this negro Stravinsky."

Cohen has found no documentation to show how much Ellington participated in shaping these campaigns. As immensely valuable as it was for him to be identified as an artist of unique genius, his definitions of his art were often quite different, and certainly had little to do with Liszt or madrigals. From the start he often distanced himself from the rubric of jazz (as later from swing), preferring to be considered "beyond category." But he showed little inclination to associate himself with the supposed prestige of European traditions. In a 1934 interview he declared: "You can't stay in the European conservatory and play the negro music. . . . Negro music is what we are working on. Not as a component of jazz, but as a definite unadulterated musical entity." He returned to the same theme many times, remarking in 1938: "There is something lasting . . . to be obtained from the Negro idiom of music. . . . Negro music has color, harmony, melody, and rhythm. It's what I'm most interested in." And again in 1939: "Our music is always intended to be definitely and purely racial. . . . Those things which we have to say, we try to express musically with the greatest possible degree of freedom of inspiration and individuality." If people heard Schoenbergian echoes in his music, he ventured to suggest, they were projecting out of their own "subconscious activity."

He pushed toward longer, more ambitious works aimed more at the concert hall than the dance floor. Here, record company executives and music critics—and sometimes audiences—alike proved resistant. When Ellington, at his epochal first Carnegie Hall concert in January 1943, presented the premiere of a forty-five-minute version of his suite *Black, Brown and Beige: A Tone Parallel of the Negro in America*, the response was disappointing. Paul Bowles called it "formless and meaningless," adding that "the whole attempt to fuse jazz as a form with art music should be discouraged"; John Hammond felt that "by becoming more complex he has robbed jazz of most of its basic virtue and lost contact with his audience." The harsh reaction, and the suggestion that he should stick to the (presumably simpler) music he excelled at, was a bitter experience for Ellington; he never recorded the complete work, which had been in process for many years, and even when he recorded an album of the music in 1958 (featuring Mahalia Jackson's magnificent rendition of "Come Sunday") he included only a portion of it.

Even the longer Carnegie Hall version failed, as Cohen explains, to convey the themes sketched in Ellington's outline of *Black, Brown and Beige*. Based, Ellington said, on his study of some eight hundred volumes on "Negro culture and its evolution," the work was meant to embrace black history from Africa to modern America, from ancient cultures—

> *In the kingdom of Songhay*
> *There flourished a system of agriculture, law,*
> *Literature, music, natural sciences, medicine*

—to contemporary Harlem:

> *Who brought the dope*
> *And made a rope*
> *Of it, to hang you*
> *In your misery . . .*
> *And Harlem . . .*
> *How'd you come to be*
> *Permitted*
> *In a land that's free?*

Along the way there were analyses of the corrosive effects of slavery on slaves and masters alike—"The master carried his fear with him"—and evocations of the ambiguous messages of the white man's religion. (Ellington interpolated passages from the Book of Proverbs, his favorite book of the Bible: "When pride cometh, then cometh shame; / But with the lowly is wisdom.") In a way that would have astonished most of the Carnegie Hall audience in 1943, he praised the slave rebellions of the "mighty men of action" Nat Turner and Denmark Vesey.

Little of this material is reflected in *Black, Brown and Beige* as performed or recorded. Most revealing is a rare moment of self-doubt:

> *And so, your song has stirred the souls*
> *Of men in strange and distant places . . .*
> *But did it ever speak to them*
> *Of what you really are? . . .*
> *How could they ever fail to hear*
> *The hurt and pain and anguish*
> *Of those who travel dark, lone ways*
> *The soul in them to languish?*
> *And was the picture true*

Of you? The camera eye in focus . . .
Or was it all a sorry bit
Of ofay hocus-pocus?

The painful questioning of the image of him that the world saw is a rare breach of Ellington's extraordinary self-control. For Cohen the doubts and conflicts surrounding *Black, Brown and Beige* expose pain and anger concealed behind his reserve, a reserve itself masked always by seemingly effortless eloquence and humor. It is true that the surviving music of the "tone parallel" to the history of the Negro seems to gesture toward another work not quite embodied, a work of overwhelming aspiration and power. Yet it is not always the finished and perfected works that have the deepest influence. In its apparently incomplete form *Black, Brown and Beige* seems all the same indispensable and pervasive, clearing a space for the expression of vast stretches of time and history.

With the rapid decline of the big band era after World War II, Ellington's days as a hit parade attraction were over. What followed—the way he sustained his orchestra in lean times and continued to compose and record exactly as he intended—turns out to be equally extraordinary. The musical sensation of the mid-1920s, variously described as "Harlem's Aristocrat of Jazz" or (bizarrely) "the Rudy Vallee of the colored race," performing at the Cotton Club for an audience including at times F. Scott Fitzgerald and George Gershwin (the latter credited with coining the phrase "jungle music"), was still, almost half a century later, pushing his music in surprising directions (listen to "Heaven" from 1969 or "Neo-Creole" from 1971), having outlived his original audiences as well as his original critics.

Ellington cared for his band as a musician cares for his voice or hands, and kept it together fifty-two weeks a year until almost the end. He explained that he needed the band permanently available so he could hear how his music sounded: "To me, music is a hobby. That is why I have to have a band. It is a sort of vanity. As soon as I hear a piece, I have to hear it played." Sometimes he called it an addiction. His energies were directed increasingly to that end—that he could compose something at three in the morning and hear it played later the same morning. To attain that luxury, he was prepared to work ceaselessly and for a fraction of the financial rewards that could have been his.

But then Ellington, it appears, was not all that interested in money. In a passage toward the end of *Music Is My Mistress* (1973)—an upbeat, generous, and for the most part deliberately unrevealing book—he gives at last a hint of the more somber assumptions underlying his art:

> After people have destroyed all people everywhere, I see heaping mounds of money strewn over the earth, floating on and sinking into the sea. . . . Money and stink, the stink of dung, the stink of money, so foul that in order for the flowers to get a breath of fresh air, the winds will come together and whip the sea into a rage, and blow across the land. Then the green leaves of trees, and grass, will give up their chlorophyll, so that the sea, the wind, the beasts, and the birds will play and sing Nature's old, sweet melody and rhythm. But since you are people, you will not, unfortunately, be here to hear it.

Yet little as he cared for commerce, he valued money as a means to retain the zone of freedom he had established—a zone that amounted to an independent polity, in which all those around him were also taken care of. (Ellington, in Cohen's summation, instead of enriching himself by investing his royalties and catering to nostalgia, "sought to support friends, family, and community, the fulltime touring of his orchestra, and, perhaps most importantly, his composing and his ability to hear his work immediately.") His goals were achieved not through meticulously laid-out plans but through a kind of unrelenting energetic improvisation in the service of deeply held convictions, doing things at the last minute because it was always the last minute, finding time and space for more than would seem to fit into a life. In talking about the Sacred Concerts he once said: "Worship is a matter of profound intent. I tried to invite everybody. It's very easy to misunderstand." That phrase—"profound intent"—could well define the whole arc of his life.

Growing Up Gaga

Vanessa Grigoriadis

One year ago this month, Lady Gaga arrived for an interview in the dark, oak-paneled lobby of the Roosevelt Hotel, a massive Spanish-style place in the tourist district of Hollywood that was supposed to make the area chic but has largely failed. "Just Dance," the lead single off her first album, *The Fame*, had reached No. 1 in Australia, Sweden, and Canada in early 2008, but in March 2009, she was still an up-and-coming artist in America: a few thousand MySpace plays, a generic website, and a short tour as the opening act for New Kids on the Block. Gaga had a video, though. "My colleagues at radio in those three countries agreed to support her if I made a video," says Martin Kierszenbaum, the president of A&R at her label, Interscope. The "Just Dance" video, shot a few miles from the Roosevelt, features Gaga shimmying with a disco ball in her hands while her friends drape themselves on a couch nearby—though most of those people were extras, not real friends. She didn't know many people on the West Coast. "I don't like Los Angeles," she told me. "The people are awful and terribly shallow, and everybody wants to be famous but nobody wants to play the game. I'm from New York. I will kill to get what I need."

Before the meeting, I assumed that someone with a stage name like "Lady" (her given name is Stefani Joanne Germanotta) was going to be a bit standoffish—that's the strategy employed by most nervous young musicians on the occasion of their first real interview, in any case. But I never thought she was going to actually *be* Lady Gaga. These days, very few artists play the media like Bob Dylan, or stay in character as Devo's Mark Mothersbaugh did in his early career. In the age of VH1's *Behind the Music*, tabloid culture, and reality television, musicians are aware that they should show themselves to journalists in as much mundane detail as they can muster. "But Lady Gaga is my name," she said, amazed that I would have thought otherwise. "If you know me, and you call me Stefani, you don't really know me at all."

This was Gaga's first interview in the U.S., and she was going to put on a show. She eased into a brown leather couch with as much grace as possible given her outfit, a stiff white jumpsuit with a jacket cut from a Martin Margiela pattern, the enormous shoulder pads stuffed underneath the fabric extending toward her ears. At five-two and 100 pounds, with her hair styled into a mod blonde bob, she looked flush from a strict diet of starvation: "Pop stars should not eat," she pronounced. She was young, skinny, and blonde, but she had a prominent Italian nose, the kind of nose that rarely survives on a starlet. (This was during Gaga's "hair-bow" phase—that would be pre-hair-hat and pre-hair-telephone—and when I asked about the bow's whereabouts, she rested her head on a pillow of her hands and said, "She's sleeping.") In the hallway near her table, families of tourists took pictures of one another with cameras, unaware of her presence, and she recoiled dramatically at every flash. "Oh, cameras," she said, shielding her eyes. "I cannot bear the cameras."

As we began the conversation, Gaga spoke carefully in a very odd accent—some combination of Madonna as Madge and a robot, an affect enhanced by the fact that she refused to remove her lightly tinted sunglasses over the course of two hours. "What I've discovered," said robo-Gaga, with a photo-ready tilt of her head, "is that in art, as in music, there's a lot of truth—and then there's a lie. The artist is essentially creating his work to make this lie a truth, but he slides it in amongst all the others. The tiny little lie is the moment I live for, my moment. It's the moment that the audience falls in love."

Gaga was very taken with her new "bubble dress" at this point, and we talked about its unreality, the beauty of the imaginary. Everyone wanted that dress, but it wasn't a dress at all—it was a bunch of plastic balls. "On my tour," she declared, "I'm going to be in my bubble dress on a piano made of bubbles, singing about love and art and the future. I should like to make one person believe in that moment, and it would be worth every salt of a No. 1 record." She dropped the accent for a moment now—the real girl, unartificed, was right underneath—and leaned in. "I can have hit records all day, but who fucking cares?" she explained. "A year from now, I could go away, and people might say, 'Gosh, what ever happened to that girl who never wore pants?' But how wonderfully memorable 30 years from now, when they say, 'Do you remember Gaga and her bubbles?' Because, for a minute, everybody in that room will forget every sad, painful thing in their lives, and they'll just live in my bubble world."

One year later, the transformation is complete: With six No. 1 hits in the last year, Lady Gaga, age 24, is the biggest pop star in the world. By definition, a pop star is manufactured—rock stars weren't, at least not until well into the seventies, and that may be part of why rock became pop—and in some ways she has benefited from a very traditional star-making model, one of the last purviews of corporate music labels. But success can have a thousand authors. Several different people have claimed credit for discovering Gaga, shaping her, naming her, making her who she is: Rob Fusari, who co-wrote and produced her early songs, sued her two weeks ago for $30 million, claiming among other grievances that he had a contract for 15 percent of her merchandising. And Gaga, of course, takes the credit herself. "I went through a great deal of creative and artistic revelation, learning, and marination to become who I am," she explains. "Tiny little lie? I wanted to become the artist I am today, and it took years."

All of them are partly right. But in another sense, she was an accident, a phenomenon that happened in New York in the first decade of a new century.

And what a happening. At a time when you wouldn't recognize the faces of the people who make most of the music we listen to (who are those guys in Vampire Weekend, again?), Gaga is visually iconic; in an age of Twitter, the remoteness she has cultivated since her first moment in the spotlight has made her an even bigger star. She completely turns the page on the last decade's era of bimbodom, taking back the limelight from women who made their careers by admitting that they had nothing to say, like Paris Hilton and Jessica Simpson. She also closes a strange era in female pop stardom, with rising talents unable to push through to superstardom (Katy Perry, Rihanna), *American Idol* contestants (Kelly Clarkson), older stars (Gwen, Fergie), tween stars (Miley and posse), and hugely popular musicians who aren't pop in their hearts, like Taylor Swift (country crossover) and Beyoncé (urban crossover). She's riveting in any language, with lyrics that compose their own Esperanto—she's effortlessly global.

Gaga's presence also introduces the formerly unthinkable idea that Madonna, another voracious Italian girl, may really, truly, finally be on her way out. Her new look is an appropriation of Madonna's circa "The Girlie Show" and "Blonde Ambition" (the darkened brows, the platinum-blonde hair, the red lips), and her music-video director, Jonas Åkerlund, is a major latter-day collaborator of Madonna's. But the two are very different: Madonna hasn't had a sense of humor about herself since the nineties, where Gaga is all fun and play. At her core, she's a young art-school student, full of optimism and kindness, childlike wonder at the bubble world. Though she may not be bisexual herself—of the many friends of hers interviewed for this article, not one of them recalls her ever having a girlfriend or being sexually interested in any woman offstage—her politics are inclusive, and she wants to promote images of as many sexual combinations as are possible on this Earth. Gaga says she's a girl who likes boys who look like girls, but she's also a girl who likes to look like a boy herself—or, rather, a drag queen, a boy pretending to be a girl. There's little that gives her more pleasure than the persistent rumor that she is a hermaphrodite, an Internet rumor based on scrutinizing a grainy video. That's not Madonna. Madonna wouldn't pretend she has a penis.

But that's the genius of Gaga: her willingness to be a mutant, a cartoon. She's got an awesome sense of humor, beaming tiny surreal moments across the world for our pleasure every day—like the gigantic bow made of hair she popped on her head last year. "One day, I said to my creative team, 'Gaultier did bows, let's do it in a new way,'" she says. "We were going back and forth with ideas, and then I said"—snaps finger—"hair-bow." She giggles. "We all fucking died, we *died*. It never cost a penny, and it looked so brilliant. It's just one of those things. I'm very arrogant about it." Her videos are global epiphenomena, like the Tarantino-flavored "Telephone," with its lesbian prison themes and Beyoncé guest appearance. "Gaga doesn't care so much about the technical part, but she's involved in every creative aspect," says Åkerlund. "We just allow ourselves to be very stupid with each other, and then you get ideas like sunglasses made of cigarettes."

Gaga also throws in our face something we've known all along but numbly decided to ignore: American celebrities have become very, very boring. (The fact that she has done this at the same time that much of the actual music she makes herself is somewhat boring is another feat.) One of her essential points is that celebrity should be the province of weirdos, like Grace Jones circa Jean-Paul Goude and her pet idol, eighties opera–meets–New Wave cult figure Klaus Nomi, who died of AIDS at 39. To Gaga, our video-game-playing, social-networking, cell-phone-obsessed culture has made all of us smaller, more normal, less interesting—and, except for odd lightning strikes like the *Jersey Shore* cast and Conan O'Brien's anointment of one Twitter fan—famous to no one, after all. "Kudos on MySpace? What is that?" she says, spitting out the words. "That's not emblematic about what I'm talking about. I'm talking about creating a genuine, memorable space for yourself in the world."

The story of Gaga is a story of being young in New York City. Stefani Germanotta grew up in a duplex on the Upper West Side, on one of the eclectic blocks between Columbus and Amsterdam in the West Seventies that are a mix of prewar brownstones, tenements, and modern condos. Her father ran a company that installed Wi-Fi in hotels, and her mother worked for a time as a V.P. at Verizon. They sent Gaga and her younger sister, Natali, 18, to Sacred Heart, a small Catholic girls' school up the street from the Guggenheim. "Sacred Heart may have been prestigious, but there were lots of different kinds of girls," says Gaga. "Some had extreme wealth, others were on welfare and scholarship, and some were in the middle, which was my family. All our money went into education and the house." Her classmates say that her family was tight-knit. "When John Kerry was running for president, Stefani supported him and her father didn't, so she joked about that," says Daniela Abatelli, Sacred Heart '05. Gaga was one of the only students with a job after school, as a waitress at a diner on the Upper West Side. With her early paychecks, she bought a Gucci purse. "I was so excited because all the girls at Sacred Heart always had their fancy purses, and I always had whatever," she says. "My mom and dad were not buying me a $600 purse."

Because her parents told her that they had sacrificed for her education, Gaga took school seriously from a young age. One of her favorite childhood memories is playing a piano concert at Sacred Heart at eight. "There was a line of twenty girls sitting in a row in our pretty dresses, and we each got up to play," she says happily. "I did a really good job. I was quite good." At 11, she began attending a full day of acting classes on Saturdays. "I remember the first time that I drank out of an imaginary coffee cup," she says, closing her eyes. "That's the very first thing they teach you. I can feel the rain, too, when it's not raining." Her lids pop open. "I don't know if this is too much for your magazine, but I can actually mentally give myself an orgasm." She hisses a little, like one of the deviant vampires in *True Blood*. "You know, sense memory is quite powerful."

By eighth grade, she had also realized that acting was a way to meet boys and began auditioning for plays with Sacred Heart's brother school, Regis High School, on 84th Street, near Park Avenue. She always landed the lead: Adelaide in *Guys and Dolls*, Philia in *A Funny Thing Happened on the Way to the Forum*. Jealous older girls stuck in the chorus began calling her "the Germ." "They always talked behind her back, like, 'Gross, she's the Germ! She's dirty!'" says a classmate. Gaga has often mentioned that she was an outcast in high school, but other than adolescent shenanigans like these, her friends from this pudding-like crowd do not share this recollection. "She was always popular," says Julia Lindenthal, Marymount '04. "I don't remember her experiencing any social problems or awkwardness."

At the time, she had a certain incipient Gaganess: She could be a little overdramatic, spoiled, brassy, but she was also a nice girl (not to say a good girl), recalled by many as kind and generous—a theater chick who was starting to express her own feelings through songwriting. A fan of Pink Floyd and the Beatles, she started a classic-rock cover band and began entering open-mike nights at the Songwriters Hall of Fame on the Upper West Side. She even cut a demo of her love ballads, and her parents gave out copies as favors at her large Sweet 16 party, at the Columbus Club. "Everyone was playing her demo, like, 'Whoa, she's going to be a star,'" says Justin Rodriguez, Regis '03. "She was by far the most talented person in high school, but she'd do so many random acts of kindness, like saying, 'Your singing has gotten so much better, you're working hard and I've noticed.' She wasn't a diva at all."

Like many private-school girls, by 15, Gaga had a fake Delaware I.D. purchased on MacDougal Street. She also started dating a 26-year-old Greek waiter from the restaurant. "That's part of why I needed a job after school, too," she says. "My dad wouldn't give me money to go out on the weekends because he knew I was going downtown and being bad." Soon, she had her first tattoo: a G clef on her lower back. ("Before I made my first big music video, I decided to turn that tattoo into a huge side piece," she says. "I just couldn't face the world with a tramp stamp.") She was still a good girl at school, even if she got in trouble with the teachers once in a while: not for short kilts but inappropriate shirts. "I was fifteen to twenty pounds heavier than I am now," says Gaga. "I would wear shirts that were low-cut, and the teachers would tell me I couldn't wear them, and I'd point to another girl who was wearing the same thing. 'Well, it looks different on her.' It wasn't fair." She shimmies her shoulders a bit. "At that time, my breasts were much bigger, and firm, and delicious." (Another high-school nickname: Big Boobs McGee.)

After the World Trade Center was attacked, Gaga cried for days and wore black, in mourning. "As she came down the aisle to get Communion at the special Mass for 9/11, her steps were in this serious cadence," says a friend. "She used to wear a lot of makeup, but she didn't have any on. I remember thinking, *Wow, she is so over-the-top.*" Gaga also had an odd habit of refusing to let cast members in plays call her by her real name backstage. "If you tried to say 'Hey, Stefani' to her, she'd put on the voice of her character, and say, 'No, I'm Ginger!'" says a friend. "It was so bizarre, because we were kids."

After high school, Gaga moved to an NYU dorm on 11th Street and enrolled in Tisch, but quickly felt that she was further along creatively than some of her classmates. "Once you learn how to think about art, you can teach yourself," she says. By the second semester of her sophomore year, she told her parents that she wasn't going back to school—she was going to be a rock star. Her father reportedly agreed to pay her rent for a year on the condition that she reenroll if she was unsuccessful. "I left my entire family, got the cheapest apartment I could find, and ate shit until somebody would listen," she says.

Gaga moved into an apartment on the Lower East Side, with a futon for a couch and a Yoko Ono record hung over her bed. In high school, she had blonde highlights and let her curls run wild, but now she dyed her hair black and began to straighten it. She started the Stefani Germanotta Band with some friends from NYU, recording an EP of her Fiona Apple–type ballads at a studio underneath a liquor store in New Jersey. "Stefani had a following of about fifteen to twenty people at each show," says the guitarist, Calvin Pia. Says her manager at the time, Frankie Fredericks, "We'd kick it, jam, get drunk. She said she wanted to have a record deal by the time she was 21."

It was a lofty goal. What was missing, almost entirely, was any idea of how to get there. Like Madonna, she had a powerful sexual charisma. But whereas Madonna had seemed to calculate every step, every coupling, every stylistic turn in her quest for stardom, Gaga's story is partly one of youthful drift, waiting for lightning to strike, for the brilliant accident to happen. Gaga, though, had something Madonna didn't have: a truly great voice.

Gaga's year off from school was set to end in March 2006—her father had set a cutoff date of her birthday. A week before, the Stefani Germanotta Band performed at the Cutting Room on the same bill as Wendy Starland, a young singer-songwriter in the mold of Peter Gabriel. Starland had been working on tracks with Rob Fusari, a 38-year-old producer in Parsippany, New Jersey, who was known for his success with R&B hits for Destiny's Child and Will Smith. He mentioned to Starland that he was interested in locating a female singer to front a band like the Strokes—she didn't have to be good-looking, or even a great singer, but she had to have something about her you couldn't take your eyes off. "Stefani's confidence filled the room," says Starland. "Her presence is enormous. And fearless. I listened for the pitch, the tone, and timbre of her voice. Was she able to have a huge dynamic range? Was she able to get soft and then belt? And I felt that she was able to do all that while giving out this very powerful energy."

Gaga erupted in giggles when Starland ran up to her after the performance and told her, "I'm about to change your life." They rushed outside the club together, and Starland called Fusari on her cell phone. "Rob said, 'Why are you waking me up?' I said I found the girl. 'What? It's really one in a million. What's her name?' Stefani Germanotta. 'Um, you gotta be kidding me. What does she look like?' Don't worry about that. 'Does she have any good songs?' No. 'How is her band?' Awful." Starland laughs. "I wasn't pitching a product. I was pitching the girl."

When Fusari first met Gaga, he didn't see the private-school thing and thought she looked like "a Guidette, totally *Jersey Shore*." Then she jumped on his piano. "She didn't have that kind of undersinging character voice of Julian Casablancas, so I dropped the Strokes thing right away," says Fusari. "I thought she was a female John Lennon, to be totally honest. She was the oddest talent." Gaga began taking the bus from Port Authority to meet him at his New Jersey studio at 10 a.m., writing grungy songs with Zeppelin or Nirvana riffs on the piano and singing her quirky Jefferson Airplane lyrics over them. "I'm a hippie at heart, and Rob and I got tattoos one day," she says. "I wanted a tattoo of a peace sign, in memory of John and Yoko. I love that they traveled the world and said 'Give peace a chance,' and when asked to elaborate, they replied, 'No, just give peace a chance.' They thought the simplicity of that phrasing would change the world. It's so beautiful."

The two of them worked on rock songs for four months, but the reaction among their colleagues was negative; they also tried the singer-songwriter route, like Michelle Branch or Avril Lavigne, but those didn't gel either. "With those kinds of records, people are looking at the source of that music, who it's coming from," says Starland. "Those artists are usually classically beautiful, very steady, and more tranquil, in a way." Stefani agreed that her name was not going to fly: Fusari liked to sing Queen's "Radio Ga Ga" when she arrived at the studio, and she says that she came up with Lady Gaga off that joke. (Success indeed has many authors: Fusari says that he made it up inadvertently in a text message; Starland says it was the product of brainstorming.)

Then, one day, Fusari read an article in the *New York Times* about folk-pop artist Nelly Furtado, whose career had stalled since her 2000 hit "I'm Like a Bird": Timbaland, the hot producer of the moment, had remade her as a slinky dance artist. "We weren't going to get past A&R with a female rock record, and dance is so much easier," says Fusari. Gaga freaked out—you don't believe in me, she told him—but, from that day onward, they started working with a drum machine. They also began an affair, which made their artistic collaboration tumultuous. When Fusari didn't like her hooks, she would get teary-eyed and rant about feeling worthless. But he was rough on her, too. Gaga wasn't into fashion at this point: She liked leggings and sweatshirts, maybe with a shoulder out. "A couple times, she came to the studio in sweatpants, and I said, 'Really, Stef?'" says Fusari. "'What if I had Clive Davis in here today? I should call the session right now. Prince doesn't pick up ice cream at the 7-Eleven looking like Chris Rock. You're an artist now. You can't turn this on and off.'"

The problem was that she didn't know how to turn it on: Though she wanted to be a star, she didn't have a clear idea of what a star was, or where the main currents in pop culture were flowing. It was at this point that she began her serious study. Gaga picked up a biography of Prince, started shopping at American Apparel, and became entranced by aughties New Age bible *The Secret*, according to friends. As a Catholic-school girl, she interpreted Fusari's remarks as a signal to cut her skirts shorter and make them tighter, until one day they totally disappeared: All that was left were undies, sometimes with tights underneath.

Starland was still part of the picture: She lived near Gaga's parents' house, and Gaga would come over, crunching Doritos on the couch while watching *Sex and the City*. But when she tried to formalize her role in Gaga's life with a lawyer, she ran aground. "I got a call from my lawyer, who said that Stefani was going to give me a very generous Christmas gift," she says. One evening, she went over to the Germanottas' duplex, where Gaga's family, including her sister and grandmother, were celebrating, alongside a new little dog that Gaga liked to put booties on for fun. In the living room, Gaga presented her with an enormous Chanel box, revealing a black quilted purse with a gold chain. This might be a *Mean Girls* moment, where Gaga sticks it to an early collaborator, but in her naïve way, Gaga thought she was giving Starland something of great worth: the kind of purse she wanted so badly when she was young.

Bursting with confidence, Gaga was ready to be transformed. The dance-music scene that she'd fallen into turned out to be a perfect fit for her highly sexualized Catholic-school energy—she was a performer, rather than purely a singer. But the business into which she was launching herself was more difficult than ever. There are only four major labels these days; EMI is teetering on the edge, and if it misses its debt payments in June, Citigroup will own a record label. By 2006, labels were asking artists for a "360 deal": Instead of financing an artist's recording and then owning the masters, they wanted to share in the rights that traditionally belonged to the artist, like merchandise, live revenue, and endorsement fees. They were wary of any artist without a proven Internet following—the bet was on MySpace stars like Paramore or Panic at the Disco!—and there was Gaga, trying to go through the front door.

But she had a good track. "Beautiful, Dirty, Rich," a song about her friends from NYU asking their dads for money, drew prospective managers to a showcase downtown—everyone had to see her live because otherwise they didn't get it. She was also invited to Island Def Jam, near Times Square. L. A. Reid walked into the room while she was playing piano and started drumming to the beat on a table. "L.A. told me I was a star," says Gaga. She signed a deal with Island Def Jam for $850,000, according to a member of her camp, but after she produced the tracks, the line went dead. Three dinners were scheduled with Reid, but he canceled on each. Finally, Gaga got a call from her A&R rep at Island Def Jam: He had played a track in a meeting, and after a couple minutes Reid made a slitting motion across his throat. (Island Def Jam did not respond to requests for comment.) She was off the label.

Gaga was devastated. "She couldn't even talk when she told me because she was crying so hard," says Fusari. Unlike most struggling musicians, she chose to decline part of her advance so that she could walk with her masters (two of her six hits are on this original record). This was the first moment Gaga had experienced real hardship—the first moment in her life she really thought she might fail. "I went back to my apartment on the Lower East Side, and I was so depressed," she says. "That's when I started the real devotion to my music and art."

In contrast to Madonna, who gravitated to the forward edge of downtown and took herself with the utmost seriousness, Gaga, following her own instinct, headed toward a scene that was inclusive and fun but not particularly hip. In 2007, hipsters were listening to creative folk-rock bands out of Brooklyn like Grizzly Bear and Animal Collective; Gaga went for hard rock and downtown art trash. She fell desperately in love with Luc Carl, a 29-year-old drummer and manager of the rock bar St. Jerome's on Rivington Street. That's where she met Lady Starlight, an L.E.S. fixture in her thirties—M·A·C makeup artist, D.J., performance artist—who still plays shows for $60 but has a vast knowledge of rock music and style history. Starlight had gone through many incarnations, from mod meets *Cabaret* to Angela Bowie to leather-studded member of Judas Priest, which is what she was rocking at that moment.

"Starlight and I bonded instantly over her love of heavy metal and my love of boys that listen to heavy metal," says Gaga. "In those days, I'd wake up at noon in my apartment with my boyfriend and his loud Nikki Sixx hair, jeans on the floor, his stinky sneakers. He'd have his T-shirt on, no boxers. Then he would go do the books at St. Jerome's. I'd spin vinyl of David Bowie and New York Dolls in my kitchen, then write music with Lady Starlight. Eventually, I'd hear a honk outside my window: his old green Camino with a black hood. I'd run down the stairs yelling, 'Baby, baby, rev the engine,' and we'd drive over the Brooklyn Bridge, dress up, meet friends, play more music."

She leans forward. "The Lower East Side has an arrogance, a stench. We walk and talk and live and breathe who we are with such an incredible stench that eventually the stench becomes a reality. Our vanity is a positive thing. It's made me the woman I am today."

Gaga started performing her songs with Starlight at small venues, and go-go dancing under a red lightbulb at Pianos—she'd wear a bikini and Luc Carl's fingerless black gloves, too big for her small hands. Dancing, diet pills, and one real meal a day was the way she finally lost weight, according to a friend. "I was naked on a bar with money hanging out of my tits and ass," she says. (Gaga has been very open about having taken cocaine during this period, but none of her friends from this time recalls any drug use; they say that she told them she only used cocaine when she was alone.) She and Starlight began opening for the glam-rockers Semi Precious Weapons; they looked like hair-metal groupies, running around the stage spraying Aqua Net on fire. "Gaga and I used to go shopping together, too," says Justin Tranter, lead singer of SPW. "Any sex store where 99 percent of the store was made up of DVDs and sex toys and 1 percent was actual clothing was our favorite place to shop. Her mom came to my loft once to pick up one Lucite pump that she left at the show the night before."

Gaga was enjoying herself, and, as usual, she spread her positive energy around. "She tried to make everyone feel good," says Brendan Sullivan, a.k.a. DJ VH1, who worked with her on some early shows. "I'd go to her apartment with my unpublished novel, and she would tell me that I was the most brilliant writer of my generation, the poet laureate of the Lower East Side. No one else was doing that for me." She wasn't talking much to Fusari—the romance was over—but he caught a show with Starlight and was appalled. "It was *Rocky Horror* meets eighties band, and I didn't get it at all," he says. "I told Stefani that I could get her another D.J., but she was like, 'I'm good.'"

But Fusari inserted himself back into the picture, in the spring of 2007, when he heard that his friend Vincent Herbert, a "hustler with a capital *H*," had landed a deal with Interscope to sign new artists.

Within a couple days, Herbert had them on a plane to Los Angeles to meet Jimmy Iovine, the head of Interscope. Gaga came to the meeting in short shorts, go-go boots, and a cutoff T-shirt, but Iovine didn't show up; they flew back to New York, then were summoned back two weeks later. Iovine, an executive from Brooklyn who made his name on gangster rap with Dr. Dre and later rode the wave of nineties soft metal, is known for his good ears, and after listening to a few tracks in his office, he stood up and said, "Let's try this."

Gaga was worried that the label didn't think she was pretty enough to be a performer—she was recording tracks with RedOne, a Moroccan-Swedish producer, but they set her up as a songwriter for the Pussycat Dolls and Britney Spears (Spears was running around Los Angeles with a shaved head, so this wasn't a plum assignment). Herbert even spent his own money to send her to Lollapalooza over the summer, and he started to think that her look was wrong—someone in the audience shouted out "Amy Winehouse," and that made him nervous. "I told her that she needed to dye her hair blonde, and she did it right away," says Herbert. "God bless that girl, she really does listen."

On vacation in the Cayman Islands with Luc Carl, Gaga picked a fight, and he told her that he wasn't sure she was going to make it. "One day, you're not going to go into a deli without hearing me," she spat back. Back in New York, she sat down at a table at Beauty Bar with Sullivan, despondent. "I'm getting a nose job," she said. "I'm going to get a new nose, and I'm moving to L.A., and I'm going to be huge." He pleaded with her to be reasonable; like a true city kid, Gaga doesn't even know how to drive. "Whatever," she said. "I have the money. I just want to start fresh."

Sullivan told her about Warhol's *Before and After I* painting of two noses, before and after rhinoplasty, with a word that looks like RAPED at the top. She went up to the Met one afternoon and stood in front of it. She bought books about Warhol, which helped her make sense of her journey while providing a new vocabulary to talk about her creations. "Andy's books became her bible," says Darian Darling, a friend. "She would highlight them with a pen."

For Warhol, stardom was its own art form, empty imagistic vividness one of the most important forces. The person behind the mask could be as seemingly sweet and ordinary as Stefani Germanotta—and still be huge. Before Warhol, however unusual, she'd been in the general category of rock chick. He freed her to invent herself, like so many before her, expand herself, make herself a spectacle. While writing a club song called "Just Dance" with RedOne, Gaga tried to broaden her surface, remaking her style as a blonde space-age queen, a fabulous chick from the Factory era. The music was global-dance-party music—faster beats, synth sounds, with an ethos that made sense to her hippie heart. "Gaga and I believe that the world needs this music, that it is a way to unite," says RedOne. It wasn't the kind of music America was listening to at the moment, but she could be broken overseas and America might follow.

Suddenly, the clouds parted. One of Interscope's big artists, Akon, an R&B singer from Senegal with a massive global following, heard the track and lost his mind about it. Iovine pushed the button. She started working seriously with a choreographer: "I heard that this was the new Madonna, so I was like, 'Okay, let's hit it, pumpkin,'" says Laurie Ann Gibson. She recorded at the home studio of Kierszenbaum, the company's A&R head, as well. "I liked that she was talking about Prince's arrangements, styling, and presentation," he says. "Interest in Prince ebbs and flows, and two years ago, it was very, very maverick. Artists were saying 'Here's my record and album cover,' not talking about putting screens on the stage." She began wearing her crazy disco outfits everywhere. "She was never out of uniform, if you will," says Kierszenbaum. She also took a personal plunge: The day that she shot the video for "Just Dance" was the same day that she finally left Carl. Her heart may have been broken, but this was her new life. (Friends say that she has not been in love since, and the ritualistic killing of male lovers in her last three videos is related to this breakup.)

The newly liberated Gaga didn't feel like she needed to express her sexuality in a typically feminine way, either, and she became obsessed with androgyny, with the look of Liza Minnelli. She loved the free expression of drag queens—she wanted to wear the same clothes as those guys, cover herself with glitter, wear a wig. Though she wasn't from gay club culture, management began sending her to small clubs around the country. She even performed at a party at the Madison nightclub in the West Twenties hosted by Kenny Kenny, for $150. "When I went backstage to say hello, she said, 'Don't look at me! I don't have my makeup on yet.'" He laughs. "I was like, 'Uh, okay.' I've seen Amanda Lepore without her makeup."

Now, Gaga thought of herself not only as a superstar—she channeled Andy himself. She adopted his round black glasses and his wigs and spouted his wisdom. "It's as if I've been shouting at everyone, and now I'm whispering and everybody's leaning in to hear me," she says. "I've had to shout for so long because I was only given five minutes, but now I've got fifteen. Andy said you only needed fifteen minutes." She even started her own Factory, or the "Haus of Gaga," as she likes to call her entourage. There's Åkerlund; Gibson; her manager, Troy Carter; and the core team of stylist Nicola Formichetti and her primary collaborator Matt Williams, an art-school graduate whom she calls "Dada" (they have dated on and off during the past couple years). In May 2009, after she released "Paparazzi," a seven-minute video—thrown off the top of her mansion by her boyfriend, she's reborn as the robot from Fritz Lang's *Metropolis*—she became the haute-fashion world's pet. "Gaga had some archival pieces from Thierry Mugler, but after 'Paparazzi,' everything changed," says a former member of the Haus. "It happened in the blink of an eye. Suddenly, every fashion designer in the world was e-mailing her images."

Like Warhol at the Factory, when Gaga likes someone, he works; when she's done with him creatively, the door is closed. When Fusari sued her for $30 million in mid-March, over recording and merchandise fees, she immediately responded through her lawyers, saying that he acted as an unlicensed employment agent in his introduction to Herbert. "I developed an artist to grow with that artist," says Fusari, his voice pained. She's changed her cell number, and most of her old friends can't reach her anymore. "You know, she used to send texts out in New York inviting everyone on the Lower East Side to her shows, and not too many people would come," says Sullivan. "And after the vocal coach, dieting, exercising, and all the rest, now everyone wants to go. She has gotten annoyed by that: 'Why didn't they come before?'" He pauses. "You know, once she blew up, and everyone wanted a piece of her, we stopped calling her Gaga. We started calling her Stef again."

This summer, Gaga will come to the United States with her arena tour, one of the only pop stars who can fill a venue that large today. She spent a lot to get here—her tour has been losing about $3 million, according to music-industry sources, because she refuses to compromise on any aspect of the stage show. "I spent my entire publishing advance on my first tour," she told me. "I've had grand pianos that are more expensive than, like, a year's worth of rent." But profits are on their way soon. "Gaga's camp knows the exact date this summer that she will turn it around and get way into the black," says a source. With her 360 deal, Lady Gaga doesn't own as much of Lady Gaga as one would think. Essentially, this is a joint venture among Iovine, Universal Music CEO Doug Morris, and Sony/ATV publishing head Marty Bandier. It's a good formula for the business: Hot looks and hot singles are the new monster albums.

These days, Gaga doesn't talk about Warhol much anymore—she's fully inhabiting the role she created. "She wants to be crazy, to make statements, make art, channel the past, experiment with performance art, try everything," says David LaChapelle, a collaborator and friend. "In Paris, she took four hours out of four days to visit museums.

That's just not done by a pop star at the beginning of a career—not when you're in the bubble, when it's all about you." She's still overly dramatic—talking about monsters, or archly trying to presage her fall by covering herself in blood and hanging from a noose at the VMAs. "I feel that if I can show my demise artistically to the public, I can somehow cure my own legend," she explained recently. She turns down most interview requests, uninterested in combating misperceptions about her work. "Andy said that the critics were right," she says, with a shrug.

It's an unlikely rise, and an unlikely name, and a totally unreal image. But what's reality? "I believe that everyone can do what I'm doing," says Gaga, spreading her arms wide. "Everyone can access the parts of themselves that are great. I'm just a girl from New York City who decided to do this, after all. Rule the world! What's life worth living if you don't rule it?"

The Mothership, lost in space

Chris Richards

This is a story about a UFO.

Not just any UFO. The Mothership.

It might be the most awe-inspiring stage prop in the history of American music and it belonged to funk legends Parliament-Funkadelic. Since the Mothership vanished in Prince George's County in 1982, rumors of its whereabouts have mutated into local lore: It burned in a fire. It was disassembled. It was stolen. Scrapped. Kidnapped. Thrown in the woods. Chained to a truck by a drug dealer and dragged to funk-knows-where. The band's most devoted followers say it flew off into space.

This is a story about trying to find it.

In concert, the Mothership was last spotted in Detroit in 1981, belching dry ice fumes and flashing kaleidoscopic light. An aluminum flying saucer, it was about 20 feet in diameter and decked out with dazzling lights. Below it stood a band of otherworldly eccentrics celebrating the hard-won freedoms of the civil rights movement in a freaky, fantastical display.

Darryll Brooks remembers the last time he saw the Mothership. It wasn't in Detroit. It was in a junkyard in Seat Pleasant. Brooks last saw it there because Brooks is the guy who threw the Mothership away.

It was the spring of 1982 and Parliament-Funkadelic frontman George Clinton and his bandmates were battling debt, drug addiction and each other. Brooks, who ran the group's Washington-based tour production company, says the only way he could pay the band's debts was to pawn its gear. With no place to store a spacecraft, he dumped the Mothership in a junkyard behind a Shell station on Martin Luther King Jr. Highway. But 28 years later, its final resting place remains a mystery.

Here's where it isn't: In that Seat Pleasant junkyard.

Here's where it *might* be: Sleeping peacefully beneath a quilt of P.G. County kudzu.

Ask Seat Pleasant residents about a missing UFO and you'll get puzzled looks and a few laughs. Tromp through the neighboring woods and you'll cut your hands on the thorny bramble. You'll also find abandoned tires, mattresses, vacuum cleaners—but no spaceships.

Parliament-Funkadelic guitarist Garry Shider resides in Upper Marlboro, not too far from where the ship disappeared. Maybe he knows where to find it.

"Aw man," Shider says. "You ain't gonna find the Mothership."

ENDLESSLY IMITATED

Throughout the '70s, Clinton and his bandmates blurred the line between escapism and empowerment with a glut of albums that have been endlessly sampled, imitated and analyzed. Look at the decades of funk, rock, techno, go-go, Prince hits and jam bands that came in P-Funk's imaginative wake—"influential" doesn't quite cut it. Without Parliament-Funkadelic, Lady Gaga would not wear ridiculous outfits and hip-hop might not exist.

Onstage, the band was a living, breathing, panting comic book—Clinton in his stringy blond wigs, bassist Bootsy Collins in his star-shaped shades, Shider in nothing but angel wings, combat boots and Pampers. It was expressive, subversive, brilliant.

"They were celebrating the intellectual breadth of the black experience and giving people a grand space to celebrate all that they had become," says California author and funk historian Rickey Vincent. "Sly Stone said, 'I Want to Take You Higher.' George Clinton said, 'Yeah, and I got the Mothership to take you there.' In a sense, he was doing what black folks had wanted to do for generations: Take themselves up."

Clinton, his 68-year-old voice rasping over the phone from Los Angeles, agrees: "We were higher than anyone else!"

Before the Mothership was built, it was a concept. Parliament released *Mothership Connection* in 1975, an album with a title track about hitchhiking to cosmic transcendence: "Swing down, sweet chariot. Stop and let me ride." Clinton started dreaming up a tour to match. After watching The Who's 1969 rock opera *Tommy*, he asked himself: "How do you do a *funk* opera? What about [black people] in space?"

He called upon David Bowie's tour producer, Jules Fisher, to help bring the Mothership to life. "This was theater. This was drama," says Fisher, a renowned Broadway lighting designer. "Current shows like U2 and the Stones—they don't provide this narrative arc."

The Mothership was assembled in Manhattan and made its first descent in New Orleans from the rafters of Municipal Auditorium on Oct. 27, 1976.

Minds were blown.

"That first night was really huge for us," Clinton says. "But we made one mistake." The band unveiled the Mothership at the beginning of the show—an impossible stunt to follow. The next night, in Baton Rouge, the ship didn't land until much later in the set.

Keyboardist Bernie Worrell remembers being unable to look away. "It was phenomenal, man. You couldn't describe it," he says. "I can play and not look at the keys. I watched it every time it would come down."

WHOLE DIFFERENT LOVE

Washingtonians greeted the Mothership with unparalleled fervor. The nation's capital had long been a stronghold for the band and in

1975, Parliament released the *Chocolate City* album, a supremely funky mash note that popularized the nickname Washington had earned for its majority-black population.

When radio personality Donnie Simpson first moved to the area, he saw P-Funk stoking a unique dialogue with the community. "As hot as I thought they were in Detroit, when I came here, it was a whole different love," he says. "A whole different appreciation for the funk."

Washington is also where Clinton first hired promoters Brooks and Carol Kirkendall for a 1977 gig at Landover's Capital Centre. "Once we started playing there, it was all over," Clinton says.

Brooks had never seen anything like it. "Here's a guy coming out of a Mothership with a mink coat and platform shoes," he says. "*And* a cane? And a fur hat? C'mon, man. Black folks been down so long. . . . It was jubilation."

Soon, Brooks and Kirkendall's company, Tiger Flower, was producing and promoting nearly all of the band's domestic tour dates. Some of the wildest shows transpired close to home. At a Capital Centre gig on April 25, 1981, Clinton stepped out of the Mothership, tossed his gold-lamé cape over his shoulder and strutted across the stage. Naked. (You won't find it on YouTube, but there's a VHS tape out there to prove it.)

"The audience went *crazy*," Brooks says. "Carol and I looked at each other like, 'We're in so much trouble. Our career is over.' But nobody said a word. I guess the officials didn't see it. The unions didn't see it. But the audience saw it."

It was also the last time a Chocolate City audience would see the Mothership in all its glory.

RAN OUT OF JUICE

Going down with the ship? In the case of Parliament-Funkadelic, the ship went down with the band.

"The volatility of the record industry at that time—the disco crash, they called it—made it really hard to subsidize that big touring group," says funk historian Vincent of the band's early-'80s collapse. "They ran out of juice and they ran out of money."

The band would later reform as the P-Funk All-Stars, and a second, less impressive Mothership would be built in the '90s, but the group never eclipsed the highs of the late '70s. Worrell rattles off the factors that dragged Parliament-Funkadelic down: "Discontent. Tired of all the unfairness. Being owed money. Lack of respect within the group. The management. Learning that money was stolen."

After the Detroit show in '81, Brooks and Kirkendall had the band's equipment trucked back to Washington for storage. Months passed. The group remained dormant and cash evaporated. Unable to pay the rent on his storage spaces, Brooks began peddling the unused gear to local go-go bands. Some of Worrell's keyboards were sold to a young Trouble Funk, cementing P-Funk's role in go-go's creation myth.

Worrell, meantime, had no idea that his fantastic machines were being snatched up by Washington's then-fledgling go-go players. "But I know that a lot of stuff I was looking for, I didn't have," he says.

Too bad go-go didn't need a spaceship.

"We had to find places to put stuff, including the Mothership," Brooks says. So he stashed it in his mom's two-car garage in Clinton, Md., for about six months—"long enough to make my mother [ticked off]."

On a cold, clear spring afternoon in 1982, she finally demanded that her son remove this piece of junk. Brooks and Bernie Walden, a young Tiger Flower employee, dragged the Mothership out of the garage, crammed it into a U-Haul truck and drove it to a tree-lined junkyard in Seat Pleasant. "We backed the truck as far as we could out into the woods and kicked it off the truck," Brooks says. "We had a bottle of something and gave it a toast."

"It was heavy," Walden says. "And I didn't want to do it."

Brooks says he regrets the decision, too, but was unable to reach Clinton or the band at that time. "Nobody was keeping phone numbers," Brooks says. "Some of them were living with *their* mamas."

Today, the group's feelings are mixed. "I thought that was pretty stupid," Clinton says of the decision to dump it. Shider disagrees, citing the massive expenses that racked up from touring with an extensive entourage, elaborate costumes, and a gigantic metal spacecraft.

"I was glad it was gone," he says. "With the Mothership came no money."

HUNTING A UFO

Today, the Shell in Seat Pleasant is a Lowest Price gas station. On a sunny weekday afternoon, the junkyard out back is busy with middle-age men poking around for old engine parts. Three guys are trying to revive a Ford sedan that wants to stay dead. Two others are searching for scrap metal they can sell in Baltimore. No one has seen any UFOs.

But they do recommend speaking with Charlie Walker, the gas station's former owner. Walker practically shouts into his telephone when he says he's never heard of Parliament-Funkadelic. But he vaguely remembers "something big and aluminum" catching on fire in the junkyard in the mid-'80s.

So the Mothership went up in flames?

"No, no, no, no, no," says Thomas Stanley, an assistant professor at George Mason University. "It didn't burn. It exists. It exists to this day."

Stanley is a true funk scholar. Along with his friends Larry Alexander and the late television writer and former *Washington Post* reporter David Mills, he wrote the book *George Clinton and P-Funk: An Oral History.* He also penned articles for *Uncut Funk*, Mills's Parliament-Funkadelic fanzine.

Stanley claims that he's recently seen the wreckage of the Mothership—*touched* it. But he doesn't want to give up the location. His reverence for this music borders on religion, but he has no interest

in sending a salvaged Mothership to the Rock and Roll Hall of Fame—
or even the Air and Space Museum.

After a cryptic conversation about how the Mothership escaped
its fate in the junkyard, Stanley e-mails some clues about its alleged
location. He also includes a plea to let it rest.

"I find it much more satisfying to imagine this sacred artifact
bound firmly in the bosom of the strong black communities that
straddle the D.C. line between Suitland and Seat Pleasant. This was
always the heart of P-Funk's base of support in Chocolate City," he
writes. "It is very important, I think, that we not seek truth at the expense of myth. Music and Myth are, after all, P-Funk's most enduring
legacy."

So is it really out there? Does it really matter? Perhaps there's no
grand cosmic truth to be found in the wilds of Prince George's County.
Just myth.

On a chilly Friday at dawn, the only thing that seems real in these
woods are the vines that strangle your ankles with every step. Swiffer
broomstick in hand, you can thwack away at the bushes for hours
without hearing a . . .

CLANG!!

The Mothership?

No. Chrome toilet bowl. Another false alarm. Definitely the funki-
est. Culverts, rusted air-conditioning units and forsaken grocery carts
make similar sounds.

But Stanley swears the Mothership is still out here with the trees
and the trash. Beneath an impenetrable blanket of weeds and dirt it
sleeps, undisturbed for nearly three decades and miraculously unde-
stroyed—rusted, rotted out and funkier than ever.

POSTSCRIPT

After reading this story about the disappearance of the original
Parliament-Funkadelic Mothership, many went searching for it, including the Smithsonian Institution. (They didn't find it either.)

However, in May of 2011, the Smithsonian announced that it had acquired a Mothership replica built for George Clinton in the 1990s. The 1,200-pound stage prop will help anchor a permanent music exhibition at the National Museum of African American History and Culture when the museum opens in 2015.

Excerpt from
How to Wreck a Nice Beach: The Vocoder from World War II to Hip-Hop
Dave Tompkins

In one word, militarism was funk.

—H. G. Wells

AXIS OF EAVESDROPPERS

I have been bugged all my life.
—Vyacheslav "Iron Arse" Molotov,
Soviet Minister of Foreign Affairs, 1955

We are clear.

It's quiet inside the Black National Theater, just above 125th Street in Harlem. Afrika Bambaataa is sitting on a defeated couch, flipping through a brochure published by the National Security Agency. He wears black sweats and fluorescent green running shoes, and there's a trainer's towel around his neck. The Thunderdome spikes, leather cape, and Martian sun dimmers have been left at home. He seems to be giving his myth the day off, looking more like a gym coach with allergies than the retired gang warlord who once borrowed his mom's records, stuck a speaker in the window and blew out the neighborhood.

Our conversation arrived at the NSA through the normal discursive channels: an old record Bam made that doesn't exist, an admiration for a British vampire soap opera, a childhood memory of sneaking to the front row to watch Sly Stone "make his instruments talk." Yet when discussing the NSA, he drops his voice into a cautious strep basso. If anything can modulate the way we speak, it's the notion of some federal protuberance listening in.

The brochure in his hands is pink and its title is not for the sore of throat. *The Start of the Digital Revolution: SIGSALY Secure Digital Voice Communications in World War II.* Bambaataa grunts and jots this down on a borrowed scrap of paper. On the cover is a dual turntable console photographed behind a nameless door in the basement of the Pentagon. Surrounding the turntables are banks of winking electronics, as if the walls are putting us on, spoofing a future that's one set of pointy ears from campy. Taken in 1944, the photo, along with the future, would not be declassified until 1976. Bambaataa is curious, having spent 1976 DJing some of the better parties in New York. By 1981, he was making people dance to German records that spoke Japanese in voices programmed by Texas Instruments.

The Pentagon turntables are now sitting at the bottom of the Chesapeake Bay. These machines were designed by Bell Labs but created by funk, back when funk meant fear, German transmitters and codebreakers under headphones. The turntables played 16-inch records of thermal noise in reverse, a randomized shush, backwards masked inside out.

Produced by the Muzak Corporation, the vinyl was deployed for the army's "Secret Telephony" voice security system, a technology that was treated with the same crypto fuss as the Manhattan Project. Installed across the globe from 1943 to 1945, these fifty-five-ton phone scramblers would be used for D-Day, the Allied invasion of Germany, the bombing of Hiroshima, and the "dismemberment of the surrender instrument"—allowing Roosevelt, Truman, Churchill and Eisenhower to discuss the world's fate with voices they barely recognized, voices not human but polite artificial replicas of speech rendered from digital pulses 20 milliseconds in length.

The wall of knobs assigned this task was the vocoder, a massive walk-in closet of cryptology invented by Bell Labs in 1928. The vocoder divided the voice into its constituent frequencies, spread across ten channels, and transmitted them through band pass filters. At the receiving end, this information would be synthesized into an electronic impression of human speech: a machine's idea of the voice as imagined by phonetic engineers. Not speech, they qualified, but a "spectral description of it."

The vocoder was sensitive, high maintenance and seven feet tall, an overheated room full of capacitors, vacuum tubes and transformers. Some engineers dubbed this system "the Green Hornet." Others called it "Special Customer." Bell Labs referred to it as Project X-61753, or "X-Ray," as if it was ordered from the back of a comic book with a pair of rubber Mad Doctor Hands. The U.S. Signal Corps called it SIGSALY, taken from children's "nonsense syllables" and used for strategizing Allied bombing campaigns. The *New York Times*, not knowing what to call it, went with "Machine that Tears Speech to Pieces," and then later, like most everybody else, decided on "the robot."

To a DJ like Bambaataa, the vocoder is "deep crazy supernatural bugged-out funk stuff," perhaps the only crypto-technology to serve the Pentagon and the roller rink. What guarded Winston Churchill's phone against Teutonic math nerds would one day become the perky teabot that chimed in on Michael Jackson's "P.Y.T." During World War II, the vocoder reduced the voice to something cold and tactical, tinny and dry like soup cans in a sandbox, dehumanizing the larynx, so to speak, for some of man's more dehumanizing moments: Hiroshima, the Cuban Missile Crisis, Soviet gulags, Vietnam. Churchill had it, FDR refused it, Hitler needed it. Kennedy was frustrated by the vocoder. Mamie Eisenhower used it to tell her husband to come home. Nixon had one in his limo. Reagan, on his plane. Stalin, on his disintegrating mind.

The Seventies would finally catch the vocoder in its double life: secret masking agent for the military and studio tool for the musician. The machine that subtracted the character from the voices of Army echelons would ultimately generate characters in itself—the one-man chorus of be all you can be. Never mind the robots: what's more human than wanting to be *something else, altogether*? Ever since the first bored kid threw his voice into an electric fan, toked on a birthday balloon, or thanked his mother in a pronounced burp, voice mutation has provided an infinite source of kicks. In 1971, that first kick was delivered to the ribs of anyone who saw Stanley Kubrick's *A Clockwork Orange*. In its big-screen debut, the vocoder sang Beethoven's Ninth to Dresden firebombings while rehabilitating a murderer who wore eyeballs for cufflinks. It was quite an association.

Soon the vocoder began showing up on records, reciting Edgar Allan Poe, and making sheep bleats. If a string section could be replaced by the synthesizer, then why not the voice? The vocoder thanked you very much in Japanese. It allowed Bee Gees to be Beatles. It just called to say it loved you. It allowed people to give themselves names like Zeus B. Held, Gay Cat Park and Ramsey 2C-3D. It could sound like an articulate bag of dead leaves. A croak, a last willed gasp. A sink clog trying to find the words. Or the InSinkErator itself, with its wiggly, butterknife smile. In Neil Young's case, it was a father trying to empathize with his son who suffered from cerebral palsy. Or it could've just been a bad idea—as I've been told, *something that punished the atmosphere.*

Shadowing the World War II model, the vocoder would have its own Axis powers: Kraftwerk (Germany), Giorgio Moroder and Italo-Disco (Italy), and Bambaataa's Roland SVC-350 Vocoder (Made in Japan). In 1976, when SIGSALY was sufficiently dated to be declassified and allowed in public, the vocoder was already well out in the open, nodding along in Kraftwerk's daydream stretch of imagination

called "Autobahn." Before the Age of Scratching Records with Bas-
ketballs, Bambaataa and his Zulu Nation DJs would use more gathered
German intelligence (Kraftwerk's "Trans-Europe Express") to make
people dance, buy synthesizers, steal ideas, make more records, and
dress like the Count of Monte Cristo. Countless electro and disco
12-inch singles owe their dance floors to the Machine that Tore
Speech to Pieces. In the early Eighties, a romance better remembered
than relived, the vocoder was the main machine of electro hip-hop,
the black voice removed from itself, dispossessed by Reaganomics,
recession, and urban renewal, and escaping to outer space, where
there was more room to do the Webbo, where the weight was taken
but the odds of being heard were no less favorable.

As the vocoder disbanded and digitized conversations in Washington, commercially available models were all over the radio, rapping
ills and blight while generating the cosmically Keytarded fantasies
needed to cope with it all. The vocoder would be used in songs about
safety, Raisin Bran, taxes, and black holes. Pods and poverty. A dance
called "the Toilet Bowl." Christmas in Miami and deep throats in Dallas.
Nuclear war, biters in the city, and the Muslim soul. Saving the children
and freaking the freaks. The ups and downs of robot relations.

The alienation of the African-American experience.

Though the military had originally wanted the vocoder to sound
human, the Germans didn't (calling it a "retro-transformer" as early
as 1951) and somehow Afrika Bambaataa ended up with the keys to
the robot. He calls the vocoder "that Joker." "I couldn't wait to get on
that Joker," he says. "We used to bring it to parties and funk 'em up
with it. Stop the turntables and I talk on that Joker. People were hearing the robot voice from the records, but the records weren't playing.
They didn't know what was going on."

A man who wanted to use the vocoder to destroy all Pac-Man
machines once said to me, "People gotta like what's going on even if
they don't know what's going on." And they did and they didn't.

Of all the World War II cryptology experts I interviewed, none
was aware of the vocoder's activities in the clubs, rinks and parks of

New York City. ("It was just analyzing breakdowns of speech energy," said the Pentagon.) Of all the hip-hop civilians I interviewed, none was aware of the vocoder's service in any war, nor were they surprised by it.

And none were aware that vocoder technology now inhabits our cell phones as a microscopic speck of silicone, allowing our laryngeal clones to sound more human, condensing the signal for more bandwidth at the expense of intelligibility in a shrinking world. The vocoder was originally invented for speech compression, to reduce bandwidth costs on undersea phone cables—the ultimate long-distance package. Now compression is back. The voices from the tower are not our own, but digital simulacra, imperfect to be real. Conversations are minutes gobbled, and songs are ringtones chirping a T-Pain hook. Auto-Tune, the pitch-correcting software popularized by the robotox of Cher and inflicted on the twenty-first century, is often misheard as a vocoder, giving the latter currency through a revival of misunderstanding. Not as a technology, but a meme. In other words, it was what it isn't.

When I mentioned this to Bambaataa, he nodded and said, "Yeahhh."

If conspiracy is your baggage, this is not unlike the way he says "Yeahhh" at the beginning of "Planet Rock," a song he recorded with the Soulsonic Force in 1982, the same year *Time* magazine replaced its Man of the Year with a computer. Stocking dance floors for the past twenty-eight years, "Planet Rock" is the first hip-hop song to say "shucks," vacuuming the sibilance, universally recognized as the white noise of secrecy. Over at Bell Labs, "shh" is called unvoiced fricatives, or "unvoiced hiss energy," pulmonary turbulence modulated by tongue, teeth and lips.

"That's bugged," says Bam, who often speaks in terms of sound effects, as if waiting for the right word to show up. It may be a while, so "bugged" will do. Though much of Bam's memory belongs to a record collection that defies mini-storage, you can always count on "bugged," a hip-hop jargonaut that has survived for over two decades, its etymology based on the act of going out of one's head through one's eyes while attended by invisible (and apparently very busy) insects under one's skin. When eyes "bug out" from their sockets, doctors call it globe luxation. Despite its provenance in pre-Industrial sanitariums, bugging out frequented military argot during the Korean War, referring to U.S. soldiers in a state of bullet-hastened egress. (Retreat was less a matter of going crazy than coming to one's senses.) Yet losing one's mind never goes out of style, and hip-hop, ever reinventing the tongue, would replace "mad" with "bugged," converting the former into a quantitative adverb, as if rightfully assuming everyone is insane.

So crazy became bugged, the bugged picked up the vocoder, rappers went under surveillance, and we listened very carefully, under headphones.

Bam continues chuckling through the NSA brochure, the towel now over his head. He hits a circuit diagram and doubles back to the Pentagon, the glowing basement and the turntables. The room looks busy yet unoccupied. He wonders where they stuck that joker. Perhaps somewhere near the world's most accurate clock. Or next to the Sumo air conditioner that kept the entire system from melting down. Or maybe behind the oven that stabilized the crystals that kept the turntables in synch 10,000 miles apart. Those capacitors have some explaining to do.

By 1943, there were two turntables and a vocoder in the Pentagon and a duplicate system in the basement of a department store in London. As the war machine kept turning, vocoders and turntables would be installed in Paris, Brisbane, Manila, Frankfurt, Berlin, Guam, Tokyo, Oakland.

Oakland?

Another one, on a barge that tailed General Douglas MacArthur around the Philippines. And another, under a mountain in Hawaii. If a satellite zoomed in on the northern bump of the African Zulu medallion hanging from Bambaataa's neck, one could see General Eisenhower checking out two turntables and a vocoder in a wine cellar in Algiers.

In the fall of 1983, the Zulu Nation funk sign began appearing on my spiral notebooks, its index and pinkie horns shooting lasers at whatever subject crossed its path. "Shazulu" became the code for "Latin Vocabulary Homework" which I did for a seventh-grade classmate in exchange for vocoder record money. (He would whisper over his shoulder from the desk in front of me: "You got that shazulu?") I would then launder the cash through Shazada Records in downtown Charlotte, North Carolina.

The Pentagon vinyl was far more rare, guarded with life but destroyed by protocol once the needle lifted. Bambaataa wonders if any of it survived. This was a world where turntables were controlled by clocks, not people. Where privacy was distinct from secrecy and a digit was referred to as a "higit." Where torpedoes were equipped with 500-watt speakers and records played thermal noise backwards behind nameless doors. Where speech must be "indestructible" and the voice wouldn't recognize itself from hello. So it's not unreasonable to think that turntables and vocoders once kept the snoops out of Churchill's whiskey diction.

Bam, often just headphones away from some version of deep space, is not surprised. He once named an album *Warlocks and Witches, Computer Chips, Microchips, and You*, his old playlists being a conspiracy theory themselves. To him, it's William Burroughs, Gary Numan and Vincent Price who are the real vocoders. In a sense, everything is bugged.

Bam mutters something about "Leviathan" and scans through the NSA appendix. There's a transcript of Bell Labs President O.E. Buckley speaking through a vocoder in Pentagon Room 3D-923, July 1943, when Special Customer was first activated:

> We are assembled here today to open a new service—
> Secret Telephony. . . . Speech has been converted into low-

frequency signals that are not speech but contain a description of it. . . . Signals have been decoded and restored and then used to regenerate speech nearly enough like that which gave them birth. . . . Speech transmitted in this matter sounds somewhat unnatural.

Bambaataa descrambles a frog in his throat, a matter of clearance in itself. *Somewhat.*

"We hope that it will be a help in the prosecution of the war," said O.E., signing off.

And so we bug.

Curiosity Slowdown

Jace Clayton

Ten years ago this month, one of the great, lazy American geniuses died, at the age of 29, from drinking too much cough syrup. His name was Robert Earl Davis Jr., and I believe he stole the technique that made him famous from the Mexicans. Under the name DJ Screw, Davis earned a living taking other people's rap songs and slowing them down. Like a good mixtape DJ, he would add EQ, subtle effects and scratches to heighten the impact of each song, but what made him special was his unrelenting commitment to syrupy slowness.

Everyone who has mistakenly played a 45rpm single at 33 knows the effect, but by dedicating himself to this process Screw turned what could have been a joke into a rap subgenre, an oft-copied process (countless Southern rap records have "chopped & screwed" versions), based on a technique so simple that it has philosophical heft.

By the 1990s Davis' style—screw—had become a genre unto itself, and his mixes were selling like hotcakes far beyond his hometown of Houston, Texas. The selling part was important: Monterrey Mexicans had been talking over and slowing down cumbia records for years before Screw came along—something he would have been likely to hear in Houston. Not all songs sound good screwed; the technique reveals a hidden face whose image can't be guessed beforehand. The effect is druggy—there's a subculture of codeine-based prescription cough syrup around screw—and occult. Once screwed, upbeat songs in a major key destabilize into eerie tonalities. Dark tunes get darker. The bass goes viscous. A screwed song urges the listener to internalize its dampened tempo, to stretch the existential qualities of the moment to match the music.

In a world where musical creations (remixes included) constantly shed economic value, the screw approach invests minimal effort into sonic transformation—yet the lazy process radically reconfigures a song. Screw dislocates body from voice—baritone rappers sound demonic, turgid, other; and female singers melt into androgyny. If a song's body is the regular-pitched version where the voice corresponds with the person it came from, then screw severs that connection. Paradoxically, screwed rap sounds more carnal than ever, yet the body is negated to expose the soul—or id, or drug-soaked semi-consciousness. Screw is the opposite of transcendence, music optimized for Houston's stuck-on-earth car culture and oppressive humidity.

DJ Screw's swamp gospel continues to spread. A clutch of new bands cite him as an influence; their damaged psychedelia—call it electronic goth, witch house, screwgaze or drag (the neologisms haven't hardened into place yet)—embraces a screw-compatible mix of murky bass and de-tuned synths. The Houston-based Disaro label's stream of CD-Rs and JPEG-artwork helped define the movement. The new crop of Screw acolytes embrace an aesthetic of visual, sonic and typographic obscurity. One of the best is Ithaca's oOoOO, who folds lessons cribbed from dubstep into the mix. There's gr†llgr†ll, Europeans who bury American pop in digital rubble. Like dreamy Swedish duo jj, gr†llgr†ll cover Lil Wayne's "Lollipop" (2008). In interviews and on record, this loose congregation of musicians constantly affirms its love for mainstream rap, disavowing an avant-garde or elitist position by implying that their work sits in a populist continuum.

Michigan trio Salem spearhead the scene. They call their screw homage "drag" (an equally multivalent term). Early Salem sounded unintentionally if unapologetically bad—their first release was 2008's

EP *Yes, I Smoke Crack*. Now that the budget is bigger their pioneering blend of cheap drum samples and mesmerizing synth lines layered with ethereal 4AD vocals remains—but now it's a well-mixed delight. The atmosphere on their debut album, *King Night* (2010), convulses between sick and soaring. Consensus describes Salem's overdriven synthpop as "dark", but the reality is much brighter. (Although this has been a good year for "dark": check albums by Richard A. Ingram, The North Sea, and Svarte Greiner). Especially from the screwed perspective: a little melodic weirdness and low-end distortion can't disguise the fact that Salem conjures up Enya rather than the boogiemen. Songs such as "Redlights" and "Asia" are yearning, catchy anthems—helped by Heather Marlatt's lovely vocals. After screw, the biggest lesson Salem have learned from hiphop is how much a sample can signify. Opening track "King Night" encapsulates their mission statement with a choral snippet from the 1847 Christmas carol "O Holy Night"—chopped up, of course. Similarly, their visuals favour Christian references done up as druggy, rust belt nihilism. Faith splinters into hymns for a weary, suspicious world where transcendence comes with a chemical aftertaste. Authenticity is not an issue, which is why Jack Donoghue's ham-fisted, pitched-down raps on "Trapdoor" and "Tair" mark the album's low points. Donoghue raps like a flunky Gucci Mane, giving the tracks a derivative feel rather than the polystylistic synthesis that originally made Salem so influential.

Like screw, drag is a pointed move away from the shared space of the club, with its possibilities of communion, lodging instead in the private: music for bedrooms and cars, insular sounds for small numbers and personal reveries. Salem's brand of darkness—expressed as murky sound, shadowy videos, and a publicist's dream back-story of drugs and prostitution—makes perfect sense in an era of over-sharing, when bloggers tirelessly unearth the obscure and personal details of the famous explode via Twitter. This is darkness as brand, an aesthetic of low information acknowledging that the mysterious is as meme-ready as pop transparency.

Perhaps the truest screw heir is Paul Octavian Nasca, a Romanian programmer who wrote the software used to create recent viral hit "U Smile 800% Slower" (2010)—a Justin Bieber track stretched to 800 percent of its original length while the pitch remains unchanged. A Florida-based electronic musician used Nasca's algorithm to smear the three-minute single into a half-hour epic of shimmering, sensual ambience. Bieber-haters and his legions of fans were equally enthralled by the transformation, which made the Canadian teen star's corn-syrup pop sound like Icelandic band Sigur Rós. In less than a month, it was heard by more than two million people, received the endorsement of Mr. Bieber (he tweeted: "this version of u smile is incredible to just chill out and fall asleep to. feels epic"), and spawned copycat slowdowns.

Nasca had heard "9 Beet Stretch" (2002), a Norwegian sound-art piece based on Beethoven's Ninth Symphony (1824) stretched across 24 hours. "I wanted to do it by myself," he explained over email, "but I couldn't find the software to do it". So Nasca developed his own, open-source version, called Paul's Extreme Sound Stretch and around 10,000 people a day downloaded it during the Bieber frenzy. Unlike screw, which bends audio downward in a linear, analogue fashion (where slower speed equals lower tones), Nasca's software uses complex formulas to extrapolate the original audio, uncoupling pitch from speed. Most of what we hear are synthesized "new" tonalities—each song's heavenly version of itself. Nasca, who prefers Goa trance slowed down by 10–15%, points out that, "if you listen carefully, you can 'feel' how the [original Bieber song] is 'frozen in time.'" Listening converges into feeling as time evaporates. Screw and drag provide corporeal experiences for people in close quarters. To sample a phrase from Charles Mingus, those slowdowns offer a look beneath the underdog. Jacked up on esoteric mathematics, Nasca's extreme stretches quite literally force songs to become more than themselves, beatified as they creep towards the infinite. As one of the many commentators streaming the 800% stretch asked: "Is this how God hears Justin Bieber?"

Meet Your #operaplot 2010 Winners

Marcia Adair with Micaela Baranello, Ralph Graves,
Josiah Gulden, James Harrington, Bryan Johnson,
Daniel Kelley, Stephen Llewellyn, and Sam Neuman

*Marcia Adair, a Canadian music journalist who blogs under the name
The Omniscient Mussel, runs an annual Twitter contest called #op-
eraplot, in which entrants are challenged to summarize the plot of an
opera in 140 or fewer characters. The 2010 edition was judged by the
celebrated young German tenor Jonas Kaufmann, who chose five winners from nearly 1,000 entries. The top five were randomly ordered
by a Twitter follower, and received prizes accordingly.*

Name: Sam Neuman (@SamNeuman), New York City

Tweet: Father is less than enthusiastic about son's love affair with
aging, bankrupt, terminally ill prostitute. Can you believe it? [*La
Traviata*]

Prize: Courtesy of Opera Theatre Company in Dublin, Sam and a guest
are heading to Ireland to see OTC's production of *The Marriage of
Figaro*. Prize includes flights and three nights at an O'Callaghan
hotel.

Bio: Sam Neuman is a 28-year-old New York City publicist whose
loves include opera, bacon, social networking, and playing Lady
Gaga songs on the violin. He is beyond delighted to have found a
practical outlet for his twin passions, Verdi and snarkiness.

Name: Micaela Baranello (@Lattavanti), Princeton, NJ

Tweet: Married girl in search of a good time accidentally causes moral collapse of Rome, influx of campy tenor nurses. [*The Coronation of Poppea*]

Prize: Wagner's *Ring* with Solti and the Vienna Philharmonic [Decca, 14 CDs]

Bio: Micaela Baranello is a doctoral candidate in musicology at Princeton University, where she is writing her dissertation on twentieth-century Viennese operetta. When not in the library or teaching, she is a frequent Met attendee and works as a stage manager and director of opera.

Name: Daniel John Kelley (@FunWithIago), New York City

Tweet: So I wrote this guy this EPIC love letter & he's like "No thanks," but now I'm married & rich & he's all "OMG I LURV U!!" WTF? [*Eugene Onegin*]

Prize: Wagner: Great Operas from Bayreuth [Decca, 33 CDs]

Bio: Daniel John Kelley is a playwright and native of Brooklyn, NY, where he lives with his girlfriend and his portrait of Verdi over his writing desk. So there's that. He is the writer and creator of the children's theatre series Monster Literature. You can stalk him at www.danieljohnkelley.com.

Name: Bryan Johnson (@BryanImmLawyer), New York City

Tweet: You'd think after so many years of planning double murders she'd remember the axe. Instead, she dances with it and drops dead. [*Elektra*]

Prize: Since Bryan lives in NYC and there's no local ticket prize, he's decided to choose the Edmonton Opera's prize pack and give it to his mother for Mother's Day. Bryan's mom will be heading to Edmonton Opera's opening-night performance of *La Bohème* on October 23, 2010, and enjoying two nights at the Crowne Plaza Chateau Lancombe.

Bio: Bryan C. Johnson is an immigration attorney in New York City. He wears big dorky headphones blasting opera, and spends an unhealthy amount of time at the Met. If you want to chat about opera, or have an immigration law question, shoot Bryan an e-mail.

Name: James Harrington (@MusicBizKid), Nashville, TN
Tweet: Idealistic poets take note: apparently "I wish to end economic injustice" sounds a lot like "just go ahead and kill me" in French [*Andrea Chénier*]
Prize: James has decided to take the Atlanta Opera up on their offer of two tickets to the opera, dinner for two at MANGIA!, passes to their VIP intermission lounge Intermezzo, and FREE VALET PARKING!
Bio: New Hampshire–born/Nashville-based James Harrington is a 2006 Berklee College of Music grad and chorister with the Nashville Opera and the Nashville Symphony. When he comes down from the shock of placing in this year's #operaplot contest, he'll return to singing, arranging, writing music-related copy, and conversatin' with the rest of Twitter's vibrant classical music community.

RUNNERS UP

Name: Stephen Llewellyn (@LeBoyfriend), Portland, OR
Tweet: Kissed the girls and made them cry. Stabbed one's dad and watched him die. Offered chances to repent, he opted to be Hades sent. Men! [*Don Giovanni*]

Name: Josiah Gulden (@JGulden), Minneapolis, MN
Tweet: Sorry 2 drop this on u babe, but I'm *technically* still married to a suicidal 16 y/o geisha & turns out she had my kid. Oops? [*Madama Butterfly*]

Name: Ralph Graves (@RalphGraves), Orange, VA
Tweet: Greek musician goes to hell and back. Wife only makes it halfway. [*Orfeo ed Euridice*]

A Pop Critic Takes on the *Ring*

Part 1, Das Rheingold

Ann Powers

Last night I put on a $20 dress I'd once worn to a party that featured an appearance by Whitney Houston, grabbed a friend, and headed to the Dorothy Chandler Pavilion to begin my immersion in Los Angeles Opera's *Der Ring des Nibelungen.* I'm a Wagner nut by disposition and regional roots—my hometown Seattle Opera company was an early pioneer in contemporary *Ring* revivals. My pal, however, was a first-timer and mostly a fan of singer-songwriters like Loudon Wainwright III. I told him he could flee at intermission if the *Sturm und Drang* bored him, having conveniently forgotten that *Das Rheingold*—the first of the four operas in the *Ring* cycle—is 2 1/2 hours of lust and deceit, gods and dwarfs, leitmotifs and arias, with no break for a glass of champagne.

I needn't have worried. Achim Freyer's staging of *Das Rheingold* is as much a pop experience as it is a classical one. That's not to say it's easily digestible. Though its elements move slowly, as if in a dream, Freyer's staging still creates a kind of over-stimulation that leads the audience to focus on the elemental aspects of Wagner's score, its sometimes startling beauty and inexorable dramatic push, instead of the emotional melodrama the opera also contains. Its rewards come closer to that of ritual than of conventional drama. But this should make it even more appealing to today's pop music fans, who relish being bombarded with images and sound, and who like their stars to transform onstage, all the way to the edge of the grotesque.

Pointing to all corners of culture, Freyer's set and costumes argue vehemently against any division between high and low. A culture maven will see what she brings to the room; his puppets, masks and elaborate tableaux evoke so many sources that playing the game of "where'd I see that before?" can distract, even from *Rheingold*'s rip-roaring plot.

A connoisseur of world folk traditions might think of Balinese shadow-puppet theater or the African ceremonial costumes also valued by the sound-suit creator Nick Cave. Avant-garde theater buffs will spot shout-outs to old favorites like Robert Wilson and Mummenschanz. There were moments when I thought of Busby Berkeley's sweetly surreal dance numbers, and others that seemed to magnify the creepy, compelling miniatures of animator Jan Švankmajer. When the huge black hat and cloak that signifies Wotan's wanderings appeared, my friend whispered, "Joseph Beuys."

At a different point, he might have murmured, "Lady Gaga." As Loge, the wonderfully emotive tenor Arnold Bezuyen wore that strange diva's signature oversized shoulder pads. His hair and makeup, on the other hand, were reminiscent of Bono as MacPhisto: this devilish trickster could command an arena-rock crowd. And then there were his Converse sneakers, the uniform shoe of indie rock musicians like Kurt Cobain. And there are many obvious nods to psychedelia and art rock: the Blue Meanies of the Beatles' "Yellow Submarine" and the giant eyeballs belonging to San Francisco art punks the Residents seem to make cameo appearances.

This interplay of high and low, ancient and cutting-edge, is one pop-wise aspect of this journey into Wagner's 19-hour opus. Pop has always been a scavengers' form, absorbing whatever glitters and glows from the street, the bohemians' salon, or even the opera house. The prelude to *Das Rheingold*, such a gorgeous and inspiring piece of music, set the stage for what would become minimalism: not only a major aspect of 20th-century classical music, but the foundation of rock bands like the Velvet Underground, ambient music pioneers like Brian Eno, and much of the electronic music of the rave era.

Das Rheingold also made clear that Freyer means to dwell in the realm of the mythic, not the psychological. This doesn't mean his gods and preternatural creatures don't feel: in Tuesday's performance, Graham Clark as Mime and Ellie Dehn as Freia sang with particularly powerful angst. Still, Freyer's use of sculptural doppelgangers and masks may frustrate some opera-goers' desire for good old-fashioned dramatic release. The traditional production I saw at New York's Metropolitan Opera a decade ago allowed for much more robe-clutching and clear facial expression, not to mention the fact that the singers' voices just came through more strongly—the biggest problem in Freyer's version is that the scrim that creates the hallucinatory mood often muffles the voices onstage. (This, incidentally, was my pop-educated companion's one complaint: he is accustomed to amplified music, and at times things were too quiet for him.)

But here's something interesting—much of today's most important mainstream and indie pop resides in a similarly fantastic realm, far from conventional emotional expression. Artists as diverse as Gaga, Kanye West, Of Montreal and Animal Collective use masks both visual and vocal to challenge the idea that human expression is ever really "natural"; these innovators are exploring how technology is changing the very ground of our consciousness. So much pop now dwells with fascination on science fiction themes, from Janelle Monae's android reveries to the astral imaginings of electronic musician Flying Lotus. Even pop tart Ke$ha wore a costume on *Saturday Night Live* that would fit right into Freyer's universe.

But what about the music? Can a pop lover appreciate Wagner? I think so. In this realm, the appeal may be less heady. Wagner's compositions are simply beautiful—especially *Das Rheingold*, which unfolds with such an organic grace. With so much to keep the eyes occupied, the pop music fan may be able to let her ears relax while watching this *Ring*, and to absorb its many subtleties.

Word

Kelefa Sanneh

Last year, an English professor named Adam Bradley issued a manifesto to his fellow-scholars. He urged them to expand the poetic canon, and possibly enlarge poetry's audience, by embracing, or coöpting, the greatest hits of hip-hop. "Thanks to the engines of global commerce, rap is now the most widely disseminated poetry in the history of the world," he wrote. "The best MCs—like Rakim, Jay-Z, Tupac, and many others—deserve consideration alongside the giants of American poetry. We ignore them at our own expense."

The manifesto was called *Book of Rhymes: The Poetics of Hip Hop* (Civitas; $16.95), and it used the terms of poetry criticism to illuminate not the content of hip-hop lyrics but their form. For Bradley, a couplet by Tupac Shakur—

> *Out on bail, fresh outta jail, California dreamin'*
> *Soon as I stepped on the scene, I'm hearin' hoochies screamin'*

—was a small marvel of "rhyme (both end and internal), assonance, and alliteration," given extra propulsion by Shakur's exaggerated stress patterns. Bradley also celebrated some lesser-known hip-hop lyrics, including this dense, percussive couplet by Pharoahe Monch, a cult favorite from Queens:

The last batter to hit, blast shattered your hip
Smash any splitter or fastball—that'll be it

Picking through this thicket, Bradley paused to appreciate Monch's use of apocopated rhyme, as when a one-syllable word is rhymed with the penultimate syllable of a multisyllabic word (last / blast / fastball). Bradley is right to think that hip-hop fans have learned to appreciate all sorts of seemingly obscure poetic devices, even if they can't name them. Though some of his comparisons are strained (John Donne loved punning, and so does Juelz Santana!), his motivation is easy to appreciate: examining and dissecting lyrics is the only way to "give rap the respect it deserves as poetry."

This campaign for respect enters a new phase with the release of *The Anthology of Rap* (Yale; $35), a nine-hundred-page compendium that is scarcely lighter than an eighties boom box. It was edited by Bradley and Andrew DuBois, another English professor (he teaches at the University of Toronto; Bradley is at the University of Colorado), who together have compiled thirty years of hip-hop lyrics, starting with transcribed recordings of parties thrown in the late nineteen-seventies—Year Zero, more or less. The book, which seems to have been loosely patterned after the various Norton anthologies of litera-ture, is, among other things, a feat of contractual legwork: Bradley and DuBois claim to have secured permission from the relevant copy-right holders, and the book ends with some forty pages of credits, as well as a weak disclaimer ("The editors have made every reasonable effort to secure permissions"), which may or may not hold up in court.

Even before *The Anthology of Rap* arrived in stores, keen-eyed fans began pointing out the book's many transcription errors, some of which are identical to ones on ohhla.com, a valuable—though by no means infallible—online compendium of hip-hop lyrics. But read-ers who don't already have these words memorized are more likely to be bothered by the lack of footnotes; where the editors of the Nor-ton anthologies, those onionskin behemoths, love to explain and overexplain obscure terms and references, Bradley and DuBois provide readers with nothing more than brief introductions. Readers are simply warned that when it comes to hip-hop lyrics "obfuscation is often the point, suggesting coded meanings worth puzzling over." In other words, you're on your own.

Happily, readers looking for a more carefully annotated collection of hip-hop lyrics can turn to an unlikely source: a rapper. In recent weeks, *The Anthology of Rap* has been upstaged by *Decoded* (Spiegel & Grau; $35), the long-awaited print début of Jay-Z, who must now be one of the most beloved musicians in the world. The book, which doesn't credit a co-writer, is essentially a collection of lyrics, liberally footnoted and accompanied by biographical anecdotes and observations. *Decoded* has benefitted from an impressive marketing campaign, including a citywide treasure hunt for hidden book pages. (The book's launch doubled as a promotion for Bing, the Microsoft search engine.) So it's a relief to find that *Decoded* is much better than it needs to be; in fact, it's one of a handful of books that just about any hip-hop fan should own. Jay-Z explains not only what his lyrics mean but how they sound, even how they feel:

> When a rapper jumps on a beat, he adds his own rhythm. Sometimes you stay in the pocket of the beat and just let the rhymes land on the square so that the beat and flow become one. But sometimes the flow chops up the beat, breaks the beat into smaller units, forces in multiple syllables and repeated sounds and internal rhymes, or hangs a drunken leg over the last *bap* and keeps going, sneaks out of that bitch.

Two paragraphs later, he's back to talking about selling crack cocaine in Brooklyn. His description, and his music, make it easier to imagine a connection—a rhyme, maybe—between these two forms of navigation, beat and street. And, no less than Bradley and DuBois, Jay-Z is eager to win for hip-hop a particular kind of respect. He states his case using almost the same words Bradley did: he wants to show that "hip-hop lyrics—not just my lyrics, but those of every great MC—are poetry if you look at them closely enough."

If you start in the recent past and work backward, the history of hip-hop spreads out in every direction: toward the Last Poets and Gil Scott-Heron, who declaimed poems over beats and grooves in the early seventies; toward Jamaica, where U-Roy pioneered the art of chatting and toasting over reggae records; toward the fifties radio DJs who used rhyming patter to seal spaces between songs; toward jazz and jive and the talking blues; toward preachers and politicians and street-corner bullshitters. In *Book of Rhymes*, Bradley argues convincingly that something changed in the late nineteen-seventies, in the Bronx, when the earliest rappers (some of whom were also DJs) discovered the value of rhyming in time. "Words started bending to the beat," as Bradley puts it; by submitting to rhythm, paradoxically, rappers came to sound more authoritative than the free-form poets, toasters, chatters, patterers, and jokers who came before.

The earliest lyrics in the anthology establish the rhyme pattern that many casual listeners still associate with hip-hop. Each four-beat line ended with a rhyme, heavily emphasized, and each verse was a series of couplets, not always thematically or sonically related to each other:

> *I'm Melle Mel and I rock so well*
> *From the World Trade to the depths of hell.*

Those lines were recorded in December 1978, at a performance by Grandmaster Flash and the Furious Five at the Audubon Ballroom, on Broadway and 165th Street (the same hall where Malcolm X was assassinated, thirteen years earlier). The springy exuberance of Melle Mel's voice matched the elastic funk of the disco records that many early rappers used as their backing tracks.

The rise of Run-D.M.C., in the early nineteen-eighties, helped change that: the group's two rappers, Run and D.M.C., performed in jeans and sneakers, and they realized that hip-hop could be entertaining without being cheerful. They delivered even goofy lyrics with staccato aggression, which is one reason that they appealed to the young Jay-Z—they reminded him of guys he knew. In *Decoded*, he quotes a couple of lines by Run:

> *Cool chief rocker, I don't drink vodka*
> *But keep a bag of cheeba inside my locker*

There is aggression in the phrasing: the first line starts sharply, with a stressed syllable, instead of easing into the beat with an unstressed one. "The words themselves don't mean much, but he snaps those clipped syllables out like drumbeats, *bap bap bapbap*," Jay-Z writes. "If you listened to that joint and came away thinking it was a simple rhyme about holding weed in a gym locker, you'd be reading it wrong: The point of those bars is to bang out a rhythmic idea."

The first Run-D.M.C. album arrived in 1984, but within a few years the group's sparse lyrical style came to seem old-fashioned; a generation of rappers had arrived with a trickier sense of swing. Hip-hop historians call this period the Golden Age (Bradley and DuBois date it from 1985 to 1992), and it produced the kinds of lyrical shifts that are easy to spot in print: extended similes and ambitious use of symbolism; an increased attention to character and ideology; unpredictable internal rhyme schemes; enjambment and uneven line lengths. This last innovation may have been designed to delight anthologizers and frustrate them, too, because it makes hip-hop hard to render in print. Bradley and DuBois claim, with ill-advised certainty, to have solved the problem of line breaks: "one musical bar is equal to one line of verse." But, in fact, most of their lines start before the downbeat, somewhere (it's not clear how they decided) between the fourth beat of one bar and the first beat of the next one. Here they are quoting Big Daddy Kane, one of the genre's

first great enjambers, in a tightly coiled passage from his 1987 single,
"Raw":

> *I'll damage ya, I'm not an amateur but a professional*
> *Unquestionable, without doubt superb*
> *So full of action, my name should be a verb.*

These three lines contain three separate rhyming pairs, and a different anthologist might turn this extract into six lines of varying
length. If Bradley and DuBois followed their own rule, they would
break mid-word—"professio-/nal"—because the final syllable actually
arrives, startlingly, on the next line's downbeat. In *Book of Rhymes*,
Bradley argued that "every rap song is a poem waiting to be performed," but the anthology's trouble with line breaks (not to mention
punctuation) reminds readers that hip-hop is an oral tradition with
no well-established written form. By presenting themselves as mere
archivists, Bradley and DuBois underestimate their own importance:
a book of hip-hop lyrics is necessarily a work of translation.

As the Golden Age ended, hip-hop's formal revolution was giving
way to a narrative revolution. So-called gangsta rappers downplayed
wordplay (without, of course, forswearing it) so they could immerse
listeners in their first-person stories of bad guys and good times.
Shakur and the Notorious B.I.G. created two of the genre's most fully
realized personae; when they were murdered, in 1996 and 1997, respectively, their deaths became part of their stories. (Both crimes remain unsolved.) As the anthologizers blast through the nineties (*Rap
Goes Mainstream*) and the aughts (*New Millennium Rap*), their excitement starts to wane. They assert that the increasing popularity
of hip-hop presented a risk of "homogenization and stagnation," without pausing to explain why this should be true (doesn't novelty sell?),
if indeed it was. There is little overt criticism, but some rappers get
fulsome praise—"socially conscious" is one of Bradley and DuBois's
highest compliments—while others get passive-aggressive reprimands
("Disagreement remains over whether Lil' Kim has been good or bad

for the image of women in hip-hop"). Perhaps the form of their project dictates its content. They are sympathetic to rappers whose lyrics survive the transition to the printed page; the verbose parables and history lessons of Talib Kweli, for instance, make his name "synonymous with depth and excellence," in their estimation. But they offer a more measured assessment of Lil Wayne, praising his "play of sound" (his froggy, bluesy voice is one of the genre's greatest instruments) while entertaining the unattributed accusation that he may be merely "a gimmick rapper." Any anthology requires judgments of taste, and this one might have been more engaging if it admitted as much.

Jay-Z grew up absorbing many of the rhymes that Bradley and DuBois celebrate. He was born in 1969, and raised in the Marcy Houses, in an area of Brooklyn from which Times Square seemed to be "a plane ride away." (Nowadays, some real-estate agents doubtless consider it part of greater Williamsburg.) "It was the seventies," he writes, "and heroin was still heavy in the hood, so we would dare one another to push a leaning nodder off a bench the way kids on farms tip sleeping cows." He was a skinny, watchful boy with a knack for rhyming but no great interest in the music industry, despite some early brushes with fame—he briefly served as Big Daddy Kane's hype man. Besides, Jay-Z had a day job that was both more dangerous and more reliable: he says he spent much of the late eighties and early nineties selling crack in Brooklyn and New Jersey and down the Eastern Seaboard. He was no kingpin, but he says he was a fairly accomplished mid-level dealer, and though he hated standing outside all day, he found that he didn't hate the routine. "It was an adventure," he says. "I got to hang out on the block with my crew, talking, cracking jokes. You know how people in office jobs talk at the watercooler? This job was almost all watercooler." Then, almost as an afterthought, "But when you weren't having fun, it was hell."

Early recordings of Jay-Z reveal a nimble but mild-mannered virtuoso, delivering rat-a-tat syllables (he liked to rap in double-time
triplets, delivering six syllables per beat) that often amounted to
études rather than songs. But by 1996, when he released his début
album, *Reasonable Doubt*, on a local independent label, he had slowed
down and settled into a style—and, more important, settled into
character. The album won him underground acclaim and a record
deal with the very above-ground hip-hop label Def Jam, which helped
him become one of the genre's most dependable hitmakers. He was
a cool-blooded hustler, describing a risky life in conversational verses
that hid their poetic devices, disparaging the art of rapping even
while perfecting it:

> *Who wanna bet us that we don't touch lettuce, stack*
> *cheddars forever, live treacherous, all the et ceteras.*
> *To the death of us, me and my confidants, we shine.*
> *You feel the ambiance—y'all niggas just rhyme.*

Too often, hip-hop's embrace of crime narratives has been portrayed as a flaw or a mistake, a regrettable detour from the overtly
ideological rhymes of groups like Public Enemy. But in Jay-Z's view
Public Enemy is an anomaly. "You rarely *become* Chuck D when
you're listening to Public Enemy," he writes. "It's more like watching
a really, really lively speech." By contrast, his tales of hustling were
generous, because they made it easy for fans to imagine that they
were part of the action. "I don't think any listeners think I'm threatening them," he writes. "I think they're singing along with me, threatening someone else. They're thinking, *Yeah, I'm coming for you.* And
they might apply it to anything, to taking their next math test or
straightening out that chick talking outta pocket in the next cubicle."

Throughout *Decoded*, Jay-Z offers readers a large dose of
hermeneutics and a small dose of biography, in keeping with his de-
served reputation for brilliance and chilliness. His footnotes are full

of pleasingly small-scale exultations ("I like the internal rhymes here") and technical explanations ("The shift in slang—from talking about guns as tools to break things to talking about shooting as *blazing*—matches the shift in tone"); at one point, he pauses to quote a passage from *Book of Rhymes* in which Bradley praises his use of homonyms. Readers curious about his life will learn something about his father, who abandoned the family when Jay-Z was twelve; a little bit about Bono, who is now one of Jay-Z's many A-list friends; and nothing at all about the time when, as a boy, Jay-Z shot his older brother in the shoulder. (Apparently, there was a dispute over an item of jewelry, possibly a ring, although Jay-Z once told Oprah Winfrey that, at the time, his brother was "dealing with a lot of demons.")

Decoded is a prestige project—it will be followed, inevitably, by a rash of imitations from rappers who realize that the self-penned coffee-table book has replaced the Lamborghini Murciélago as hip-hop's ultimate status symbol. In his early years, Jay-Z liked to insist that rapping was only a means to an end—like selling crack, only safer. "I was an eager hustler and a reluctant artist," he writes. "But the irony of it is that to make the hustle work, really work, over the long term, you have to be a true artist, too." Certainly this book emphasizes Jay-Z the true artist, ignoring high-spirited tracks like "Ain't No Nigga" to focus on his moodier ruminations on success and regrets. (The lyrics to "Success" and "Regrets" are, in fact, included.) Readers might be able to trace Jay-Z's growing self-consciousness over the years, as his slick vernacular verses give way to language that's more decorous and sometimes less elegant. In "Fallin'," from 2007, he returned to a favorite old topic, with mixed results:

> *The irony of selling drugs is sort of like I'm using it*
> *Guess it's two sides to what substance abuse is*

Bradley has written about rappers "so insistent on how their rhymes sound that they lose control over what they are actually saying." But with late-period Jay-Z the reverse is sometimes true: the ideas are clear and precise, but the syntax gets convoluted, and he settles for clumsy near-rhymes like "using it"/"abuse is." For all Bradley and DuBois's talk about "conscious" hip-hop, the genre owes much of its energy to the power of what might be called "unconscious" rapping: heedless or reckless lyrics, full of contradictions and exaggerations (to say nothing of insults). If you are going to follow a beat, as rappers must, then it helps not to have too many other firm commitments.

One day four years ago, Jay-Z was reading *The Economist* when he came across an article bearing the heading "Bubbles and Bling." The article was about Cristal, the expensive champagne that figured in the rhymes of Jay-Z and other prominent rappers. In the article, Frédéric Rouzaud, the managing director of the winery behind Cristal, was asked whether these unsought endorsements might hurt his brand. "That's a good question, but what can we do? We can't forbid people from buying it," he said, adding, slyly, "I'm sure Dom Pérignon or Krug would be delighted to have their business." Jay-Z was irritated enough that he released a statement vowing never to drink Cristal again, and he started removing references to Cristal from his old lyrics during concerts. (He eventually switched his endorsement to Armand de Brignac.) In Jay-Z's view, Rouzaud had not only insulted hip-hop culture; he had violated an unspoken promotional arrangement. "We used their brand as a signifier of luxury and they got free advertising and credibility every time we mentioned it," he writes. "We were trading cachet." (Actually, the book, not free of typos, says "cache.")

It's hard not to think about Cristal when Jay-Z insists that his lyrics should be heard—read—as poetry, or when Bradley and DuBois produce an anthology designed to win for rappers the status of poets. They are, all of them, trading cachet, and their eagerness to make this trade suggests that they are trading up—that hip-hop, despite its success, still aches for respect and recognition. It stands to reason, then, that as the genre's place in the cultural firmament grows more secure its advocates will grow less envious of poetry's allegedly exalted status.

Another great American lyricist has just published a book of his own: *Finishing the Hat* (Knopf; $39.95), by Stephen Sondheim, is curiously similar in form to *Decoded*. Sondheim is just as appealing a narrator as Jay-Z, although he's much less polite. (While Jay-Z has almost nothing bad to say about his fellow-rappers, Sondheim is quick to disparage his rivals, subject to a "cowardly but simple" precept: "criticize only the dead.") But where Jay-Z wants to help readers see the poetry in hip-hop, Sondheim thinks poeticism can be a problem: in his discussion of "Tonight," from *West Side Story*, he half apologizes for the song's "lapses into 'poetry.'" And where Bradley and DuBois are quick to praise rappers for using trick rhymes and big words, Sondheim is ever on guard against "overrhyming" and other instances of unwarranted cleverness. "In theatrical fact," he writes, "it is usually the plainer and flatter lyric that soars poetically when infused with music." Most rappers are no less pragmatic: they use the language that works, which is sometimes ornate, but more often plainspoken, even homely. (One thinks of Webbie, the pride of Baton Rouge, deftly rhyming "drunk as a fuckin' wino" with "my people gon' get they shine on.") Maybe future anthologies will help show why the most complicated hip-hop lyrics aren't always the most successful.

It's significant that hip-hop, virtually alone among popular-music genres, has never embraced the tradition of lyric booklets. The genius of hip-hop is that it encourages listeners to hear spoken words as music. Few people listen to speeches or books on tape over and over, but hip-hop seems to have just as much replay value as any other popular genre. Reading rap lyrics may be useful, but it's also tiring. The Jay-Z of *Decoded* is engaging; the Jay-Z of his albums is irresistible. The difference has something to do with his odd, perpetually adolescent-sounding voice, and a lot to do with his sophisticated sense of rhythm. Sure, he's a poet—and, while we're at it, a singer and percussionist, too. But why should any of these titles be more impressive than "rapper"?

In the introduction to *Finishing the Hat*, Sondheim explains that "all rhymes, even the farthest afield of the near ones (*home/dope*), draw attention to the rhymed word." But surely rhyming can deëmphasize the meaning of a word by emphasizing its sound. Rhyme, like other phonetic techniques, is a way to turn a spoken phrase into a musical phrase—a "rhythmic idea," as Jay-Z put it. *Bap bap bapbap.* Rapping is the art of addressing listeners and distracting them at the same time. Bradley argues in *Book of Rhymes* that hip-hop lyrics represent the genre's best chance for immortality: "When all the club bangers have faded, when all the styles and videos are long forgotten, the words will remain." That gets the relationship backward. On the contrary, one suspects that the words will endure—and the books will proliferate—because the music will, too.

Why We Fight #5:
Why Risks are Risky
Nitsuh Abebe

This is years ago now: I'm standing with a friend outside a venue in Manhattan. There's a line and it's fall and we're waiting to go in and see CocoRosie perform. "I *like* them," I'm saying. "There's just certain stuff I'm not sure about. Also I feel like they have some kind of weird thing about black people. Or 'blackness.' I'm not *saying*, I'm just saying."

My friend is a fan. She's looking at me very, very skeptically. I'm sure someone behind me in line is, too. There is a slight gender issue involved: The band I originally wanted to see tonight has, in this conversation, been described as "boy music." So now I probably sound like I'm looking for a reason not to enjoy the show.

"It's not a criticism," I say. "There are just a lot of . . . *things* with them. One possibly involving black people. But mostly just others in general." And now I'm shrugging hopelessly, because I don't know how to feel about any of this.

My friend still looks skeptical, or maybe exasperated, or maybe disappointed in me.

These days I still like CocoRosie, and I still haven't figured out how to feel about certain "things." Maybe that's the reason I like them. As for the rest of the world, the Casady sisters and the music they make are still classically divisive. They're undeniably successful: they have plenty of fans, here and abroad. They fill sizable venues and have been featured in places like the *New York Times Magazine*. But they also get everything from vigorous disinterest to rabid abuse. (And let's not kid ourselves: if you're women doing this stuff, at least *some* of that abuse is going to get a lot more rabid than it would otherwise.) Critics have fallen on both ends of the spectrum and throughout the middle. Reviews of their newest album, *Grey Oceans*, tended to revolve around finding a ratio for how much the record was beautiful versus how much it was boring or irritating. Some ended with shrugs. It's to CocoRosie's credit that they have no apparent issue with being confounding like that.

Last week, Stereogum ran a feature in which a group of likeminded artists talked about loving CocoRosie. It's a great idea for a piece, and great reading, with contributions from Antony Hegarty, Yoko Ono, Jamie Stewart, and others—plus a lovely metaphor from Nico Muhly, and a particularly killer text sent in by Annie Clark. So far as I can tell, there are two main threads running through the whole thing. One is praise for how the Casady sisters are "unafraid" and "take risks," how they're "bravely naked" and "utterly uninhibited"— all great qualities that completely make sense for other musicians to admire. The other thread is speculation about why CocoRosie don't get more respect or critical attention. There are suggestions, here and elsewhere, that it's about gender, or queer aesthetics, or a rock-guy habit of undervaluing everything that sits outside a narrow, boyish sense of art.

That speculation puts me in a fix, because I agree with the principle—the principle practically gets me cheering. I do wish certain parts of the music world embraced strangeness and artifice more readily, especially when it's not a pre-approved and boyish variety of strangeness. (I like plenty of boyish things, but the day I believe indie has just become straight-ahead rock for straight-ahead bros is the day I'm out.) At the same time, it's sort of up to you to decide which of this group's risks you find valuable and which ones aren't worth much to you—always a tricky distinction. Is it possible some of these artists are congratulating CocoRosie on bravely taking risks, and then trying to erase some of what makes those risks brave in the first place? This is the whole point of risks, right? They're risky. And if I ask myself what keeps CocoRosie from getting even more attention, I can hear a few answers right on their records. They sing in affected voices modeled on scratchy old jazz records, and occasionally enunciate like black singers from the tail end of the Depression. Their songs feel loose and formless, which is sometimes gorgeously charged, and sometimes just messy. Contributors to the Stereogum piece talk about how the music is irregular, irritating, dangerous, controversial, frightening, and sometimes ugly. Even their cover art, always eye-opening, is not built to inspire confidence in a majority of potential listeners.

This is purposeful. Bianca Casady has said her fashion sense is "to put on the things you like the least, the things you hate the most. Things that give you pain. It's the same thing we do with the language we use in our songs: making ourselves use words we hate." Sierra Casady, who studied opera, has talked about treating pop as a space of uninhibited freedom, a counter-reaction to the extremely rigid structure of classical singing. They chose the braveness and nakedness and painful things. And so they might wind up writing a seductive song like "By Your Side," which takes the idea of devotion and pulls it slowly, slyly in the most uncomfortable direction—from "I'll always be by your side" to "I'd wear your black eyes" to "All I want with my life is to die a housewife."

Sometimes this is awesome: I love a lot of these qualities, and there are others I'm still enjoying being mystified by. What is definitely *not* a mystery to me about this act is why a lot of people wouldn't care for them. I'd guess, in fact, that some people read the Stereogum piece and just saw a bunch of arty types blowing smoke at each other about how brave they are. That attitude is probably unfair and disrespectful toward art and artists. But praising a group for taking risks and then questioning the idea that those risks didn't pan out—it's possible this is unfair and disrespectful in the other direction, toward listeners and audiences. Listeners aren't just puerile children who need to be provoked into thinking; often they're smart enough to decide *your* point is the thing that's facile and childish. Or, perhaps, they just don't care for how your music sounds.

So you wind up with one of these vexed and "divisive" conversations where everyone's trying to infer everyone else's motives, and someone's continually insisting that it's not *that*, I'm just responding to the actual music—really! honestly!—and maybe this was the undertone of the conversation I was having with my friend, the one where I considered myself agnostic and she probably felt like I was undermining something special, something *she* found special. Maybe it's the undertone of my writing this and your reading this, waiting for some kind of catharsis—some part where I either slam the music as irritating drivel or slam the audience for not appreciating real art.

What's funny is that if you put on one of the group's records, there's a good chance you'll think it doesn't sound nearly as weird— or else, not nearly as interesting—as all of this makes it sound.

So my friend and I are inside the venue now, and CocoRosie are just taking the stage, and my friend turns to me and says: "Ohhh." I think she's in the process of agreeing with me about the blackness thing.

The Casady sisters themselves, as I understand it, are Cherokee, Syrian, and white. (It's not super-clear and I don't mean to lock them in a particular box.) You might not care a ton—this might just be a small thing I have personal reasons for noticing, the way that "black eye" line might stick out to someone else—but here are some facts that led me to decide there was something complicated happening between CocoRosie and the idea of blackness.

Their first album contained a well-meaning song called "Jesus Loves Me," which used a notable racial slur a half-dozen times—and later, Sierra Casady would say it was "really shocking" that anyone would hear that and "wonder if we were being offensive."

Bianca Casady was quoted in a newspaper article about "Kill Whitie" dance parties, where—to put it charitably—mostly non-black crowds maybe ironically reveled in ideas you might call "racially charged." (For instance, free admission if you bring fried chicken.)

And I assume the reason my friend is saying "ohh" is that the sisters are taking the stage in head-to-toe Sean John, hair in cornrows, the rhythm loops on their records replaced with beatboxing; there are a few black musicians in their touring group.

They look nice—obviously there's no reason anyone shouldn't wear Sean John or cornrows. (No idea whether or not this falls under their rubric of "putting on the things you like the least.") They also sound wonderful. Sierra's vocals are like a Theremin singing opera. One of the most fascinating things about the music is the way they use *beats*— odd versions of house beats, hip-hop beats, drum'n'bass beats—in contexts and against productions where you might not expect them to make sense. It's strange to hear beats like that in songs that feel so fluid and primordial, and it's even better with the beatboxing. The music we're hearing can send shivers around the room, even with a bad mix; with a few songs I'm watching a band do gorgeous, inexplicable things I'll never see anyone else do. With other songs the spell breaks and it's just a tiresome mess, a wreck. I shouldn't have said anything about my reservations on the way in, because now, during the messy parts, I get the feeling my friend has to hear it through "bad ears"—that sudden hyper-awareness of everything I might be finding bad or embarrassing about it. I worry I spoiled the fun.

But here lies this whole other thing I've never been able to decide on about them. The best I've ever done is to imagine myself as a psychiatrist, scratching my chin, steepling my fingers, and saying: okay, CocoRosie, this is interesting. You are maybe interested in something having to do with blackness. But beyond that, who knows: is this wonderful or creepy or even worth mentioning? Occasionally it just seems *European*—they're based in Paris. Or else "arty"—they're playing with identity, they're using the racial slur to suggest a point—but what if the point's too silly or banal to justify it?

Jamie Stewart, of Xiu Xiu, thinks it's worth mentioning. Here's what he has to say in that Stereogum piece, *sic* throughout:

"Cocorosie has always had what John Darnielle—a huge fan of theirs—described as race issues, but they seemed to deal with race as just that, an issue. not like fake Ivy League Afropop rip-off assholes who are, as their wealthy grandparents before them, plundering race without any consideration for the implications. Coco race [*sic!*] dives into race in a way that—as I said—scares me. Scares me because it is so insane and so bold and it also feels respectful and true."

I'm not sure what to say about the weird Vampire Weekend slam in the middle. (I like Stewart's work a lot, but the best I can figure is either (a) he's working through his own issues about grandparents and borrowing from east-Asian music, (b) he's been doing some creepy stalking to learn about things like the fortunes of the Batmanglij family under the Shah, or (c) he is living in kind of a glass house in terms of calling other people assholes.) I agree with him, though, about the existence of a race issue. And I agree that, like a lot of things about CocoRosie, it seems complex, messy, evocative, and potentially scary. But these are musicians who claimed to be shocked—straight-up flabbergasted—that using a grade-A racial slur in a song might raise a few questions for some Americans. One of them felt comfortable talking to a newspaper reporter about those parties. This is bold and honest, absolutely, but I'm not sure "consideration for the implications" is even on their list.

Remember, this is the whole quality some people love about them—the nakedness, the lack of inhibition, the risk-taking. The desire to dig into tough things, or confront ideas they hate. The way it seems brave and *unpremeditated* when they do it, like they're past sitting around thinking over implications. But there's a sense of luxury in Stewart's being able to enjoy scariness and insanity about race. For others of us, if you take a risk on this front and you don't make it work, there is no big pat on the back for trying—you're just going to look, at best, pretty stupid. And while the issue is a lot clearer when it comes to something like race, the same might go for other types of risks, too. The whole reason there's "risk" involved is that art, contrary to what some people might tell you, is not some magical safe space where nothing matters beyond pouring out your true self. Other people get to look at and think about what's pouring out, and they might not like what they find—just as you might read this column and decide you hate everything I have to say. If we couldn't do that, then art and speech wouldn't even *matter*; it would just be mumbling to yourself.

I don't mention this to suggest to you that the Casady sisters are bigots or grotesquely racially insensitive—I don't think that for a second. But it's a good example of how, when you make something a concern in your music, listeners get to work through their own concerns in the opposite direction. We're not passive sponges; we're involved, we're thinking back. Maybe we'll appreciate the process. Maybe we won't be interested. Or maybe we'll think you're doing a crappy job.

Of course, it's exactly the fear of that fact that can make music narrow and boring: everyone afraid to do anything unusual, to take on any quality listeners might actually *react* to. "Straight-ahead rock for straight-ahead bros" gets to duck the question entirely—blend in with a boyish pack whose status as "normal" tends to go unchallenged. Sometimes that's where fear leads.

Judging by the voices the Casadys pull on their records, I'm guessing they know their Billie Holiday far better than I do. There's a song Holiday sang called "Ain't Nobody's Business If I Do," and it starts like this:

> *There ain't nothing I can do, or nothing I can say,*
> *that folks don't criticize me*
> *But I'm going to do just as I want to anyway*
> *and don't care just what people say.*

Maybe this is a little like CocoRosie's approach. It's a great one—an important one—and I'm impressed by how well they've adopted it. I hope they don't change a thing. I hope more bands take that stance. And I'd be happy if a lot of CocoRosie's qualities—riskiness, femininity, artifice, queer aesthetics, formlessness—didn't get quite so many reactionary eye-rolls in the indie world. But the difference between singing those Holiday lines about life and singing them about art is that, in the latter, it *is* somebody's business if you do. I get the feeling CocoRosie know that. They can do what they do because they *don't* require more people to like it, don't require more critics to praise it, don't require the conversation between artist and audience to always end in a "victory." Which is terrific of them.

Tour Diary Day Four:
Rock and Roll is Dead

Amy Klein

Midway between Ottawa, Canada, and Ithaca, New York, we stop to buy gas. In the truck stop parking lot, I see an elderly woman getting out of the driver's seat slowly, limb by limb, the way a jellyfish might squeeze itself through a narrow break in a coral reef. She's at least 75, and her legs shake slightly as she maneuvers them onto the street, but she still has that kind of awkward languor about her, that same animal grace. It's like she's moving perfectly normally, and instead, the whole world around her has slowed down. She's wearing a big blue jean jacket with an American flag patch sewn onto the shoulder and "SUPPORT OUR TROOPS" emblazoned in gold lettering on the back, and a skirt with a bold floral print, and socks adorned with pink and red hearts. Her mouth is a thin, taut slash of bright red lipstick gripping the end of a cigarette. I pass her as I walk into the building—moving in another, faster system of time, like one star passing a planet light years away.

Inside the truck stop, it smells like old hot dogs and gasoline. The guys browse the contents of the tiny magazine rack, which seems to be mostly made up of porn. I see them poring over the cover of a magazine with a naked woman on it, and look away, instinctively feeling that this is not my scene. However, my curiosity gets the better of me, and I walk closer to see what's going on. My suspicions are confirmed: There's a naked woman on the cover. But it turns out that I'm wrong in assuming the guys are looking at porn, because the magazine is *Rolling Stone.*

After the guys have gone back to the van, I peruse the pages of the latest edition. I see a lot of photos of guys playing guitars, and ads for guys who play guitar featuring other guys playing guitars, and a photo of Lady Gaga wearing pasties and not much else. I begin to feel increasingly alienated by this magazine. Once again, I've got a suspicion that's rooted in the back of my mind—that the issue will not contain a single image of a woman holding an instrument of any kind. Perversely, I want to see if I'm correct. The sensation of knowing what I will find is already sad. It's like discovering a letter in which the guy you're crushing on declares his love for some other woman, and still, inevitably, reading the whole thing down to the last painful line.

Of course, *Rolling Stone* contains only one image of a "token" woman holding an instrument. It's Taylor Swift, dressed in a diamond studded ball gown, holding a matching silver diamond acoustic guitar. Good for her! As America's large-scale concert industry pretty much collapses around her feet, she's single-handedly (okay, alongside Justin Bieber) holding down the fort. Other than Taylor, the closest thing I can find to a woman with an instrument in *Rolling Stone* is a tiny photo of Cat Power holding a microphone at Lilith Fair, the image wedged into a short write-up way at the bottom of the page. There is also a photo of two women in their late thirties or forties called the Wilson Sisters, one of whom is holding something that looks like the neck of a guitar down below her waist. The guitar itself has been cut out of the photo. Besides them, and Lady Gaga, and the naked, air-brushed star of *True Blood* on the cover, who incidentally, is pictured with a guy grabbing her boob, I can't find any other women in the whole magazine. This means that Taylor Swift, Cat Power, and the Wilson Sisters are not only the only women that *Rolling Stone* depicts as musicians, but also the only women that *Rolling Stone* depicts as wearing clothes.

I know that the magazine industry is failing and is doing everything it can to sell copies, and I know that it's not easy to come up with content that will sell, and I know that sex sells, and that pop music in its purest form has a lot to do with sex, but dammit, *Rolling Stone*, can't you try to be a little more fair to us? We are, after all, people too. We have purchasing power. We buy magazines. By we, I don't just mean feminists, but women. We deserve to buy into this glorious image that you call music these days just as much as straight males do. We deserve to see ourselves as present in pop culture in some capacity that does not totally dehumanize us, and overly sexualize us, and turn us into objects for the straight male consumer to ogle. And since there are women fucking DOING incredible things in the music scene these days, we deserve to see images of women DOING things, alongside men, and not just passively posing, semi-naked, for those men's titillation. Got that? Okay!

Feminists have been railing against the images of women in magazines for ages. But the thing is, it's become such an old story that people frequently forget how vital the issue is. Nowadays, most adult women know that photographs of women in magazines are airbrushed into perfection, and some feminist organizations have started bugging the media about the unhealthy images of women that appear in the pages of magazines, but the magazine industry has largely failed to respond to feminist challenges of its content. Why is this important? I mean, why is it important that girls and women be able to open a magazine and see pictures of women doing things? Why is it so vital that media portray women as participants in culture? Well, let me tell you a little story.

When I was fourteen years old, my friends and I discovered women's magazines. Fascinated, we pored over the images of slightly older teenage girls doing what teenage girls are supposed to like to do—shopping, dating, dieting, dating, and shopping. Reading the magazines always brought on a kind of nausea, an awful sinking feeling in the pit of my stomach that made me feel like I was sitting on an airplane and powerless to stop it from dropping out of the sky.

For some reason, the feeling was addictive, and I always came back for more: All the candy-colored costumes, that shiny lip gloss, that bright future that the magazines promised us within their pages, and time after time failed to provide. I was pretty much in an abusive relationship with magazines. And why? I guess I was optimistic. I was looking for some kind of validation, as all teenagers are, when they are growing up. I was looking and looking for a picture of a woman who looked like me, a slightly older teen who I could identify with, a person I could see myself becoming when I grew up.

Did I find that person in a magazine? Of course not! What I found was hundreds and hundreds of denials of my self, and hundreds of disappointing statements about what women are supposed to be—statements which I immediately internalized, and which my brain chemically converted into ten years of serious anxiety and depression. In all those years, did it ever occur to me to open a copy of *Rolling Stone*? No, of course not, because I knew, even from looking at the cover, that *Rolling Stone* was not for me. The idea of *Rolling Stone* conjured up images of Mick Jagger stroking a phallic guitar and wearing a ridiculous hat, or of the guys at guitar center with their long grey beards and their technical talk about digital effects pedals. There were no pictures of women with guitars on the cover of *Rolling Stone*. There was no one in that magazine who looked like me. I knew from which scenes I had been excluded.

A few months ago, I had a talk with a friend named Emily, and she told me something about her life that has stuck with me for a long time. The conversation came up after somebody tweeted something about me and my performance during Pitchfork fest. "Saw Titus Andronicus," wrote the dude. "They still have that girl trying to play guitar who can't play guitar." The nausea in my stomach that appeared suddenly resembled the sinking feeling I had discovered in looking at women's magazines as a teen. Although I know, as a performer, I'm subject to bad reviews, and people are not always going to like what I do, this guy's comment had a definitively sexist ring to it. "Why is it," I asked Emily, "that women who try anything at all seem to be subjected to unfair amounts of criticism, just for trying! It's like society is encouraging women not to put themselves out there! What on earth is wrong with trying something and struggling with it, and not being perfect? Well, nothing! Except if you're a girl. Then you have to be perfect, and perfect by standards that men get to set and enforce. And if you're not that, then people think you're nothing at all."

Emily responded with a story about her life. She stated that she'd been confused as a teen too, and didn't really know where she fit in. Then she discovered independent music. For her, the music was important; she later became a music reviewer, and still has an impressive knowledge of indie rock. But for her, the music was something more; indie rock was a gateway into a way of thinking about the world—a kind of independent viewpoint that allowed her to approach our culture from a critical perspective. Today Emily is an activist who fights to empower urban communities. She is interested in history, and wants to change it, and knows that, if she tries hard enough, she can. I identified with this story, because independent music did the exact same thing for me. I remember discovering my sister's CDs by Liz Phair and Bikini Kill, and listening to them, and feeling like some secret knowledge was being conveyed to me by a neural network buried deep within my brain. Although I didn't quite understand what Liz Phair was talking about when she talked about sex, I knew what she was talking about when she talked about power. I knew about the image of a girl washing dishes in a frat house, and standing way too tall for her height. Listening to punk and rock and roll and indie taught me that there were scenes outside the mainstream—that there was a secret history hidden beneath the surface of the America we learned about in school, and it made me want to become a part of that secret world, to stand alongside those female superheroes who were so strong and brave they might as well have been from another planet. I remember the first time I read a zine, which my sister had hidden in her top desk drawer, and found—yes—a real interview with Liz Phair. How honest her comments made her seem! I aspired to be that honest with myself one day.

What we're doing when we exclude women from rock and roll, and from the sense of rebellion that rock and roll promises, is disallowing women that independent perspective. We're never giving them the chance to think critically about the world, and about the systems that oppress them. When we take women out of the arts, and take them out of art's ability to critique the way things are, we're making sure that women keep swallowing the status quo, day after day, and it's the status quo that keeps us down.

When I went to Japan, I met a woman named Ayumi. She worked a boring job as a secretary in a big office, and found her life to be unfulfilling at best. One day, she saw a certain photograph—that is, the photo of Kathleen Hanna on the cover of a certain CD in which Ms. Hanna wears a pair of short shorts, and spreads her legs wide in a V, and screams into the microphone as if her voice is a laser beam about to destroy the earth. That image was all Ayumi needed to change her life. She quit her job and started her own magazine, about female musicians, and then started her own record label releasing music by Japanese girls bands, and then started a blog, and began running her own shows and events. That picture seriously changed her life, and when I heard this, I was not shocked, because, all the way across the world, at the same time, that picture changed my life too.

This is why it's important for the media to portray women who are powerful, women who are confident, and women whose actions are culturally significant. It's not just because of what these women are doing, it's because of what these magazines are failing to do. The mainstream media is failing to allow girls into its cultural castle. It's keeping girls on the outside, and alienating them, when it could be—with a single image—changing these same girls' lives for the better. Does a business have social responsibility? Well, it doesn't have to, if people will buy the magazine anyway. But what if we decide not to buy magazines that don't portray women the way they really are? There are countless magazines out there that portray women in a positive light. Try *Venus Zine*, for women in indie and DIY culture, or *Bust*, for fashion shoots that feature women of all different shapes and sizes, or *Bitch*, for articles written by women for women about women's issues. Or better yet, check out the zine table at your local punk show, or read some blogs, and find out what women are self-publishing these days.

This is not an article about *Rolling Stone*. *Rolling Stone* is not guilty of anything, except of being complicit in a larger system that governs the way our country exists. But *Rolling Stone*, at its purest form, was meant to be about rock and roll, and rock and roll is about rebellion, and if we let that spirit die, then we are missing out on everything the genre has to offer. Are we going to patrol the borders of American culture so as to admit only straight, white males? Or are we going to open our culture up to challenge oppressive systems of race and class, and privilege, and gender, and sexual orientation? This is what rock and roll was meant for, and what the spirit that captures the collective imagination of youth can accomplish, if it is funneled constructively into the future. How many things can you get young people excited about these days, besides music? What else breaks the apathy of large crowds and causes them to dance together, and sing the same words, and not want to fight everyone who's different from them, for once? If our culture's "rebellion" actually belongs to those in power, and continues to belong to them, then it's not a real rebellion at all anymore, and therefore rock and roll is dead.

Is it so wrong of me to want to believe that the spirit of rock and roll is still alive, and that all those 1950s teenagers who became infatuated with the Beatles, and that before that, America's blues and gospel traditions, and after that, Riot Grrrl in the '90s, all meant something in the sense of a grand historical continuum—that they were leading our country somewhere, and not just entertaining the crowds as the whole damn ship began to sink? What is there left for us to do, and for that old lady at the gas station who has probably lost a son in Iraq, when the economy is failing and our education system sucks, and the media is dying, and we're all escaping into a parallel universe online—what is there left for us to do but try to right the wrongs that have befallen us? What does some magazine's airbrushed idea of beauty have to do with that old woman's life, and what does it have to do with mine?

To me, that crazy old lady is America. She may be old and poor, and she may be struggling to move, and she may have lost her sons to that war we're always fighting far away, but dammit, she's still got that feisty, red-lipsticked mouth on her. She's a rebel through and through. She doesn't give up.

What on earth are we doing with ourselves, with our culture, making sure that women are not going to reach their potential, and that at least half of the country's populace is not going to attain the American dream? This is an article about America as it exists today, and if we exclude women from our culture, from our opportunities, and from our collective conscience, then our country is going nowhere fast. The cycle through which those in power remain in power and exclude the dis-empowered from the system is no longer viable. It is now vitally apparent to me that, unless we let everyone participate in this country equally, then we are all going to fail.

Jetlagged Manifesto

Jeremy Denk

I woke at 3:32 and stumbled over my open suitcase towards the kitchen, neither awake nor asleep, floating in time-purgatory. A slice of slightly crusty Monterey Jack from the back of the refrigerator did not bring comfort. All sorts of anxieties bubbled out of my last hour of sleep: even they were groggy, dazed . . . maybe a bit crabby.

In other words, a classic jetlag situation where you confront the weird empty hour thinking what the hell am I going to do with you? I stared out the window at nothing, and my mind helped itself to a ridiculous and comically dark train of thought, which (for some reason) I can't help sharing:

> Sometimes performances bring pieces to life, but sometimes they (I, we) kill them instead. Performers (and this seems obvious, inevitable, we're human, we're all culpable) are sometimes complicit in the Death of Classical Music.

Ouch! But fasten your seatbelts, it gets darker yet:

> If the concert is sometimes a "murder" of what should be a living work, program notes are the chloroform rag we use to numb the victim, before dragging it to the scene of the crime.

Ha! Yes, I realize it's unfair to carp about program notes at 4 a.m. just because you're grumpy about being awake and stressed about practicing Ligeti Etudes! But this program note thing had been on my mind for a while.

It seems regrettable that a writing style called Program Note Style ever came into existence. It's hard to define, I suppose; you know it when you read it, by a slight heartburn of the soul. When I start to compose program notes, I feel the Siren of this Style, calling me. The words clump into clichéd paragraphs, habits learned from hundreds of programs, perused in waiting moments . . . You begin with a few dates, then you slip in the curious historical tidbit: "while he composed X in 18xx, curiously he didn't publish it until 18xx . . . " The tidbit that makes it seem authoritative, knowledgeable, yawn yawn . . . Agh! Select All. Delete. Contemplate blank screen with relief.

I would like to enumerate the Deadly Sins of program notes.

The first one is **HISTORICIZATION**.

I've never been a big fan of the "imagine how revolutionary this piece was when it was written" school of inspiration. For my money, it should be revolutionary now. (And it is.) Whatever else the composer might have intended, he or she didn't want you to think "boy that must have been cool back then." The most basic compositional intent, the absolute ur-intent, is that you play it NOW, you make it happen NOW.

If you've ever been pestered by a composer to play their music, you know what I mean.

Now, history and understanding are delicious, essential! At the same time, I don't think program notes should rub your face too much in the NOT NOW. It certainly doesn't help classical music's "age problem." I'll confess: historical context is good for me (context me good, baby!) mainly to the extent that it creates a kind of suspended now in which the work can exist again—present, perpetually different. There's generally not room for that sort of context in a program note; instead, a thicket of dates and boring circumstances tends to evoke an officious wall between us and the living work, reminding us for no good reason that the composer is dead, conjuring his coffin, a notched timeline. Consider this opening to a program note:

> The world was changing in the late 18th and early 19th centuries. The authority of monarchies, no matter how enlightened they might be, was challenged: the American colonies against England, Hungarian peasants against Austria under Joseph II, the people of France and Louis XVI. Economic power was shifting away from the landed aristocracy to an urban middle class that included bankers, lawyers, merchants, and factory owners.

This note is for the "Trout" Quintet. You, listener: get serious, be studious and pensive for the urban middle class specimen you're about to hear! If the performer's aim is to recreate the piece in the present, immediate, alive, why do so many program notes make that so much more difficult?

The second sin is **MAKING GENERIC**: the sausage-like conversion of extraordinary musical moments into blobs of generic prose. Think of the program note as a field of battle on which the great defining characteristics of a work of art lie strewn, wounded by flying bullets of blandness.

Generic-ization is a very understandable sin; there's nothing worse than a program note writer who goes hogwild with subjective and silly adjectives, like me. (I hate my own notes, for the most part, but I can't help writing them!) To avoid this, the "typical program note writer" holds back, purging description of individuality. For instance:

> The last movement takes up the motives of the first in varied form.

Now, it's not that this sentence isn't true, or isn't a valid, cogent structural observation about the Stravinsky Piano Concerto. But this phrase "varied form" sticks in my throat—generic, indigestible. It seems a wasted opportunity. Varied how? To what purpose? I mean variation is nearly everywhere, it's like the amino acid or DNA of music: a replication process which allows life to happen.

In fact, in this particular piece (the Stravinsky Concerto for Piano and Winds) the last movement visits some particularly grotesque, comic transformations on the ideas of the first. And as it turns out, the first movement is a set of inventive rethinkings of Bach and the Baroque: so, the last movement is a transformation of a transformation! While the first movement has ragtime mashed in with its toccata-Bach, the last allows Bach to head towards vaudeville, towards the Charleston, or the Foxtrot. The main thematic material is good crusty Baroque fare: full of pointed, jagged intervals, evoking an academic abstruse fugue, food for angular counterpoint . . . to allow this to become roaring '20s jazz is a punning leap from the cloister to the cabaret. The composer is grinning, he's courting sacrilege; it's a wicked, almost brutal mashup. Perhaps you feel my description goes too far. But would you say . . .

"Picasso in his Cubist period takes up the motive of the guitar in varied form."

No, I didn't think so.

Sin #3: **INSIDER'S CLUB**.

Included in many program notes are tidbits of historical information.

It's amazing how canonical these tidbits can become. I played Beethoven's First Concerto a number of times last season and every single program note noted that while the First Concerto is called number 1, it was actually composed **second**, after the Second Concerto, which was actually **first**. Now, as a performer and person, I am theoretically glad I know this, in the larger context of the Beethoven story, but, finally: YAWN. In fact, double yawn! Yawn times infinity plus one! Suppose you as a listener and program note reader do not know the Second Concerto, and you're just looking for help to appreciate the work before you: this seems like a pretty "meta" piece of information to help you out; it seems like what a kind of tedious museum guide would say. Ironic, because of all Beethoven works the First Concerto is **not** "meta": from the moment the piano enters, its simplicity requires no insider information. Beethoven takes care to speak to you with obvious grammar, with clear rhetoric, almost Phrasing for Dummies. And he takes you dummies through an epic tale nonetheless, using the harmonic equivalent of "see Jane run" as a doorway to shaded, subtle corners of tonality.

When I find these tidbits in program notes, I get an unshakable mental image: a group of gentlemen in smoking jackets, smoking cigars in a private club, exchanging "I say, old chap, did you know that the first concerto was actually composed second"? They're chortling to each other, but their back is to you; through the knowledge they share, they exclude the larger group. The tidbits of knowledge are a badge of belonging, even though they do not particularly or centrally illuminate the work in question. For some reason these tidbits have become a habit, even a required element of program notes: I have no idea why.

And the last sin: **DOMESTICATION**.

These works are not our pets. They are not *tchotchkes* to be set upon the shelf for occasional amusement and decoration. But certain turns of phrase in program notes seem to reduce tremendous originalities down to size, seem to want to put composers' innovations in their place. I found the following in a program note for the Stravinsky Piano Concerto (again):

> *Although Stravinsky moved very far from his earlier "Russian-period" works in the Piano Concerto, we may recognize him, among other things, by his fondness for asymmetrical rhythms, which is evident in all three movements of the work.*

A "fondness" for asymmetrical rhythms? FONDNESS? You may as well say "Proust has a fondness for discussing the passing of time," or "Beethoven has a fondness for exploring the relationship between tonic and dominant," or "Shakespeare has a fondness for observing character traits." It's the fatal understatement, the polite absurd word that stops meaning in its tracks.

Stravinsky's attack upon, and reinvention of, rhythm is obviously core to his life's work, core to his whole revolution of musical time, which has haunted and inspired much of the twentieth century. It is not a fondness, but an artistic essence, the grammar of a thrilling, unsettling new language. Program notes should avoid this mistake; and yet, it is the very human, natural mistake of someone wandering too long through an art museum, fatigued by one great canvas after another, trying to know what to say. Sometimes, sadly, you don't have the option to say nothing!

Through the grimy kitchen window (I really should get that cleaned!) there was a gradual increase in the green and now yellow and blue stripe of dawn. I'm a sucker for quickening colors. My anxieties began to blow away, leaving reality sitting on the table: a hunk of sweaty cheese. Having written down my rant, I realized I wasn't upset at any one program note writer; I was upset at the construct, the genre, and its expectations.

I perversely Googled one last program note, for the Archduke Trio. It began:

> *Despite the considerable contributions of Haydn and Mozart, it remained for Beethoven to give the piano trio an importance it had not enjoyed before.*

I mean, I can't argue with it, it's depressingly true—but somehow the word "importance" gets on my nerves. The piece is very important to me. But the sense of the word "importance," in this context, seems violently different from that personal importance. I scrolled down to see what the author said about my favorite movement:

> *The serene slow movement . . . is a series of variations on a hymnlike melody. ["hymnlike": true, but GENERIC] (After Beethoven's death it was gratuitously adapted to a choral setting of verses by Goethe.) [HISTORICIZATION, INSIDER'S*

CLUB] There are four variations, of great melodic and rhythmic interest [GENERIC: what interest? how?], and of growing tension and complexity, but after the fourth the theme is restated in its original purity [GENERIC: not exactly, crucial changes are made], to be followed by a dreamy coda which extends as a bridge to the finale (yet again as in Op. 59, No. 1—and numerous other works of its period). [INSIDER'S CLUB, DOMESTICATION]

I found all my enumerated sins. Of course I was evilly looking for them. "Dreamy coda which extends as a bridge to the finale"—it's accurate, but upsets me. It absorbs one of my favorite moments in music, absorbs it into terminology which seems too comfy, too prosaic . . . like putting caviar on mashed potatoes.

I wasn't being objective, I admit that. This Archduke note is just fine, it's even quite good; it is well-written, and what's more, it doesn't force any particular vision. But . . .

What is it about these variations, why do they make me so happy? Maybe they have what I feel I lack? Patience, reliance on the beauty of a few tried and true harmonies, on color itself, and time: all of these givens, given space to breathe. The cumulative effect of all this space and breathing and inevitability is a kind of love expressed in tones, not the potiony feverish love of *Tristan* but—I'm embarrassed to say it, I suppose—love for the universe, love for things as they are, or if not that either, love for just being. Felix Galimir, the famous violinist and teacher, at my first lesson on the piece, said that it was "the only truly beautiful thing ever written for the piano." (Haha.) Yes, in its profound color-thinking at the piano, the exploitation of the overtones, registers: it was (is, continues to be) a new kind of prayer to sound, sensual sound as a sign of love. Of course, you cannot say "prayer to sound" in a program note; that would be ridiculous. It's so much safer to say "series of variations on a hymnlike melody," don't you think?

Making Pop for Capitalist Pigs

Jessica Hopper

M.I.A.'s third album, /\/\ /\ Y /\, arrives piled high with the pre-conceptions of its audience. But let's set aside Lynn Hirschberg's *New York Times Magazine* profile/takedown and those infamous truffle fries. Let's forget about whatever meaning we extracted (or didn't) from M.I.A.'s "Born Free" video, with its simulated land mines launching little-boy legs sky-high in a cloud of vague polemics and computer-assisted movie magic. Let's pretend for a bit we can separate her from her own image, even though in many ways that image is her real art, the daily emanation of a Warholian figure ghost-riding the zeitgeist. Maybe it's still possible to simply talk about the thing that got people interested in M.I.A. in the first place—her music.

/\/\ /\ Y /\, officially out July 13, is like a transmission from the ultra now—an e-mailed camera-phone video compressed till it's cruddy and degenerated, a live-tweeting of capitalist culture's fore-closure proceedings on the tar-blotched shores of American apocalyptica. This is not pleasure pop—it's an allergic reaction to it, an involuntary spasm full of exploding, hissing, and banging, all un-comfortably close. For most of its duration /\/\ /\ Y /\ is a barrage, mimicking modern information overload, but its crowded jumbles of jarring, ugly sounds are broken up by scary expanses of what-if—a sort of creepy, hookless drift that gets at her dystopian vision from the opposite angle.

The album starts with the clicking of fingernails on a keyboard, but in lieu of the modem handshake that would follow if this were the '90s, we get drilling and clanging—the sound of something mechanical being pieced together. The first track, "The Message," is less than a minute long, a stage-setting vignette that touches on a topic she's been rolling out in recent interviews, like the cover story of the current *Nylon*—the claim that the CIA monitors or even invented Google. Here as there, she doesn't elaborate much, instead just laying it out as nursery-rhymed fact: "Head bone connects to the headphones / Headphones connect to the iPhone / iPhone connects to the Internet, connects to the Google, connects to the government." It's less a well-argued thesis and more the sort of conspiracy theory you might hear in a dorm room after someone's had a few bong rips.

On /\/\ /\ Y /\ M.I.A. doesn't connect dots. She recites lists, mixing brand names with heavier signifiers—CIA, Google, Obama, Allah—in a flat, staccato rap. It's hard to tell whether she's genuinely trying to convince anyone of anything or just using what's now basically the default setting in contemporary fiction and Top 40 hip-hop: relying on the audience's understanding of the connotations of certain brands or products instead of doing any real character development. We get a portrait of a consumer, not of a person, via symbols like champagne, cars, Izods, and iPods.

The CIA is of course shorthand for the sins of American power, and that's the focus of this album—America, or M.I.A. in America. (She settled in the Brentwood area of Los Angeles early in 2009.) Her previous albums spanned the world in sound and vision, setting their sights on the havoc globalism wreaks, but /\/\ /\ Y /\ is myopic by comparison. It's as though she's been sidetracked into responding to personal provocations, real or imagined. On "Lovealot," when she tauntingly says "They told me this was a free country," you almost expect to hear a bedroom door slam and a stereo crank up. She sounds petulant, like a pissed-off teenager. When she raps "I fight the ones that fight me," it's hard to tell if she's singing as America or as herself.

Despite its statement songs and bombastic production, /\/\ /\ Y /\ often lacks gravitas—it's so overloaded, and tries to do so many things, that it ends up feeling dilettantish and lightweight. M.I.A. gets on a roll, her music and her message pulling together, and then derails herself with misguided attempts at pop like "Teqkilla," a hook-free tribute to whatever's in the red Solo party cup you're holding in the air. The chorus: "I got sticky sticky / Icky icky / Weeeed!" (Yes, really.) It feels long after two and a half minutes, and its actual length—six minutes and 20 seconds—represents a grievous overes-timation of listener patience. Much of the rest of the middle of the album is just as aimless: "It Iz What It Iz" with its sour sung notes, "It Takes a Muscle" with its treacly synth-reggae uplift and some Auto-Tune to make it sound truly inconsequential.

/\/\ /\ Y /\ gives us a little of everything, and it feels like the potluck it is. M.I.A. worked piecemeal with six different producers across the album (and more on the editions with bonus tracks). The cuts with British producer and dubstep poster boy Rusko are inter-esting—his low-gear grind is pretty dazzling in any setting—but he doesn't compose well for singers. His dark, wub-wubbing electro is so full of detail and WTF twists that it's best taken on its own; despite his awesomely claustrophobic (claustrophonic?) sound, M.I.A.'s Bomb Squad he ain't. The tracks were edited into song forms from record-ings of epic jam sessions, and you can tell. With the exceptions of al-bum highlight "Born Free," which samples Suicide's "Ghost Rider," and "XXXO," a straight radio-pop construction, /\/\ /\ Y /\ sounds like something roped down from the ether and pasted together.

"You know who I am," she sings on "Steppin Up," and now and then it feels like we do. /\/\ /\ Y /\ is as close to a treatise on her personal brand as she's ever gotten—there's a lot more about M.I.A., a lot more first person. Or at least about M.I.A. as she wishes to be known: a world-weary pop terrorist, a truth-telling Robin Hoodrat here to dis-abuse us of our first-world ignorance, a siren singer who's seen the rewards of pop-chart success and is alternately burdened with and enchanted by them. "You want me to be somebody who I'm really not," she sings on the hook to "XXXO," but who is she talking to?

Throughout the album she broadcasts her ID: immigrant, refugee, Pope hater, enemy of the bourgeoisie. Unsurprisingly she leaves out the part where she's engaged to Ben Brewer, aka Benjamin Zachary Bronfman, son of Warner Music Group CEO Edgar Bronfman Jr. and heir to the Seagram fortune—but she can't leave out the part where she's an international celebrity, even if she'd prefer to. ("I don't wanna talk about money, 'cause I got it," she sings on "Born Free.") She is perhaps more than ever doing as Robert Christgau wrote in 2005: making art of her contradictions. They're what make her compelling, and why her rebel-girl image—calculated and genuine, with both halves magnified in the limelight—is so hard to take at face value. M.I.A. confounds us as a pop star and political artist, a slippery shape shifter moving easily between two positions we've learned to see as incompatible: she's an enemy of America even as she makes pop for Americans.

The Underground Rises

Morad Mansouri

With assistance from Dan Geist

For those engaged in the musical crafts in Iran, the very term "underground music" sparks controversy, for they realize that its provenance—coined to express the rebellion of Western musicians against the commodification and banality of music in their own societies—ill suits it to the Iranian context.

In Iran, "underground music" denotes something vastly different: not a protest against market norms imposed by a constrictive and domineering music industry, but rather a *samizdat* art form in a country whose rulers abhor music altogether and have consigned most expressions of it to the realm of the forbidden.

In a place where music diverging from the state's tight bounds of propriety is forced underground to survive, and where that scene has far more adherents than the state-endorsed music it challenges, it is inapt to classify the underground music that has emerged over the past decade as a Western-style, self-defined purist movement eschewing mainstream success in favor of artistic integrity or creative independence. Instead, I propose to examine how this music reflects the symbiotic bond between Iran's underground subculture and shifts in mainstream social consciousness.

Starting roughly eight years ago, the authorities in Iran were faced with something radically novel. The music blaring out of taxis, spewing from apartment windows, or pumping out of their own children's jukeboxes was unlike anything they had heard before.

Until then, musical trendsetting had been the exclusive preserve of an aging clique of Los Angeles-based Iranian pop singers exiled by the Revolution. In the cultural ferment of the pre-revolutionary '70s, many of these singers, then young, audacious, and innovative, had helped pioneer a musical revolution of their own, deftly fusing traditional Iranian styles and melodies with modern Western rhythms and instruments, with results at once avant-garde and authentically Iranian. This flush of syncretic creativity, and the promising genres of music flowing from it, were stamped out by the Revolution and nearly forgotten over two decades of theocratic stasis.

Once in exile, shorn of the atmosphere and community that had fostered their skill, the singers did not regain their poise. Their talents stagnated and their music gradually devolved into vulgar, lowbrow kitsch.

In revolutionary Iran's stifling social milieu, where neighbors and family often took perverse pleasure in enforcing the state's grim code of conduct, Iranians would dance furtively in private gatherings to this imported potboiler music—a guilt-ridden, awkward release inhibited by fear of being discovered, chastised, ostracized. The merit of the music itself was of scant interest to hounded revelers.

The homegrown music that began to crash the scene was as impoverished and vulgar as the Los Angeles music it was displacing, but it did introduce novelties in sound and lyric that guaranteed a rapturous audience. A strong beat, lilting tempo, and heavy electronic synthesis, married to the popular 6/8 compound meter, animated listeners into a dance much freer of inhibition and reserve. Incoherent, disjointed, raunchy lyrics mimicked Western hip-hop, breaking taboos by delving hotly into sexual topics. Most were composed with painful shoddiness using a single desktop PC, a keyboard, and a solitary mike.

The authorities were staggered: where was this seditious music coming from and, more pointedly, why was it so immensely popular?

Short answer to that pointed query: state oppression, and social reaction to it. My longer explanation follows.

This underground music was not as spontaneous and rootless as our blinkered authorities imagined it to be. It followed in the wake of, and in tandem with, broader currents that preceded it into the mirthless still of postwar Iranian society. In the years of gradual liberalization following the end of the Iran-Iraq War, many youngsters had eagerly sought tutoring in music. Conservatories were established—with much trepidation at first, but they gradually found their bearings and started to proliferate. Computers and CDs eased access to all variety of Western music, from trailblazing giants like John Lennon and Roger Waters to bad-boy maestros such as Johnny Rotten and Metallica, on to Eminem and Snoop Dog. Talented pop artists who won rare official permits added a handful of good local songs to the brew.

Many teenagers would take to the Elburz mountains north of Tehran on weekends, trekking up high, well past the morality police and Basij enforcers stalking the foothills, to play the guitar and sing for friends and lovers in the seclusion of nature. Back in the urban jungle, scores embraced heavy metal, punk and grunge, together with the affectations of dress and hair that went with those renegade musical styles. A few studied and practiced the masterpieces of Pink Floyd and the Beatles. Legions more spent time, in class, on the school bus, and at home, composing new verse for rap.

Rappers and hip-hop DJs would gather in remote cloisters of public parks and in deserted car lots to practice and flaunt their talent, while punks and heavy metalists set up studios in the basements of their homes. The rappers eventually became more popular, as they practiced their craft in the native Farsi language, lived the gang lifestyle more convincingly, and had the wind of a worldwide musical trend at their backs. Rap finally came of age in 2004 with the widespread success of hip-hop artist Soroush Lashkari (aka, Hichkas) and his group, 021.

As underground studios proliferated, hard rock and heavy metal artists began to discover each other and form bands to produce serious music. In 2003, the website TehranAvenue, run by a group of avant-garde artists and progressive social critics, held its first Underground Music Contest (UMC) for Iranian rock and heavy metal artists, with around 20 bands prequalified to compete. The recording quality of submissions was pitiful, but as the event coincided with the explosion of blogging and Internet use in the country, its reception among Iranian youth was nothing less than spectacular.

Meanwhile, Tehran's rap scene was also in ferment. Individual rappers formed bands, took stage names, adopted gang insignia and distinctive clothing styles, faced off in rap duels with rival bands in Tehran's public parks, and collected hordes of fans and groupies. They even began recording diss tracks against each other.

Websites dedicated to Iranian rap popped up constantly, introducing a rash of new artists. Aping Western role models, their typical formula was to extol drugs, denigrate women, and cram as many obscenities as possible into the span of each song. Some artists stood out with better music and passable lyrics—albeit without shedding the profanity.

TehranAvenue organized more contests in 2004 and 2005, attracting a much wider spectrum of styles. The standard hard rock and heavy metal fare was now supplemented with a repertoire of punk, pop, and rap.

Significantly, some entries in these contests offered serious, technically proficient attempts at fusing Iran's regional melodic formulae with Western electronic, jazz, and percussion styles. This, in turn, stimulated youthful interest in more mainstream musicians who had spent the previous decades drawing on the rich lode of Iranian traditional music and poetry to compose innovative and powerful pieces.

A sex scandal that rocked Iran in 2006 exposed deep moral fissures in society, helped widen them, and proved seminal in clearing a path for mainstream acceptance of underground music.

Shortly after the conclusion of the popular TV mini-series *Narges*, a home video emerged of popular cast member Zahra Amirebrahimi engaged in passionate sex with her lover. Within days it went viral, becoming the lead topic of gossip at parties and gatherings for months in this avowedly pious and prudish nation, where outings of far lesser indiscretions had led girls to suicide or forced them to flee their homes in permanent disgrace to live as social outcasts.

But now, parents and teachers were vying with their children and students to prove that they had watched the rousing "Zahra" video in all its lurid detail. A huge stigma had been shed, at great cost to the young star's prospects. The longevity of the scandal, and the bold discussions it kindled, helped unravel social inhibitions, causing a liberal shift in attitudes toward relations between the sexes.

While public sentiment was still a disquiet mix of voyeurism, empathy, and scorn, TehranAvenue's timely intervention helped cast Zahra's status as an iconic martyr for a society fed up with its own moral sanctimony. An editor, Hamed Safaee, posted a beautifully crafted video on the website, animating a time-lapse sequence of stills he had taken of a solitary Zahra walking down a rainy alley, staring pensively at the camera, smiling happily at the clearing sky, sipping coffee alone in a tiny, abject kitchen. The music he chose as background was Mohsen Namjoo's recent "Zolf Bar Baad" (Unbound Tresses), whose lyrics, originally penned in the 14th century by Iran's great classical poet Hafez, are the crazed admonishments of a man consumed by jealousy to the object of his cloying, possessive love:

> *Free not your tresses lest I come unmoored*
> *Bestill your charm lest my foundation shatters*
> *Drink not the cup with everyman lest I drown in envy*
> *Bridle your thirst lest I cry unbridled to heavens*
> *Lock not your tresses lest my heart be bound*

Zahra's story, coupled with Namjoo's edgy musical delivery, gave added poignancy to the coy double entendres of Hafez's medieval Persian verse.

The impact was immediate and cathartic. The video went viral much faster than the notorious sex tape had earlier, and it was downloaded hundreds of thousands of times in a matter of weeks. Zahra was no longer social menace, object of pity, or public spectacle. She was a normal, brave, resilient human being, deserving of sympathy and regard—everyone's daughter and sister. And young Mohsen Namjoo, already a rising star in Tehran's music scene and a UMC contestant in 2005, became a celebrated household name in the remotest corners of Iran.

Namjoo was a classical Persian vocalist and *setar* virtuoso who had developed a unique form of protest music by fusing Persian poetry and the traditional *maghami* music of northeastern Iran with the melodic templates and lyrical styles of Bob Dylan and Jim Morrison. In so doing, he had to forfeit some of the allure of Persian poetry and part of the richness of *maghami*, but the synthesis he achieved was mesmerizing and without precedent in Iranian music. He would add stanzas to the classic poems, satirize the original verse, or distort his vocal delivery in such a way as to load his songs with heavy political and sexual innuendo, intoxicating the listener with a playful mix of tragic sentimentality and cynical sarcasm.

In 2006, yet another scandal rocked the country. Hundreds of rappers, rockers, and fans had organized a huge night-time bacchanalia, a secret Woodstock of sorts, in a sprawling country estate on the outskirts of Karaj, immediately west of Tehran. The police raided the party and arrested scores.* State media gave wide coverage to the event and concocted all sorts of labels for the unfortunate detainees: libertines, cultists, drug addicts, debauchees, corruptors of youth, even Satanists.

Both media and state realized the pervasiveness of the underground music culture in Iran, but trapped in the solipsism of religious ortho-

---

* Bahman Ghobadi's award-winning documentary film, *No One Knows About Persian Cats* (2009), was inspired by the raid on the Karaj bacchanalia. Focusing his narrative on a micro-trend and two musicians captured in the raid who now burned with the desire to emigrate, he seems to explain away the whole underground music phenomenon as an expression by repressed Iranian youth of their desire to escape the country en masse.

doxy, they could not fathom the movement's origins, grasp the reasons for its widespread allure, or understand the messages of the social commentary it conveyed. Conferences were sponsored by the government to discuss this apparently unstoppable phenomenon, with Mohsen Namjoo and Hichkas invited to perform for the attendees. Comically, the audience did not pick up on the taunts in Hichkas's lyrics against the police or the barely concealed ridicule of religious dogma in Namjoo's songs.

The cognitive dissonance presaged the epochal drama of June 2009, where the most regressive government since the war was caught totally off guard by the cresting of public fury at the surreal vote tallies announced for the presidential election.

More than a year after the crushing of that popular revolt, many underground musicians have fled Iran, but not at a rate outstripping the creation of new talent inside the country.

Now rappers and rock artists, both male and female, exist in every Iranian city, large and small, studying and experimenting with classic Western styles and developing their own. With no hope of obtaining licenses for concerts and records, they perform in basement studios or in the countryside. They are resilient and resourceful. When studios are raided, musical instruments confiscated, and fines levied, they start again from scratch.

There are some who have surrendered to state orthodoxy. The government coddles and promotes musicians who adhere to the rules and concoct the most hackneyed and vacuous music imaginable. Yet even these untalented quislings crudely mimic the stylistic elements of the far more progressive and innovative underground music, if only to stay marginally relevant to society. For it is in the very act of protesting and transgressing norms that music becomes creative and exciting and worthwhile, especially when those norms are enforced by the repressive machinery of a killjoy state.

Pantha du Prince

Philip Sherburne

*Who . . . has witnessed the terror and majesty of the Alpine
storm, when the very rocks seem to shake with the wind,
and the lightning seems to laugh with the pride and glory of
its power? These things cannot be really communicated.
They are the unique possession of those who have
experienced them. It is only very dimly that words can give
to the outer world some distant glimpses of the glories that
the eye has seen and the tongue is stumbling to tell.*
—Harold Spender, "In Praise of Switzerland" (1912)

On a crisp day in 1816, the villagers of a town in the foothills of the
Swiss Alps may have looked up, startled, as a flock of birds exploded
from the rocks and trees, taking spontaneous flight. They would not
have had much time to reflect on this occurrence, however, as the
mountain above came tumbling down, burying the town in boulders
and a pall of dust.

On a late autumn day in Kreuzberg, with the cheerful sounds of a
children's playground drifting up to Hendrik Weber's third-floor studio, that event couldn't seem farther away. But it has been resonating
here for months, as Weber finished *Black Noise*, the third album released under his alias Pantha du Prince.

"Black noise is a frequency you can't hear," explains Weber, "that
happens in a landslide or an avalanche or earthquake." It's bass at the

tectonic level, a sound only animals can perceive. As an album title, it makes a perfect fit for an artist known for infusing his music with sweeping, almost gothic gravitas. But it's more than a metaphor, in this case.

Weber spent several weeks in the Swiss Alps gathering the sounds for the album, accompanied by his friends Joachim Schütz (a member of the Arnold Dreyblatt Trio) and Stephan Abry (of Workshop). "I wanted to collect source material," says Weber, who has long used a combination of acoustic samples and digital synthesis in his music, imperceptibly fusing the two into a rich, electro-acoustic mixture. "To collect sounds that actually have a physical source, an original moment. You have these split seconds that you use in a sample bank, but they're not just sounds. They tell a story. I know where they came from, I know the moment they were recorded. I wanted them to be able to lead me back to certain moments."

Sleeping and working in a wooden mountain cabin, the trio spent their days wandering and recording with portable field recorders, capturing the crunch of dried leaves underfoot, the crackle of loose stones, the plinking of kalimbas that they carried with them and played outdoors. Back in the cabin, Weber came across a text commemorating the landslide, and he realized that they had unwittingly been recording atop a mass grave. "I had had the idea to do something with black noise for a long time," he says; it turned out that it was all around him, encoded in the rocks like an echo frozen in the geologic record.

"This idea of a mountain that fell and left all these stories and fragments buried beneath the stones—that is somehow there when you listen," says Weber. With the sounds chopped up, edited and reduced to "homeopathic doses," they inject his music with something essential, even animistic, he thinks. "The whole idea of black noise is that it's something that you don't hear, but you feel it, because it's there. This was basically what the whole album should be about. When you listen closely you hear stories that don't need words to be told, because they have sounds."

But in the case of Pantha du Prince, natural forces find a different outlet than they do in the work of more austere sound artists like Chris Watson, Francisco Lopez, Thomas Köner, even Biosphere. Through an intricate process of transubstantiation, Pantha du Prince's music filters natural inputs into four-to-the-floor techno tracks, rich with brooding melodies, that fall into a lineage stretching back through the dance-music traditions of Cologne, Detroit and Chicago.

Weber discovered dance music as a young teenager living in a small town near Kassel, where in the early '90s big-city DJs would play parties en route from Frankfurt to Berlin; later, living in Hamburg, he became fascinated with the DIY ethos of Detroit pioneers like Mad Mike and Underground resistance. Weber is something of a polymath: widely read in cultural theory, he trained as a carpenter, a skill he applied towards setbuilding for experimental theater projects in Hamburg. He also played bass in the indie band Stella (alongside Elena Lange, producer Thies Mynther and Egoexpress' Mense Reents), taking advantage of the band's gear to begin experimenting with his own solo recordings. It was at L'Age D'Or, the band's record label, that Weber met a young intern named David Lieske (aka Carsten Jost), who in 2000 would establish Hamburg's Dial label with Paul Kominek (Turner) and Peter Kersten (Lawrence, Sten).

"David was the only guy [at L'Age D'Or] listening to Studio 1 records and DHR," recalls Weber. They quickly bonded over their love of experimental electronic music, with Lieske constantly badgering Weber to share his solo productions with him. Around the same time, Weber met Kersten at a Hamburg drum 'n' bass party where, somehow, the two ended up performing a drunken tag-team DJ session utilizing only the run-out grooves of their records, blending "tschk-tschk-tschk" rhythms for hours. He officially joined the Dial family in 2002 with *Nowhere*, his first EP as Pantha du Prince, and followed up in 2003 with an ambient album, *Das Schweigen der Sirenen*, released under the name Glühen 4.

The next year found Dial developing its identity across releases from Pawel, Lawrence, Sten, Efdemin, Carsten Jost and Pantha du

Prince. Pantha's album, *Diamond Daze*, felt in many ways like a perfect distillation of the Dial sound, with muscular bass lines and crackling, rock-steady percussion providing stable ground beneath billowing arrays of chiming keyboards, fluttering choral samples and layer upon layer of bell tones.

Bell tones played an even greater role in Pantha du Prince's 2007 album, *This Bliss*, their pealing overtones adding an unsettling layer to the music. They suggested a fusion of the sacred and the profane, of church and nightclub. And, trembling at the limits of temperament, hovering on the border between tuned frequency and atonality, they imbued Weber's compositions with a feeling at once melancholy and brightly optimistic—sorrow with just a hint of a wink.

Weber's studio is a small, one-room apartment that feels at once cluttered and strangely empty, like a flat whose resident began the process of packing up and moving out, and then got distracted somewhere along the way. Suggestive of an artist's Left Bank garret from the '20s, the clutter fits Pantha du Prince's Romantic, Bohemian persona like a kind of biographical diorama. Stark black and white clothing lies folded on sagging shelves. Rows of records extend across the floor like jetties, and the visible sleeves suggest the scope of Pantha's own sound: Tin Man, the Sundays, Bach, Joan Baez. Ben Watt's 1982 album *Summer Into Winter*, featuring Robert Wyatt, lies on one of two Technics turntables, although no mixer is readily apparent. An electric bass guitar leans in the corner next to an old Vermona drum machine, formerly the property of Moritz von Oswald. Its matte grey casing and rickety faders appear perfectly attuned to the dusky, makeshift music for which Pantha is known. And then there are the piles of books, each title more suggestive than the last: Marc Augé's *An Anthropology of Non-Places: An Introduction to Supermodernity*, Slavoj Žižek's *Lieb Dein Symptom wie Dich selbst!*, Georges Bataille's *Dark Star*. Atop all of these, *Sensations: A Time Travel Through Garden History* rubs up against a Snoop Dogg DVD.

"I fall asleep sometimes during the day, when I'm not working," admits Weber, gesturing to the unmade bed. He is drinking tea, recovering from a weeklong fever, and yet he looks little different from his on-stage appearance, clad in a long, flowing, knit black cardigan, a demure scarf knotted tightly around his throat. "When I'm waking up I always have the best ideas—that's why I'll always have a bed in my studio. I think it's the most important thing."

Weber does not work in his studio every day, and in fact, much of the work on any given recording takes place anywhere but here. "How I work is very nomadic," he says, pulling out a small cloth bag stuffed with contact microphones, a field recording device and other bits of gear. Indeed, aside from the bass, the Vermona, and a rack of heavy, glistening brass bells, there's little in the way of physical music-making devices in his studio. Weber is particularly fond of sampling other musicians' studios—for instance, the former studio of Can's Michael Karoli, owned by a friend of Weber's. "I record a lot when I'm going to places with synthesizers," says Weber, "places like [Karoli's] that have a certain atmosphere you want to catch, which you can't in your own studio."

Black Noise contains two notable collaborations. On "The Splendour," Tyler Pope (!!!, LCD Soundsystem) plays electric bass. The two musicians had met at Hamburg's Golden Püdel club; recording together was a spontaneous affair. "I had this track in my head with kalimba and crazy feedback," says Weber. "I played Larry Heard's 'Miss You' while he jammed over it playing bass guitar. Then I stopped the record and he kept playing this bassline for about 15 minutes, and I made sounds along with it. That is how I wanted the whole album to work: you have this split second when something is happening without you noticing. It's just a moment you capture."

Animal Collective's Panda Bear (Noah Lennox) sings on "Stick to My Side," his multi-tracked harmonies and cryptic lyrics lending a compelling touch of woozy, psychedelic pop to Pantha's focused blast of synth bass, drum machine and dissonant bells. This is not the first time Weber has worked with Animal Collective. He remixed their song "Peacebone" in 2007, after having struck up a friendship with the band on a visit to New York. (It was Pantha du Prince's first New York club gig, and several members of the band were in the audience; one spent the entire night in front of the DJ booth, eyes closed, enraptured. "I was like, what's going on, who are these people? They're great!" remembers Weber.) Earlier this year, he toured with the band, opening for them on more than a dozen dates across Europe, solidifying their friendship, challenging him artistically—both acts decided to switch up their set list every night, forcing Weber to spend hours on the bus each day, retooling his live set—and, crucially, giving him a crack at 1,000-person venues with top-notch sound. The sound was crucial: Weber prefers to include bells, contact microphones and live sampling in his gigs, but muddy, bass-heavy sound systems often force him to curtail the subtler sonics in favor of heavier, groove-based tracks.

"It went so smoothly," says Weber. "When I played in rock bands and was on tour you always had personal conflicts, but with Animal Collective, it was easy. I could have gone on like this for the next ten years, it was so natural."

The gigs, paired with one of America's best loved indie bands of the moment, certainly didn't hurt Pantha du Prince's profile, and neither will the label releasing *Black Noise*, Rough Trade. It was Geoff Travers, head of the iconic English label, who reached out to Weber, asking by email, "Could you imagine doing an album for Rough Trade?" For Weber, who not only grew up with plenty of English guitar rock but also absorbed Hamburg's Anglophila, the offer—a non-exclusive contract that doesn't interfere with his relationship with Dial—the answer was easy.

"For me it always happens like this," he says. "Like the remixes, it came at a moment I was thinking about stopping music. Like, *This Bliss* sold this amount of copies, you've traveled the world for a few years, you've experienced a lot—go on and do something else. Go more into visual art, or do film or documentary or something. Then Geoff Travers writes an email and you're doing an album for Rough Trade! It's a gift."

Weber's multi-disciplinary interests make sense in the context of his work, which is all about making connections between disparate phenomena. Behind all the sampling and field recording lies a process of mutation or transubstantiation by which Weber replaces "real" acoustic samples with their synthesized equivalent. On *Black Noise*, he says, many tracks are structured as a seamless fade from field-recording to a synthesizer patch modeled upon it, a kind of acoustic illusion carried out at house tempo, sneaking the sounds of the forest into the heart of the dance club—a space Weber refers to as "the forest of the city," a space of contained wilderness.

He gestures to a painting hanging above his bed. Depicting St. Bartholomä Kirche on Bavaria's Königssee, it serves as the album's cover art. "You see this painting on the cover of the album, and what is it? It is a painting or a reproduction of a painting? Is it digital or analog? That's the process of the recordings," which fade seamlessly from "natural" to "unnatural" sound, upending the idea of "naturalism" in the process. Hence the choice of St. Bartholomä church as the cover, with its strong associations of German Romanticism undercut by a musical process caught up in a simulacral tug-of-war—its kistchy landscape crushed by a wave of black noise.

There's certainly something melancholy about the concept, even more so given the minor-key melodies and pensive chord progressions of *Black Noise*, with its mossy caverns of reverb contrasting with its hard, sharp tones, glinting like limestone in the sunlight. But "that's just an atmosphere," says Weber. "I think my music is not so melancholic and dark as people think, it's just the pictures that come with it. Sometimes I listen to it and I think it's happy music!" He prefers to speak in terms of *Sehnsucht*, a concept he has difficulty explaining to me in English, but I've heard enough about the term to understand how it relates to his music. "It's this whole Romantic concept, this idea of longing—you look over there and see something, and you want to go there, but you can't . . . " I get it: it's the same feeling I've gotten staring out the plane window over the mountains and forests of the western United States, the same sense of nameless yearning buried in the brushtrokes of a Caspar David Friedrich painting. And it's there in the wending chord progressions and ringing tones of Pantha du Prince's music.

To the extent that *Black Noise* places itself in the German Romantic tradition, it follows Wolfgang Voigt's recently revived Gas project and Uwe Schmidt's curious, delightful *Liedgut* album from 2009. Weber, who grew up in the region of the Brothers Grimm and spent much of his youth in the woods, is keenly attuned to this darkly Romantic streak. "It has a lot to do with being German, which I always try to deny," he concedes. "But let's not get into the German issue—I just see myself as a cosmopolitan. But I still have my roots, and it's the woods, for sure, a place I always need to go before I go crazy."

True story: the day after our interview, in a second-hand shop in Neukölln, a painting catches my eye. It is St. Bartholomä Kirche on Königssee, with its distinctive, rounded towers and the same snow-capped peaks looming behind. A coincidence, sure—just a bit of flea-market kitsch, a dime-a-dozen landscape of the sort that fills Flughafenstrasse's second-hand shops like debris from a landslide. But the coincidence feels more than a little uncanny, as well, given the way that the image on the cover of *Black Noise* implies a process that pulls us farther and farther from "nature"—even as the sounds themselves tap nature's very waveforms, like a fiber-optic pipeline connected to the essence of being. Like a movie spoiler, or identifying the rare soul record behind a white-label disco edit, seeing the painting feels a little disappointing, anticlimactic. It's the melancholy that comes, I suppose, with any repetition, because repetition, like mechanical reproduction, replaces longing for the event with a longing for its unique, unrepeatable quality; it replaces longing with longing for longing itself. Maybe that's the need at the heart of *Sehnsucht*. Thus Weber's process of tunneling back through sound, his quixotic attempt to capture the aura in a fragment of recorded sound—crushed, by definition, by the very process of recording. Black noise.

Wormrot, Defeatist, Mutant Supremacy, Psychic Limb and Curandera— October 3rd—The Acheron, Brooklyn

Mike Turbé

Metal is sprouting out of every rancid nook and cranny of New York City. On Sunday night, grindcore spewed from a joint called The Acheron, and it was another in a long line of venues I'd not yet patronized. Situated in a veritable warehouse wasteland in Brooklyn, The Acheron closely resembles the trash compactor of the Death Star. The deep, narrow room has high ceilings and claustrophobia-inducing walls. The concrete floor is ideal for life threatening mosh pits, replete with a strange side door that opens directly into the melée. At some point during the night, the place started to fill up with water. No shitting. On the bright side, The Acheron has a nice, high stage and an excellent sound system. In a world of brutal basement shows, those last two features rank The Acheron amongst the elite.

Curandera blasted us with a dazzling display of muckified grind, frequently shifting velocity and generally making good use of the high quality sonic accoutrements. Next, Psychic Limb devoured every inch of the narrow stage with a cacophonous and spastic noise attack. Singer Brian Montuori's antics teased out smiles from the rapidly expanding and imbibing crowd. The band's vicious and intriguing tunes incited a pit into which I accidentally stepped. One quick taste of the brick wall was enough for me. I retreated to safer ground, but there's not much in the way of secure real estate at The Acheron.

Between the first two sets I made the acquaintance of Mutant Supremacy's gregarious front man, Sam Awry, as well as drummer Robert Nelson. No rock star bullshit here—just nice guys willing to talk it up with fans. No one seemed the least bit fazed by the insertion of killer death metal into the middle of a genuine grind-fest. *Infinite Suffering* is still in heavy rotation, so I was really looking forward to this set.

Mutant Supremacy made good on the promise of their recorded music, absolutely annihilating the crowd with a hypnotic performance. "Extinction" started things off full throttle, instantly giving my neck a workout and demanding I scream along. Mutant Supremacy didn't have the most articulate mix from the soundboard. I would have liked to hear a bit more of Sam Awry's guitar in there, but it didn't detract from the destruction.

The set transported me back a good fifteen years to my early concert-going days. The ripping death metal vibe reminded me of shows at long-closed clubs with line-ups chock-full of shredded carnage; Mutant Supremacy would have fit right in. I felt the same drooling jealous awe I did as a kid, witnessing professional musicians rip off complex riffs without breaking a sweat. Mutant Supremacy kill.

The Mutant Supremacy pit raged unchecked and reached its apex when the band tore into a cover of Death's "Zombie Ritual." The guy in the *Scream Bloody Gore* shirt was certainly pleased. I don't have the slightest idea why Mutant Supremacy aren't signed to a label and touring the world amongst the elite.

Speaking of elite, Defeatist ratcheted up the evening's absurdity with a mind blowing display of grind warfare. The Acheron seems built to channel the sonic ethos of three-piece bands. Defeatist sounded infinitely clearer than they did when I saw them last at Cake Shop. Once again, Joel Stallings stole the entire evening with an ungodly display of drumming. He and Josh Scott comprise the most dynamic and explosive rhythm section you'll find anywhere. (Incidentally, the duo have an incredible side project called Radiation Blackbody that showcases those dynamics.) Aaron Nichols' vocals weren't particularly high in the mix, but his deceptively complicated guitar riffs sang loud and clear. The slide-stepping slaughter of "Death Holds Her Brood" sent the crowd into hysterics. Righteous.

Finally, Wormrot burnt The Acheron to the ground. Everything about this set was twice as precise, twice as fast, and twice as potent as the Bowery Electric show in September. A month on the road has transformed Wormrot into an inhuman grind machine. The crowd was berserk throughout the entire set, stage diving and otherwise beating the hell out of each other. The claustrophobic confines of The Acheron were magnified, as if someone had switched on the Death Star trash compactor in an attempt to grind us to bits.

The split with I Abhor again comprised a good chunk of the setlist, with a sweet selection of *Abuse* tracks rounding out the menu. The new song Wormrot debuted last month has coagulated into a thing of beauty. The band played for a good long while, leaving a bruise that will not soon fade. By now their tour is over and the 'rot are on their way back to Singapore. Safe travels, come back soon.

On a side note, I apologize for the lack of visual aides. I managed to leave my camera at home on this night. I'm not sure I would have caught anything but a blur, in any case.

Giant Steps
The Survival of a Great Jazz Pianist

David Hajdu

Influential artists sometimes click in the public consciousness only after the rise of the movements they have influenced. A school of creative work emerges—seemingly spontaneously, its origins obscure at first. Then, with attention to the artists in that school comes recognition of their influences, their antecedents and their mentors. After Pollock, de Kooning and their peers in postwar American art established Abstract Expressionism, the precursory importance of prewar iconoclasts like Kandinsky became clear. After the Ramones, the Sex Pistols and the Clash blurted forth punk rock in the 1970s, a rude vision became apparent in the noise of '60s garage bands like the Seeds.

A new movement in jazz has surfaced over the past few years—a wave of highly expressive music more concerned with emotion than with craft or virtuosity; a genre-blind music that casually mingles strains of pop, classical and folk musics from many cultures; an informal, elastic music unyielding to rigid conceptions of what jazz is supposed to be. It's fair to call it "post-Marsalis," in that it leaves behind the defensive, canon-oriented musical conservatism of '90s jazz (as both Branford and Wynton Marsalis themselves have done in their best work of the past decade). Among this music's most celebrated and duly admired practitioners are the pianists Brad Mehldau, Ethan Iverson (of the trio the Bad Plus), Jason Moran and Vijay Iyer.

And singular among the trailblazers of their art, a largely unsung in-
novator of this borderless, individualistic jazz—a jazz for the 21st
century—is the pianist and composer Fred Hersch.

Never a grandstander, unconcerned with publicity, Hersch has
been a fiercely independent but unassuming presence on the New
York jazz scene since he moved to the city at age 21 in 1977. He has
made more than 45 albums as a solo performer, composer, bandleader or duo partner since 1991, when he released his first record of
original material, a collection of unclassifiable songs composed for
jazz rhythm section, tenor saxophone and cello, aptly titled, *Forward
Motion.* His body of work is clearly recognizable as a manifesto of
contemporary jazz. "Some people think I sound like Fred," says
Mehldau, who like Iverson is a former student of Hersch's. "That's
because Fred was a major influence on me and on a lot of the players
around today. Fred's musical world is a world where a lot of the de-
velopments of jazz history and all of music history come together in
a very contemporary way. His style has a lot to do with thinking as
an individual, and it has a lot to do with beauty. I wouldn't be doing
what I do if I hadn't learned from Fred, and I think that's true of
quite a few other people."

Jazz—a music energized by the tensions between tradition and
innovation, between collaborative cooperation and individual expression—has gone through multiple phases over the years since
Hersch started playing professionally more than 30 years ago: a craze
for jazz-rock fusion; a celebrated rediscovery of the work of iconic
masters (chief among them, Louis Armstrong, Duke Ellington and
Charlie Parker, exemplars of swing, orchestral jazz and bop, respectively); a retro lindy-hop fad; an arty "downtown" kick; and a leaning
toward world music. Hersch has concerned himself with none of
them. Hardly a straight-ahead bopper or a swing revivalist, a player
too romantic for the avant-garde and far too serious for the lounges,
Hersch is an artist indifferent to genre and unbeholden to musical
fashion. The jazz tradition he best connects to is the unshakable
iconoclasm of Thelonious Monk, Charles Mingus, Ornette Coleman

and others like-minded in their disregard for like-mindedness. Hersch's music—luxurious, free-flowing, unashamedly gorgeous jazz—is idiosyncratically, unmistakably a creation of his own. As Ben Ratliff described him in a *New York Times* review of a Village Vanguard performance in 1997, Hersch is "a master who plays it his way."

His determination to do things the Fred Hersch way has intensified considerably since the early '90s, when he made public his diagnosis of AIDS. Indeed, Hersch's range and prolificacy are such that he has needed half a dozen record labels for as many purposes: Nonesuch for Hersch the solo pianist; Sunnyside for his unorthodox quartet, the Pocket Orchestra; Palmetto for his quintet, the Fred Hersch Trio +2; Naxos for his hybrid jazz-classical concert music; various labels for his duet projects with singers as varied as Janis Siegel of the Manhattan Transfer, the veteran Brazilian vocalist Leny Andrade and the classical soprano Renée Fleming; and Concord for his concert at the Maybeck Recital Hall.

"Fred is one of those rare musicians who can do many things well and never tries to sound like anyone else," says Seth Abramson, who books the Jazz Standard. "It's interesting how many other pianists who come into the club remind me of Fred." That is to say, jazz has come around to doing it Hersch's way.

While the sensibility he pioneered has flourished, Hersch himself has been heard from only sporadically over the past two years. The reason is that he has, on and off during this period, been gravely ill, so sick from AIDS and a severe bout of pneumonia that the people closest to him—his partner, Scott Morgan, and his brother, Hank, as well as his parents—thought, on the worst of his many very bad days, that they had seen him for the last time. Early in 2008, the HIV virus migrated to his brain, and Hersch developed AIDS-related dementia. He lived for a time in mental and physical seclusion, hallucinating under the delusion that he had the power to control time and space and that everyone around him was plotting his demise. In fact, he came so close to dying that his paranoia seemed practically justified. At his sickest, late that year, Hersch fell into a coma and remained unconscious for a full two months. While incapacitated, he was bound to his bed in St. Vincent's Hospital in New York. He lost renal function and had to undergo regular dialysis, and he required a tracheotomy. He was unable to consume food or liquids of any kind, including water, for eight months. He could not swallow a thing or speak above a faint whisper. As a result of his prolonged unconsciousness and inactivity, he lost nearly all motor function in his hands and could not hold a pencil, let alone play the piano.

Today, at age 54, after many months of rehabilitation and therapy, grueling effort, effective medical care, an almost irrationally defiant refusal to accept his problems as anything less than temporary distractions from his music and a considerable amount of good luck, Hersch has achieved full recovery. Last year, he released two albums: a concert performance of his Pocket Orchestra CD, issued in the spring, and a solo piano record, *Fred Hersch Plays Jobim*, released (to immediate acclaim) in the summer. He has three completed works as yet unrecorded: a song cycle about art and photographic images, which he wrote with the poet Mary Jo Salter (some pieces of which were performed in a tribute to Hersch's music at Jazz at Lincoln Center a few years ago); a collection of jazz tunes honoring a quirky range of artists (musicians, writers, dancers) whom he admires; and a suite derived from themes by Tchaikovsky. On top of this explosion of Hersch music, a documentary about him—*Let Yourself Go: The Lives of Fred Hersch*, directed by the German filmmaker Katja Duregger—also came out last year.

In the fall, Hersch began work on a major new project, a long-form work that will deal explicitly with his recent traumas in words and music. The piece is an attempt to make art from the only life he knew for months, to give musical form to the dream images and cryptic narratives he still recalls vividly from his days and nights in a coma.

"I've been through a lot, and I want to make something of it, musically," Hersch said one afternoon in October. He had just finished giving a private lesson to a young pianist named Jeremy Siskind in the SoHo loft that has served as his professional headquarters and his New York residence for 30 years. For a while in the '80s, Hersch used the loft as a recording studio. In the corner of his parlor, a tiny, half-octagon-shaped room-within-a-room betrays its past as a drum chamber. He has brightened the almost lightless space by choosing splashy, Southwestern-ish pastel fabrics for the furnishings, and by placing, here and there, whimsical decorations like the toy piano on the top of the bookcase. Seated on the stool of the toy, prepared to play a four-handed duet, are painted carved-wood sculptures of a cat and a parrot. Facing the sofa is a 1921 Steinway grand piano at which Hersch, a jazz cat who has lived several lives, just gave a lesson to one of his many emulators. The piano—the real one—once belonged to Hersch's paternal grandmother.

"I never wanted to be a classical pianist, because that takes a lot of discipline, and it takes chops, and I don't particularly like to practice, and I don't care very much about chops," Hersch said. "To me, chops are just the ability to spin off and rattle off stuff. When you listen to somebody with a lot of chops, you say, 'Wow!' But you don't really come away feeling very much."

Hersch looked cheery in a pale-lemon, open-neck, wide-collar sport shirt from the '50s. He has a thing for vintage clothes, which provide him with a way to dress with flair, economically but without slavishness to the fashions of the season; as such, they connect loosely to his music, down to his work's winking humor and element of homage to musicians he admires.

Growing up as a child music star in Cincinnati, Hersch was composing little pieces by age 7, and by the time he was 10, he was appearing weekly on a local Sunday-morning kids' program, *The Skipper Ryle Show*. "The fact that he was on TV and had this prodigious talent gave him a lot of confidence," recalls his only sibling, Hank, an editor at *Sports Illustrated* who is about two years younger than his brother. "In fact, he was always a bit of a prima donna." Also at age 10, Hersch composed a musical play about Peter Pan for his elementary school and rejected the faculty's demand that he cut or amend the music.

Around the same time, he entered a musical competition and showed up with only a short sketch; he announced that he would play an original composition titled "A Windy Night," improvised most of it and won first prize. "Fred," says his father, Henry Hersch, an attorney, "was and is, um . . . "—pause—"a somewhat, I don't know . . ." —longer pause—"I don't want to use too loaded a word, but I'd say 'high-strung' or 'mercurial' or whatever. He has what some people call an artistic temperament."

After a term in general studies at Grinnell College in Iowa, Hersch dropped out and moved back to Cincinnati for a year and a half. He concentrated on his jazz education, gigging around town with local players, learning the music and its culture. Invigorated, he went back to college for music, enrolling in the New England Conservatory, where he studied under the jazz pianist and composer Jaki Byard. Graduating with honors, he moved to New York for the postgraduate education of sideman life.

Few jazz musicians in Hersch's generation rose as fast as he did. "Fred was way out in front," says the tenor saxophonist Joe Lovano, a fellow Ohio native three years older than Hersch. "A lot of the giants were still on the scene, and it was the great dream of the young cats like us to play with them, and Fred was one of the first ones to make that big jump."

When I first heard of Hersch, in the mid-'80s, he seemed to be in all the best places a jazz pianist could be—playing one night with Joe Henderson, another night with Stan Getz or Lee Konitz or on his own at Bradley's, the club on University Place where many of the most respected pianists in jazz played and congregated to hear, support and pilfer from one another. Hank Jones, Tommy Flanagan and Jimmy Rowles all used Bradley's as their base, and each of them was at least 25 years older than Hersch. "Fred is unique among pianists his age as a musician who really paid his dues as a jazz player," Ethan Iverson says. "I can't even imagine what it was like to play night after night with Joe Henderson or Art Farmer and to play at Bradley's in front of the most horrifyingly heavy judges, juries and executioners. The way that pianists of my generation have learned about the music is through the sort of artificial world of records and scores, and not really natural assimilation. Fred absorbed the whole jazz tradition in the deepest possible way, and that's only the foundation of his playing. It was just his starting point. For a lot of other pianists, that would be the end point."

What I recall most vividly about Hersch's playing from his early years is its striking technical facility; I found him impressive—though not as moving as I would find him years later. Over time, the physics of Hersch's musicianship inverted; he gave up impressing and worked, increasingly, to move. "Jazz musicians didn't have stylists and publicists," Hersch said, sitting straight-backed on the sofa in his loft. "You could hang out at the bar, and there was Art Blakey, smashed and hitting on the woman next to him. I wanted to play with the greatest players in the world, and I was probably pushy, but that's how I achieved what I did."

While he worked closely with other musicians, as jazz demands, he labored to protect the secret of his homosexuality. "I was leading a dual life—being gay and being a jazz musician and not knowing how those were going to meet," Hersch said. "Jazz music, by its very nature, is intimate. You're trusting other people—there's an intensity and shared emotion of creating something together, and I felt that if people knew that I was gay, they would mistake my intensity for sexual attraction. I didn't want it to stand in the way of achieving what I wanted to achieve. If you were sincere and you had talent and you're the kind of guy people want to play with, they didn't care what color you are—you could be purple—but gayness was a different matter."

Around the time Hersch recorded his first album as a trio leader, *Horizons*, for Concord, in the mid-'80s, he found out he was HIV-positive. "So my whole career as a leader has had this cloud over it," Hersch said. "I was in that who-knows-what's-going-to-happen? land.

A lot of my friends"—many of whom had full-blown AIDS—"were hopping off."

One afternoon, Hersch had a rehearsal scheduled with Stan Getz in Hersch's loft. After Getz rang Hersch's buzzer, Hersch found himself scooting to his bathroom to hide his boyfriend's toothbrush. "That's when I realized, What the hell am I doing?" he recalled. "This is my home. This is my life. I decided I was going to open up about everything and just be myself, and the period of coming out was the beginning of my gaining confidence as a composer. I felt like I had to get it out there while I still had time."

Hersch paused abruptly, and said, "Hold on—I need to keep hydrated." He took a long gulp of iced tea and swallowed, with a bit of difficulty. "I thought every album I did was going to be my last album," he went on. "Being sick and knowing my time is precious has made me want to be totally myself in my music. I decided that I wasn't interested in playing hip music for hip cats. So I don't pander to an audience. I'm completely comfortable with what I do, and I just don't care what other people are doing." He coughed a bit of iced tea into a paper napkin.

"It's kind of a miracle that I'm here at all," he said matter-of-factly. "It's interesting—I had to learn to work with a more limited palette, technically, as a pianist. At the same time, I felt stronger than ever, creatively. I found that I had more interesting things to say musically. I had more to express, and what I had to say didn't require pyrotechnics. The way I deal with the disease is, even though it has the power, I am not going to acknowledge that it has the power to mess with me."

In October, Hersch started working intently on what he sees as his "most personal and probably most ambitious" effort: "the coma project." As he conceives of it at this early stage, it will be a concert-length piece with words, music and perhaps multimedia elements, to be performed by a midsize ensemble of a configuration to be determined as the music takes shape. Hersch is developing the new work with Herschel Garfein, the librettist and sometime composer best known for his collaboration with the composer Robert Aldridge on the opera *Elmer Gantry*. "I was still alive for all that time I was unconscious, but the only life I had was in my dreams and nightmares, and they were incredibly strange and sometimes horrifying and sometimes beautiful," Hersch said. "I was in a lot of physical pain and discomfort. I found out later that I had been restrained—I was strapped to the bed, and the dreams I had were unbelievably weird and mysterious. I've been trying to come to terms with what I went through, and the best way I know is to try to express it in music."

What form will that music take? "It was an incredibly bizarre and sometimes terrifying experience," Hersch said. "There are no words to describe it. I'm hoping music can."

To many jazz fans, Fred Hersch is perhaps best known as a gay jazzman—or the gay jazzman, despite the fact that the jazz world, like every sphere of human endeavor in and out of the arts, has always had a homosexual population. Indeed, Hersch's identity as a gay man—and one with AIDS—has shaped the way his music has been perceived by many people, including his own partner, Scott Morgan. On a cool Saturday morning last summer, Morgan relaxed on the deck of the nice vinyl-sided house he and Hersch have built on the side of a hill in the Pennsylvania woods, and he reflected on Hersch's image as a gay artist. "One of the reasons that I was attracted to his music was not just his music but the fact that he was an out, gay musician early on—I had him on a pedestal as a musician and as a person," said Morgan, who has studied both piano and voice and can play standards in the manner of a good rehearsal pianist.

"It impressed me that he was willing to go against the grain from a career perspective," Morgan went on. "He's got this incredible core of what he wants and who he is that is kind of amazing to me. I think Fred's music has an expressiveness and a lyricism that is his own. People say that's because he's gay, and I see how people can read into that and say, 'Well, I hear this sense of emotion, this depth, this lyricism'—you hear some of that in some of his compositions. Clearly, we are gay, but our lives are not defined by the 'gay community' or by being gay."

If anything has inhibited the ability of Hersch's music to achieve the broader acceptance that, say, the work of the Marsalis brothers has achieved, it may be the subtlety and sheer loveliness of it—its warmth, its quality of melancholy, traits that Americans conditioned to equate "edginess" and "darkness" with gravity can be slow to take as seriously as music that hits the ears more assaultively. His openness as a gay man is no help here and has surely conspired to feed hoary stereotypes of Hersch and his music as light stuff. As the pianist Jason Moran points out: "Because Fred's playing is so beautiful, some people don't take it as seriously as they should. I think some people hear only flowers, but there's deep soil there. They don't really understand everything that's going on. Maybe if he gyrated and groaned and squinted his eyes and made it look hard when he played, they would get it. But Fred doesn't go for theatrics. Fred at the piano is like LeBron James on the basketball court. He's perfection."

Hersch, among the most sensitive of jazz pianists, is acutely sensitive to the proposition that his sensitivity makes his music "gay." I took up the subject on a walk with him along the gravel path behind his country house. We heard hummingbirds in the beech trees and got to talking about nature and the conception of beauty as a value in gay culture. "I wouldn't quite say that's bull, but it's a very dangerous idea," Hersch said, slowing his gait. "The compliment I get the most often is, 'My, you sounded really beautiful.' I used to think, I want them to say something else, because I felt like that was a kind of, Oh, yeah, you're gay—so of course you play lyrically and you're one of the great ballad players. Of course. But now I just don't care at all what people think. I think music should be beautiful. There's nothing wrong with beauty. I'm attracted to beauty and lyricism, but I don't play the way I do because I'm gay. I play the way I do because I'm Fred."

If his music is sometimes mistaken for soft, its composer never is. Among musicians and other professionals in jazz circles, Hersch's clarity of purpose and fierceness of will have contributed to his reputation as a fearsome taskmaster. Jo Lawry, the Pocket Orchestra vocalist, remembers as the "foundation stone" of her relationship with Hersch his phone call to her the day after he first saw her sing. Hersch told her that the way she swayed to the beat onstage was a distraction from the music and that she was "jumping all over the place" in her improvisations rather than fully developing her musical ideas.

At a Pocket Orchestra rehearsal in his loft, which I attended early last summer, Hersch ran the group through a piece called "Free Flying" at a vertiginous clip. The piece called for Lawry to precision-scat a wildly complicated melody in unison with the piano, and she flew through it. "Now let's do it at a preposterous speed," Hersch announced; the group did, and Lawry got through it surprisingly well. "Now, let's do it even faster, and I'm not going to play the melody with you anymore," he said, and Lawry survived being pushed beyond reasonable limits.

Janis Siegel, with whom Hersch has recorded several albums, has come to rely on Hersch's scrutiny and candor. "Fred has pushed me to become a better musician, a better singer—in ways, a better person," she says. "He doesn't have time to goof around. If I want some straight-ahead feedback, I go to him. People will tell you what you want to hear, or they'll be not-quite truthful, because they don't want to hurt your feelings, but Fred's allegiance is to the music."

In the recording studio, "Fred always knows what he wants," says his longtime engineer, Michael MacDonald, with whom Hersch has made more than 40 albums. "If you ask him a question, he'll never say, 'Oh, I don't know.' He always has an idea." Twenty-five years ago, MacDonald says: "Fred was a petulant, stubborn, incredibly talented egomaniac eccentric who would dominate a recording session. He was always playing brilliantly, but it was a whole lot more egocentric. Since his illnesses, he's matured musically and also emotionally, in saying, 'Everything I do has to have meaning and has to be my best game, because I don't have a lot of time.' I've seen a huge change in him with the illnesses—just the stop fooling around, stop wasting time.

"Fred's ego is enormous," MacDonald adds, dragging out the word. "But when he's sitting at the piano, you don't hear the ego. You only hear his humanity."

Hersch played a handful of gigs in New York last year as he grew stronger, and one was a run at the Jazz Standard with the Pocket Orchestra, to introduce the group's first CD. In addition to Hersch's piano, the instrumentation of this orchestra includes trumpet, percussion and voice. Like a great many things in Fred Hersch's life and work, the Pocket Orchestra defies expectations.

"He looks good," said Fred's brother, Hank, who left a busy late night at work to go to the Jazz Standard with their mother, Flo Hoffheimer (who is divorced from her sons' father and remarried). Now 80, she flew in from Cincinnati that day for the occasion. The club was packed. Twenty or 30 people without reservations huddled outside the entrance hopefully, and the house manager waved some of them into the bar area as Hersch shuffled onto the bandstand with the Pocket Orchestra.

As he took his seat at the piano, Hersch fluffed the back of the silky mushroom brown shirt he was wearing, so the bottom of the fabric draped over the bench as the tails of a tuxedo would. He glanced at the audience for a second when he did this, and gave a little smile. He shook his shoulders loose and wiggled his bottom into a position he liked. Then he began to play, constructing a tight pattern of dense, repeating chords. He lowered his head slowly till it hovered just half a foot from the top of the piano, and he appeared to shrink into his clothes. Hersch, slim all his adult life, was about 15 pounds under his usual weight. His cheeks were hollow, and his skin was gray, though his eyes were bright and his playing was strong. In fact, in its emotive urgency, expressive range and beauty, Hersch's music had rarely been so potent.

After the second number, a lightly bopping composition called "Lee's Dream," which Hersch wrote in tribute to the alto saxophonist

Lee Konitz, Hersch's mother leaned back in the corner banquette where she was sitting with Hank and a few others, and she said, to no one in particular, "Fred was such a fat little thing."

At the end of the set, she elaborated: "When Fred was a boy, he was the most beautiful, chubby little thing you ever laid eyes on—he was a blimp with appendages. And one day when he was 3 years old, I was pushing him around in a cart in the grocery store, and a woman—a stranger, I had never met her before—saw Fred, and she stopped in her tracks, and she looked at Fred, and she said, 'And who do you belong to?'

"And Fred looked at her, and he said: 'I don't belong to anybody. I belong to myself.'

"That was Fred," his mother said, "and it still is."

Will.i.am and the Science
of Global Pop Domination
Chris Norris

Many years ago, a great American shared a dream that one day our nation's children might sit at the table of brotherhood, that justice and freedom might ring through the land, and that a 35-year-old black man in leather pants and glitter boots might lead 73,000 Texans as they sing in one voice: "Whatcha gonna do with all that junk—all that junk inside your trunk?"

That day is here at Houston's Reliant Park, which pulses with the lights, sounds and smells of the 78th annual Houston Livestock Show and Rodeo, concert site for giants from Elvis Presley to Miley Cyrus. Tonight's headliners, the Black Eyed Peas, appear after the six-year-old sheep riders of "Mutton Bustin." Midway through their first smash hit, 2005's "My Humps," singer Fergie struts the stage catwalk in a skin-tight metallic suit recalling the sleek android of Fritz Lang's *Metropolis*, only with hair and the song's titular "humps." "I drive these brothers crazy," she raps as Peas Apl.de.ap and Taboo strike street-ogler poses. "I do it on the daily."

When the chant returns, eight giant video screens flash the broad, beard-fringed, and enigmatic grin of the song's author and master Pea, Will.i.am, who pauses to thank the group's followers: "Houston, we thank you from the bottom of our hearts to the depths of our souls. In 2005, we put out a record called *Monkey Business*," he says, then names two outlets that drove it to 10 million sales: "Tower Records and Virgin. They don't exist anymore." The crowd roars. "Last year, we released our latest record and it's because of you it sold—"

"I wanna say something!" Fergie says, cutting in. "Hi, Mom and Dad!"

The nation's largest rodeo is merely one of the last dominoes to fall in Will.i.am's global campaign to build the world's most ubiquitous music brand. In the 15 years since forming the Peas, Will.i.am has toured the world a dozen times, sold 27 million albums and done ads for Apple, Pepsi, Target, Verizon and the president of the United States. "He's a real force," says Bono, who enlisted Will.i.am to work on U2's 2009 album, *No Line on the Horizon*. "He's got the biggest songs on Earth right now, he's the most wonderful spirit to be around, and he's interested in the macro as well as the micro."

So macro, in fact, that Will.i.am is unlike virtually any musician that preceded him. To Will.i.am, songs aren't discrete works of art but multi-use applications—hit singles, ad jingles, film trailers—all serving a purpose larger than music consumption. Creatively, he draws no distinction between writing rhymes and business plans, rocking arenas and PowerPoint, producing albums and media platforms, all united under a clear-eyed mission to unite the largest possible audience over the broadest range imaginable. It's a mission he communicates with a combination of Pentecostal zeal and Silicon Valley jargon, suggesting a hybrid of Stevie Wonder and Steve Jobs. In conversation, he has a tendency to drop koanlike pronouncements that, like his songs, often go from moronic to brilliant with repeated listening. A journey through the mind of Will.i.am follows a twisty trail, but if you pay close attention certain themes emerge. . . .

MAKE ART WORK IN SQUARES

Backstage in Houston, Will.i.am has changed out of his costume into street clothes: a black Jedi-ish shawl-collared shirt, punkish low-slung trousers and a shoulder satchel made of recycled soda flip tops.

While dancers, managers and band mates chatter behind him, Will.i.am starts breaking music and commerce down to subatomic particles. "It's about frequency, currency," he says. "The words 'current' and 'frequent'—what do they mean? Time. If currency also means something you can spend, that means it's fluid—a current. If I'm currently doing something and keep doing it, I'm doing it frequently. And if I change my frequency to being positive, I attract currency."

Will.i.am speaks quickly, stands a bit too close, and keeps his wide-set eyes fixed on yours like a boxer's cornerman, psyching his fighter up. "Every time music was put out on circles, it was successful," he says. "When records came out, you had 45s, then 33s, then 12-inches—all multiples of three, all circles. As soon as tape decks came out and there were 8-tracks—square. Didn't work. A cassette is a rectangle—didn't work. CD came out—through the roof. The iPods and laptops put music on rectangles—doesn't work, can't monetize it. You have to figure out how to make art work in squares."

After taking a call from Interscope chairman Jimmy Iovine, Will.i.am returns and gives a quick summary of their conversation. "'Hey, Will, it's Jimmy,'" he says in Iovine's hoarse Brooklynese. "'Blah-de-blah, congratulations, blah-de-blah, through the roof, blah-de-blah, game-changing, blah-de-blah, one billion.'"

"'One billion?'" asks Will.i.am.

"'One billion,'" says Iovine.

"'Yes,'" says Will.i.am.

"'OK,'" says Iovine. "'Bye.'"

Will could easily be a stand-up comedian, with his uproarious, infectious laugh and spot-on impersonations of everyone from ad execs to Aussie ravers to Michael Jackson, all recent members of a calling circle that now includes Bono, Quincy Jones, Oprah, Hugh Jackman, Diddy, a founder of YouTube, Prince, the CEO of BlackBerry and—as a sheer mathematical certainty—Kevin Bacon. Unlike most fans, Will.i.am learned of Jackson's death in Los Angeles not from CNN but from 20 text messages he received while DJing in Paris, whose conflicting information he sorted out with updates and eventual confirmation in a phone call with Quincy Jones—who was in Moscow.

CONTROL THE CLOUD

While Will.i.am's producing credits read like a playlist on shuffle—Nas, Sergio Mendes, Celine Dion, the Rolling Stones—his influence now stretches into the boardrooms of BlackBerry, YouTube and other companies that consider the MC a tech visionary. "He'll sit with Evan Williams at Twitter or Chad Hurley at YouTube and give them ideas for their business," says legendary Silicon Valley venture capitalist Ron Conway, whose startup investments have included Google, PayPal and—most recently—Will's own social-media platform, Dipdive, which is kind of like a cross between Facebook and Hulu (but as of now seems mostly to exist to promote the Peas). "Corporations use words like 'cloud computing' and 'data cloud,'" Will says. "This thing we all communicate with is in the clouds, on a tiny bandwidth that very few people control."

Will intends to be one of them. With Dipdive, he plans to build an entire distribution system—from singer's voice to user's earbud. Selecting artists from various fields on a "dopeness" criteria, Will.i.am says Dipdive's filtered, curated social-media platform will unite millions of "partners" and play a role somewhere between ad agency, record label, radio and TV network. "That's coming in 2013," says Will.i.am. "The biggest artist is going to do it all: play, produce, remix and distribute music. The next Jimi Hendrix or John Coltrane will play the whole system. He's coming by 2013."

WHOEVER CRACKS DANCE MUSIC WINS

On paper, the Black Eyed Peas sound like the worst band you can imagine: one brainy leader, one break dancer/martial artist, one Filipino

MC who learned English at age 14 and one rock chick/ex-meth addict. Like a true visionary, Will flipped these deficits into a global-domination scheme. "I go to Brazil, they think I'm Brazilian," he says. "I go to Panama, they think I'm Panamanian, because I speak Spanish." In Sweden? "They like Fergie. We'll put her in front. South America? Taboo, you get in the front, be Latin! Southeast Asia? Apl, go! Speak Filipino!"

In 2008, Will.i.am found the final key to claiming a global audience. He was in Australia shooting a co-starring role as the teleporting mutant John Wraith in *X-Men Origins: Wolverine* when he had one of those everything-you-know-is-wrong insights: After asking some friends to bring him to a hip-hop club, he was told, "'Ip-'op's daid, mate. Electrow.'" He returned to the States possessed. "I came back hollering, 'Dance music, Jimmy [Io-vine], dance music! Whoever cracks dance music wins.'"

Will approached *The E.N.D.* less as an album than as a DJ set—and even hired the French superstar DJ David Guetta himself to produce the second single, "I Gotta Feeling." "The only reason I see to make an album is to occupy an hour with a mood," Will says. "If I'm a doctor and you say, 'I just want to dance,' I prescribe this." Hence, 15 midtempo, upbeat tracks, light on gray matter and heavy on good vibes. Of critics who impugn their simplicity, the Peas say that such people aren't using *The E.N.D.* as directed: "It's meant as escapism," says Fergie. "We specifically wanted people to forget about their money problems, losing their jobs, their homes."

ADAPT EVERY TUNE TO A SPECIFIC USE

To Will.i.am, songs are fluid, free-floating entities that function in various frequencies. In some of those frequencies—like frequently played ads—that function tends to bring currency. Lots of it. For nearly a decade, the Peas have been perfecting a music style that works seamlessly in commercials. In 2003, they rereleased the modestly performing "Let's Get Retarded" as the NBA theme, "Let's Get

It Started." That same year, the band broke in America, largely thanks to Apple's use of "Hey Mama" in an iPod commercial. In 2009, the group debuted "I Gotta Feeling" months before its official release as the theme song to CBS's summer prime-time lineup—and that was just the beginning. The Peas performed outside Oprah's studios, then went on to play *Dick Clark's New Year's Rockin' Eve*, Super Bowl weekend, the Grammys and a live set in Times Square shot by James Cameron's company, to be released as a 3-D concert film. By 2010, the Earth was Planet Pea.

In a way, this was a macro version of what Will does everywhere he goes. "If we go to a party, I'll just be chilling in the corner, absorbing everything," says Apl.de.ap. "I'll look over and see Will talking with Prince." Two years ago, Prince invited Will.i.am to sit in with him at a show in Las Vegas. Will asked if he could invite a singer-songwriter he was working with—Michael Jackson, who Will says had a beef with Prince running back to a 1983 misunderstanding at a James Brown concert. Jackson showed. "I told Quincy, and he was like, 'I can't believe you got Mike to go there,'" says Will.i.am. "Prince and Michael Jackson? Come on, dude. That's connecting worlds."

Of course, connecting worlds often does wonders for the connector. In a 2009 Pepsi commercial, Will.i.am rapped over Bob Dylan's "Forever Young" while a digital montage branded him the successor to rock's greatest songwriter. A year earlier, he took a chunk of Barack Obama's stump speech, added a guitar part played by actor Bryan Greenberg, tapped a friends list that included Scarlett Johansson and Kareem Abdul-Jabbar, and released a video—watched 26 million times—that helped sweep a one-term black senator into the White House. "Yes I Can" didn't exactly hurt Will.i.am's profile either, making him the songwriter of America 2.0.

SELL YOUR MUSIC TO THE AUDIENCE, THEN SELL THE AUDIENCE

Will's unorthodox views on blending art and commerce—a bit extreme even for hip-hop—stem from an outsider perspective he's had since childhood. He grew up in the mostly Mexican projects of East L.A. and was bused daily to a magnet school in prosperous Pacific Palisades. To survive, he had to learn how to be a chameleon. "Being a black guy in an all-Mexican neighborhood who went to an all-white school—I don't give a fuck what anybody says," says Will. "There's a reason why I am who I am, that upbringing and conditioning. 'Why you dressed like that, *ese*?'" he says, channeling a cholo neighbor. "Then I'd go to school with Brett and Brent," he says, going white boy. "'Hey, *William*.' Today, people are like, 'Where you from, London?'" says Will. "'No. That's an East L.A.-and-white-boy accent.'"

Initially a break dancer, Will had switched to MCing by high school and formed the De La Soul-inspired hip-hop group Atban Klann with fellow breakers-turned-MCs Apl.de.ap and Taboo. Will scored his first record deal in 1992 by winning a Hollywood freestyle battle against Twista, the Chicago MC who would light up his and Kanye West's "Slow Jamz" and who once claimed the Guinness World Record for speed. Asked how he slew such a dragon, Will.i.am says, "My thing was, I do what you're doing better than you." By pursuing just that strategy, Will.i.am built a Black Eyed Peas that delivers: pumping excitement, giddy spectacle and a message of peace, love and pan-inoffensiveness. As it happens, those are the exact qualities ad agencies seek for selling just about anything—a fact that has blurred the boundaries between song and ad as the Peas' fame has continued to rise. *The E.N.D.*'s rock song "Now Generation," for instance, doesn't just bear a close titular resemblance to a Pepsi jingle, it sounds like one: a defiant declaration of young consumers united by a taste for the new. The fact that Will is also a Pepsi-sponsored artist who wrote a 2007 song called "More" specifically for a Pepsi ad makes things even more nebulous. Do the Peas make songs? Or jingles?

To Will, the very question is so 20th century. "Since the 1960s, it's been a taboo for bands to fuck with brands, like they should only sell music," he says. "But music was never the product. When you played in a bar, music drew people in to sell a ticket and drinks. The first music industry was publishing, because they sold sheet music."

Beethoven? Verdi? "They were selling aggregation, the ability to bring people to a concert hall."

REAL GANGSTAS DON'T RAP

Until he was 14, smart, music-obsessed William James Adams Jr. wore a Mom-enforced dress code of suits and an Afro. When this was repealed in ninth grade, he chose the flat-topped style he wears today, the Gumby, which perfectly complemented the harem-pants ensemble he wore to his first live concert: a 1989 USC performance by a man he still calls an inspiration. "People are going to shit on me for saying this, but it's the fucking truth," says Will.i.am. "MC Hammer opened the door for all of us. Without Hammer there wouldn't be Puffy, there wouldn't be me."

But he owes just as much to the founders of gangsta rap. Atban Klann's first record deal was with Ruthless, founded by N.W.A's Eazy-E. While Eazy's 1995 death from AIDS derailed the project, the gangsta rapper confirmed something Will already knew. "I'm from the fucking projects, and the gangsters, the real niggas—they're out doing shit," he says. "They're out calling shots, ain't got time to rhyme. It's the little soldiers that want to be like that dude: Those are the gangster rappers."

Despite first appearing on an Eazy-E single called "Merry Motha-fuckin' Xmas," Will says his progressive, pan-racial vision was in place from the beginning: "On our first underground record, *Joints and Jam*, we said, 'We're about mass appeal, no segregation / Got black to Asian and Caucasian. . . . ' It was part of the plan. My first album was *Behind the Front*. Which meant, 'This is what I truly am, behind the front.'"

ALWAYS LISTEN TO THE GIRLS

Shortly after entering a Black Eyed Peas afterparty at a velvet-rope Houston club—where Jay-Z's "Empire State of Mind" is followed by a string of Black Eyed Peas songs—Will.i.am pronounces the vibe wack, lets a few drunks blast him with digital-camera flashes, and ducks out into a waiting car. He's headed to an after-afterparty where he'll DJ what he promises will be "some real underground shit." On the ride to the spot, Will asks the club's promoter what kind of music the crowd likes. "Oh, they'll like whatever you play—Top 40, hip-hop, dance," says the young white dude, whose girlfriend cuts him off, saying, "Electro."

"Always listen to the girls," Will.i.am says later, a theorem with the corollary "Hook the 14-year-old fan." "Why? Because I fell in love with music when I was 14, and you couldn't tell me anything—I thought I knew what was going on. I built my personality off of music I listened to at 14."

Minutes later, amid the flashing lights and jackhammering beats, Will sets up a MacBook and a rectangular interface with illuminated knobs and buttons. As the crowd screams, he pulls on a pair of orange headphones and picks up a mike. "Yo—Houuuuuuuston," he calls out, triggering a dramatic orchestral synth chord from a David Guetta record. "Y'all ready to rock?"

With a hand-chopping flourish, Will kicks in a pounding techno beat, then sets into a live performance of rapping, chanting and cross-fading between four channels on a system he calls "iTunes on steroids." His shades and fade suggest Wesley Snipes' vampire hunter Blade, as he weaves his own beats with "remixes of other people's remixes of classic records," drawing from a massive hard drive of tunes.

"On to the next, on to the next, on to the next," he chants, as he segues from Basement Jaxx's 2001 "Where's Your Head At" into the opening of Nirvana's "Smells Like Teen Spirit" and into Pat Benatar's "Hit Me With Your Best Shot," whose chorus he merges into that of the 2009 hit "Shots" by the electro group LMFAO, whose MCs Redfoo and Sky Blu he has known since high school and whose father and grandfather, respectively, is Motown founder Berry Gordy. "If you're a DJ at the top of your game, you got 80,000 people in the middle of Los Angeles in the hood," says Will. "Eighty thousand cats. No Rihannas, no fuckin' Beyoncés. DJs."

THE WHOLE SONG SHOULD BE A CHORUS

As a songwriter, Will.i.am ascribes to Moore's Law, the software principle whereby increasingly smaller devices hold increasingly more information. "Right now, every chorus is getting shorter and shorter," he says. "Soon we'll be listening to blips. Nowadays, the more complex things sound, when you break them down, all the veils and sheets are just disguises." On the other hand, an apparently simple song, like "Boom Boom Pow," is actually downright avant-garde. "It has one note," says Will.i.am. "It says 'boom' 168 times. The structure has three beats in one song. It's not lyrics—it's audio patterns, structure, architecture. Lots of people say, 'Black Eyed Peas shit is simple,' and I'll be like, 'No, fool, it's the most complex shit you even could fathom, that's the reason it works everywhere around the planet.'"

Will.i.am can apply this kind of thinking to any tune. So how would he rewrite the national anthem? He suggests a simple approach. "There wouldn't be no verse and chorus," he says. "The whole song should be a chorus. It should be about a minute and have highs and lows able to be sung by males and females in all keys." The mix to shoot for, he says, is "We Are the World," for its ingenious simplicity, and the Dolly Parton–penned Whitney Houston hit "I Will Always Love You," which ruled the charts for 14 weeks—a feat matched by the Peas' "I Gotta Feeling." The new anthem, says Will, "should tell our stories, say we've done bad things, that we've suffered and grown, and we care about the future. The Whitney Houston song has all that—humility and passion and pain and joy and love all at the same time. You take those two approaches and marry them—that's power. That's how America should talk to the world."

GO STRAIGHT TO JOY

In the cold reality of the marketplace, networking, promotion and synergy do a fine job of making the mediocre popular every day. The rarer successes, those that truly win hearts and minds, work an alchemy even Will.i.am hasn't quite wired, one he discusses without mentioning brands, audio patterns or BPMs. "What is the easiest emotion to act?" he asks. "Anger. What is the hardest? Joy. That's 'cause joy is complex. It's somber, sad, happy, heartbroken, hopeful—it's all these emotions in one. What you hear in 'I Gotta Feeling'? To me, that's joy. You're in pain, but tonight's going to be a good night. You can't feel happy when you've been pissed off the whole week. You have to go straight to joy."

He thinks back to an insight he got from Bono. "Bono said, 'Our music gets to people closer than you ever can be: You're in their ears, they put us in their head.' That changed my whole view on things. Someone consciously put you this close to their brain. That's serious."

Within two weeks of that conversation, Will was back at his home in Los Angeles. It was a year after he had stood on the steps of the Lincoln Memorial next to the new president, a moment during which his mind raced with thoughts about his childhood, his hour-and-a-half bus ride to school, his grandmother. "I was thinking of her watching the inauguration of a black man as president with her grandson onstage—all those thoughts running through me," he says. "I was up there and I was like, 'Why me?'"

And within an hour he wrote "I Gotta Feeling," a song that nails every single note of a state-of-the-art, multi-user, good-time delivery system—although its intended use, its reason for existence, may be just as significant to its success.

"Nobody asked me to write 'I Gotta Feeling,'" says Will.i.am. "It just came."

Notes from a Wedding

Lauren Wilcox Puchowski

On a muggy Saturday afternoon, longtime wedding performer and bandleader Kenney Holmes stood in the middle of a private dining room in a restaurant in Northern Virginia. "They want us catty-corner," muttered Holmes, mopping his forehead with a handkerchief and squinting at the space he was arranging as a stage. A cluster of lights and speakers bunched awkwardly, like wallflowers at a dance, at the far end. Suddenly he strode across the room and, seizing a large silver tureen from behind a speaker, moved it to the other end of the room. "I have a phobia about playing next to garbage cans," he said. "I think I'm afraid that I will be identified with garbage."

For some 15 years, Holmes and his band, Showbiz, have made an excellent living playing events on and around Capitol Hill, from weddings to Rep. Bennie Thompson's fish fry, bringing in as much as $500,000 a year. But these are leaner days. Where Holmes was once booked solid every weekend of the wedding season, he has played only a handful of gigs this year.

Like most career musicians, Holmes cut his teeth playing anywhere that would have him, and he prides himself on his ability to create a party under even the humblest of conditions. (He said he was once the top act, measured in liquor sales, on a regular gig playing the club car of an Amtrak bound for Montreal.) By comparison, an engagement such as this, a wedding reception in the Koi Room of the restaurant 2941, overlooking the Potomac River, might seem a particularly refined and relaxing way to spend an evening.

But for Holmes, who is 56 but whose unlined face and round spectacles give him the look of a schoolboy, playing a wedding can be a kind of Faustian bargain. On the one hand, weddings—besides being extremely lucrative—are an oasis of good cheer and freshly cut flowers in the often dingy and unromantic world of paying gigs. On the other hand, they rely on an elaborate sleight-of-hand: the creation of a fantasy, a bride's favorite songs brought to life with a carload of speakers and coaxial cable and a handful of part-time musicians.

This was a particularly high-dollar gig, and, for Holmes, the evening was fraught with potential disasters that, though minor, threatened the illusion. Dancing and dinner were in separate rooms, which compromised Holmes's ability to control the energy of the party, or, as he calls it, "putting them on the roller coaster." "Once we get them on the floor," he says, "we keep them on the floor." And there were others: the seasonal allergies that weakened his singing voice, the short life of the batteries in his cordless microphone, musicians who might ignore instructions to enter via the loading dock and instead steer their towering carts of equipment around guests sipping cocktails in the lobby.

"Be early," he had reminded his band in an e-mail, in bold blue font, a few days before. "Overcome obstacles before you get to the gig."

By 6:30 p.m., an hour before showtime, two of his three musicians had arrived via the loading dock: keyboardist Bruce Robinson, a slight, dapper man with a mustache; and drummer Sam Brawner, tall and broad-shouldered and wearing a gold ring in the shape of a lion's head on each hand. Still missing was saxophonist Atiba Taylor. "You look like a new shilling," Holmes said into the microphone to Robinson, who had already changed into his tuxedo.

As with most of the weddings he played, Holmes would emcee the evening's events in addition to singing and playing guitar. At 6:45 the wedding planner, Joan Sacarob, wearing a cream-and-peach tweed suit and peach heels, clicked across the parquet dance floor for a run-through of the agenda. It was Holmes's first time working with Sacarob, a petite woman with a neat bob who said she had been named a "top pick for Jewish wedding planners" by *Washingtonian* magazine. She flipped the schedule open to the dinner, which included a blessing over a loaf of challah. Perhaps 80 percent of the weddings Holmes plays are for Jewish clients; he considers them a specialty of his, and he learned the Hebrew words to accompany the hora years ago to help ensure his marketability.

"*Chah*-lah," Sacarob was saying to Holmes, leaning into the syllables.

"Chah-lah," repeated Holmes. Sacarob narrowed her eyes.

"Okay, the blessing over the bread, don't even use the word 'challah,'" she said. "Do you mind? Just say, 'Blessing by Margaret Fisher and Carol Greco.'"

"I can say 'challah!'" Holmes said to the room after Sacarob left, waving his finger in the air in mock indignation. "I can say that word!"

By 7 p.m., Holmes had fired up his laptop, on which he keeps his library of songs, and he, Robinson and Brawner were noodling around an instrumental version of "Papa Was a Rolling Stone." Holmes, who had donned a cream-colored dinner jacket, fiddled with some levels on his mixer. Sacarob returned to check on the placement of some urns. Behind them, visible through the floor-to-ceiling plate-glass windows, the wedding party posed for the photographer on the far side of the koi pond.

"I do a lot of work here," said Sacarob, gazing at the pond.

"Well, I'd like to do a lot of work with you," Holmes said pleasantly.

At 7:15, 15 minutes before Kenney Holmes & Showbiz were due to begin their dinner set, Sam Brawner cocked his head at the front walk, where Atiba Taylor was threading his way around guests with a couple of cases slung over his shoulder. "That's how all the sax players are," Brawner mused. "I only know two sax players that come with the rest of the band." Holmes shook his head but said nothing.

Taylor had his reed softened up in time for the opening bars of "Killer Joe," a Quincy Jones tune that Holmes likes to use as background music, which the band played with spark and feeling to an empty dance floor as the guests dined in the adjacent room. The band had the well-oiled, nimble sound of musicians who are used to listening to each other, and the launching of each successive number was like the ascension of some complicated flying machine, alive with internal machinations, drifting lightly around the room. Holmes's voice is not extraordinary, but it is rich and soulful; he has a knack, useful for a wedding singer, for fully inhabiting someone else's song while giving it a little something of his own. The musicians smirked to themselves at each change and solo, as though at some private joke. When Holmes sang a line of scat, Brawner pressed his knuckles to his mouth and shook his head happily.

By the second set—after Holmes had announced the bride and groom at dinner, and introduced the blessing over the challah without using the word "challah," and led his musicians through a rousing version of "Hava Nagila"—the party had found a groove. He coaxed the guests into a conga line, spearheaded by the bridesmaids, with "Hot Hot Hot," and sent the bride sashaying out onto the floor in the middle of "Mustang Sally." There was a lull as dessert was served in the other room, and then the bridesmaids returned to do the Electric Slide, and the floor slowly filled back up.

At the end of the evening, the bride and groom came over to thank him. "When you got my dad on the dance floor—you've got a friend in the D.C. Court of Appeals," the groom said. Holmes, however, was not as pleased. The dance floor had emptied for several stretches during the night, and he had struggled with his voice on some of the numbers. And he was not happy with Taylor, whose lateness had not caused any major problems but who had cut it too close for Holmes.

"This was a hard gig," Holmes said, shaking his head, as the musicians began breaking down their equipment.

"But they danced, though," Taylor said encouragingly.

Holmes reminded the musicians about their next wedding a month later, at the National Republican Club of Capitol Hill, for which they would be joined by a trumpeter and a new vocalist, a woman Holmes was eager to debut.

Taylor, as saxophonist, traveled the lightest, and he finished packing while the others were still loading their carts. He walked over to say goodnight to Holmes, and the two shook hands and slapped each other on the back.

"I hope I made up for myself," Taylor said.

"No, you didn't," Holmes said.

It was never Kenney Holmes's intention to become a wedding singer. The grandson of West Indian immigrants, Holmes was raised in Gordon Heights, on Long Island, in what he calls "a small black community founded by like-minded thinkers," families of immigrants and Southern blacks who, as Holmes says, "didn't come here to fool around" and who handed down to their children their own keen sense of ambition.

"We grew up in that kind of atmosphere," he says, "of positive thinking, of getting educated, whether or not you had a degree."

Like any red-blooded American boy in the 1950s and '60s, he was fascinated with popular music: He listened to the area's one radio station, which "mostly played Sinatra"; sometimes in the evenings, with a coat hanger stuck into the top of his portable radio, he could pick up a faint signal from WWRL, a rhythm and blues station in New York City. When he was a teenager, his brother brought home a guitar. "I was 16, it was a Sunday night," he says. "I sat down and played 'I Can't Get No Satisfaction.' I was addicted."

While he was not a virtuoso, he was, he discovered, good at making money at it. He learned three songs—"Satisfaction" by the Rolling Stones, "And I Love Her" by the Beatles, and "Shotgun" by Junior Walker and the All Stars—and formed a band with a few friends. "We went out and sold it," he says. "We could play those three songs all night. We got pretty popular on the island, playing battle of the bands, fire halls, high school proms, for $10 a night."

Still, a career as a musician was not what he, or his family, had had in mind. Over the next few years, he says: "I did everything I could not to be a guitar player. I went to college not to be a guitar player." Thinking he would be a psychiatrist, he took pre-med classes at Stony Brook University and at Suffolk County Community College but didn't complete a degree. Along the way, he continued playing nightclubs and parties.

In his mid-20s, when he was visiting his brother in Washington, "I was standing on Georgia Avenue when I saw a black man driving down the street in a Rolls Royce," Holmes says. "Now, I'm a very simple thinker. I thought, 'I've never seen that in New York City.' And I sold my house and moved down here."

Washington may have looked, to Holmes, like a good place to be an ambitious, career-minded black man, but it also had a thriving music scene in nightclubs and hotel lounges, and the next 15 years played out as a sort of tussle between his creative pursuits and his more business-driven impulses. Trying to work his way up in the music scene, he played five and six nights a week in nightclubs and wrote his own music. He started a recording studio called Sound Ideas, which trawled local talent for the makings of a hit song, but he found the pickings slim.

The club scene, after a long while, began to wear on him, as well. Holmes has been married four times, which he has come to see as an occupational hazard for a club musician. "Most musicians I know went through a lot of wives or a lot of women. Suppose your husband was coming home every morning at 5 a.m. drunk, with lipstick on his collar?" he asks, more or less rhetorically. Plus, although Holmes had become a popular club act, his gigs had not made him a star, and neither had his songwriting. By this time, he had a daughter from his first marriage. Unwilling to resign himself to the life of a starving artist, when an agent approached him in the early '90s about specializing in wedding and private parties, Holmes decided to try it.

It was a revelation. "I could make in one night what I used to make in five," he says. And "it changed the culture of what I was doing. It was no longer cool to get drunk onstage."

Holmes was well-suited for the role of event bandleader. His production skills helped him control his band's sound, and his familiarity with country, big-band and classical music made him popular with audiences who wanted, as he says, "a tango or a Viennese waltz," as well as Wilson Pickett.

Because business ebbs and flows with the seasons and the economy, Holmes, who lives in Upper Marlboro, has always kept a variety of sidelines, including a job driving a limousine for nine years to put his oldest daughter through a private high school and college. These days, at gigs, he hands out a stack of million-dollar "bills" printed with his image and his current enterprises: bandleader, commercial mortgage broker, hard money lender (slogan: "Hard Money with a Soft Touch").

Holmes uses as many as eight musicians and two singers for weddings. He accepts turnover as a fact of running a band, but his current core lineup has, in the mercurial world of part-time performers, been fairly steady. Brawner, the drummer, and Taylor, the sax player, have played with him for three and four years, respectively, and Robinson, the keyboardist, has played with him for 15.

This is perhaps partly because Holmes insists on making music. During performances, he lets his musicians take the lead and uses specialized, stripped-down tracks, called digital sequences, to set the tempo and fill in musical parts when necessary, ultimately preferring the messy alchemy of live music to something more canned. The musicians say that this is in contrast to other bandleaders they've worked for, who often rely heavily on recordings and use musicians more as visual props. Holmes's respect for the music endears him to his musicians, all long-time veterans of the club scene, who return the favor with their performances. "These guys play from the heart," says Robinson. "They're not just trying to get through the gig."

Still, as manager, Holmes is quick to draw a line between him and his employees, who, he says, don't always cleave to the more rigid codes of commercial work. He fines for transgressions such as tardiness and sloppy dress, and while he tips good behavior, he keeps wages competitive but not lavish. Raising wages, he thinks, only creates divas. "I learned the hard way, because I ruined some good people."

A month after the wedding at 2941, Holmes stood at the second-floor railing of the National Republican Club in the early evening, watching as guests milled around the lobby below. The bride and groom were from Tennessee and Texas, and the crowd skewed tall, tanned and blond; the bride had been attended by 10 bridesmaids in floor-length black gowns. "As a wedding planner I know once said, this is not a Southern Maryland fire hall wedding," said Holmes. He flipped through a copy of the evening's itinerary. "A lot of moving parts," he murmured.

Holmes's new female vocalist, Teri Swinton, had arrived earlier in a low-cut black dress and silver lamé jacket and was sitting at a table in the room where the band would play, under a portrait of Gen. Douglas MacArthur. Swinton was a club performer whom Holmes had hired for her voice as well as her stage presence. "I try to encourage my female singers to be feminine, to be a songbird," he had said earlier. "I think that's why people want a female singer, to bring some softness to the band." (Holmes, who says that female singers can be the hardest to manage, also calls them "a necessary evil.")

"We're probably going to start with 'Saving All My Love,' Teri," Holmes said. Swinton grimaced.

"I don't like that song," she said. "Kenney makes me sing all these songs that are, like, aarggh." She made a gargling noise in her throat.

"Sometimes you got to sacrifice something for a higher power," Taylor told her.

"Sacrifice," said Holmes, indignantly. "I like that song!"

In addition to the singer, Holmes's core band—Taylor, Robinson and Brawner—was joined by Curtis Pope, a trumpeter who had once been Wilson Pickett's bandleader, a big teddy bear of a man wearing a skintight black shirt with little silver spangles on it under his jacket, and playing a horn partly clad in burl wood. The dinner, on the floor below, was running long. The musicians sat around one of the party tables waiting.

"I wish my father could hear me play," Taylor was saying. "My father was a gospel singer—well, he was a bricklayer, but in the evenings and on the weekends, he sang gospel. I can't wait to get to heaven, so we can have a band." In the foyer outside the dining room, the elevator doors opened with the first of the guests.

"Okay, boys," Holmes said, "let's go to work."

Live music at weddings is an age-old tradition, but the wedding band as we know it today is a more recent phenomenon that grew out of a couple of converging trends. In the late 1980s, the once-vital live-music scene in nightclubs and lounges began to wane, says Jan Davis, a former singer and bandleader who now runs her own event consulting agency in the Washington area, Jan Davis Entertainment and Events. "When I started," Davis says, "you could drive around the Beltway and hit every hotel and find live music. . . . Everybody had a pianist in their lobby playing beautiful music. Now you have a couple of D.C. hotels doing that, and the rest of them have those pianos that play themselves." Bands used to working five nights a week soon began looking elsewhere.

At the same time, the small business of weddings was rapidly becoming a full-fledged industry, with a lengthening list of specialized components. Brides who previously might have been content with an evening of pop ballads now wanted a specific music for each portion of the evening. Bands began to expand their playlists, and thus was born "this animal called the wedding band," Davis says, " . . . that could play everything from big-band swing to Beyoncé." Like a catchier version of Muzak, the wedding band was the great equalizer, turning six decades of pop into danceable numbers for a crowd of all ages.

But recent times have not been kind to these bands. There is the poor economy; live music is often one of the first things trimmed from a tighter budget, and Holmes and Davis say they have never seen business this bad. "I used to have one to two inches of contracts in my book, and now I have just one or two in there," Holmes says.

Technology has also changed the profession. Davis says business is booming for DJs, whom many brides are finding an adequate, and far cheaper, substitute for the wedding band. (Brides can expect to pay about $3,500 to $10,000 for a live band, depending on the number of musicians, says Davis, and from $600 to $1,500 for a DJ.) While a good DJ ostensibly does the same thing as a good band—playing the songs that keep people on the dance floor—Holmes maintains that the connection between live musicians and a crowd is finely tuned and impossible to create with recorded music.

"[The DJ] can't tell the bass player, 'Kick it,'" he says. "He can't tell the drummer, 'You've got a solo now. Let's work 'em.'" And Davis, whose business represents both DJs and bands, is unwilling to call the era of the wedding band over. The interaction between a band and a crowd, she says, is "a rapport that you can't get any other way." If playing at a wedding is creating a fantasy, she believes the fantasy still has traction: "Walking into a beautifully set room, and you've got this good-looking band on stage, with the tuxes and the gowns, and they're singing this wonderful music—there's nothing like it."

At the National Republican Club, Holmes, Swinton and the musicians were positioned a hair's breadth from the dance floor, and the number that they used to kick off the dancing, a nondescript instrumental, was like touching a match to a tank of gas. By the time the band was halfway through it, the square of parquet floor in front of them was all but obscured by the scrum of bodies. "We want everyone to have a good time tonight," Holmes called to the crowd unnecessarily. The father-daughter dance, propelled by the momentum of the music and the ecstatic response of the crowd to the appearance of the bride, began without the father; the mother-son dance began without the son, until the groom was extracted from the crowd and delivered to the middle of the floor.

Swinton debuted on "Oh, What a Night"; her voice was so piercing and golden that she might have been mistaken for a studio recording. But partway through, in the middle of a verse, she trailed off, lost. Holmes glanced at her, and she mopped her brow, smiled into the middle distance, and picked it up at the chorus.

The party that the band proceeded to create, for the guests of the Wheaton-Greaves wedding, was sort of a Platonic ideal of wedding receptions. Holmes led his troops through an escalating series of feel-good oldies and disco tunes, "Brown-Eyed Girl" to "Give It to Me, Baby" to "Brick House" to "Ain't Too Proud to Beg." Their sound was big and turbulent, and number after number, the crowd matched them with a spiraling frenzy of dancing: foot-stomping and formally perfect. Old-timers two-stepped. Rogueish-looking Southern boys with heads full of pomade spun their dainty girlfriends, Astaire-Rogers style, and dipped them until their hairdos touched the floor.

Holmes, with sweat pouring down his face and his glasses slipping to the end of his nose, reined in the party enough to emcee the cutting of the cake, and the tossing of the garter and the bridal bouquet. At the end of the evening, when it was time for the send-off, with sparklers, of the happy couple on their Jamaican honeymoon, the crowd lingered, unwilling to leave. "Ladies and gentlemen, as part of the send-off, go downstairs. That means leave the room," Holmes admonished them, in the same patiently bossy voice he used to reprimand his musicians. "That means go downstairs."

When the room was mostly empty, Holmes began breaking down his equipment. Although Swinton had fumbled for the words on other songs, and occasionally sung too quietly, looking down at lyric sheets, Holmes was content to chalk it up to inexperience. He was, he said, very pleased with how her first performance had gone.

It was after midnight. Holmes had two cartloads of equipment to pack into his gold Ford Explorer, but he hoped to get home by 1 or

1:30. The last few guests were chatting on the dance floor. The groom and one of his friends stood in the middle, swaying slightly.

"Can we get one more last dance?" the friend asked Holmes.

"Can we get one of those DJ songs?" the groom added.

Holmes cued up a CD that the bride and groom had given him to play during breaks, and Barry White's familiar voice came growling out of the speakers. "Can't get enough of your love, babe," White crooned. At the back of the room, Holmes zipped his guitar into his case. Softly, under his breath, he sang along.

For the Record

Jason Cherkis

Five years ago, as often happened, Ian Nagoski was stuck behind the counter of his True Vine record store in Baltimore one afternoon when a set of burly men showed up at his door carting a box of records. The box was not filled with obvious collector's bait. The vinyl did not shimmer like fresh store stock. The discs were just old 78s in wrinkled brown paper sleeves. The box had been marked as trash.

The men were part of Baltimore's eviction economy. They worked hauling out the left-behind junk of the foreclosed, the kicked-out, the newly imprisoned and the dearly departed. If they found old records, they brought them to Nagoski, hoping he'd be enough of a softie to want to save them. He didn't always take everything, but he did have one rule: If the records were not in English, he had to buy them.

This box, Nagoski noticed, contained very old Greek records. He paid $5 for the box, roughly 10 cents per record. When he put them on his turntable, he didn't know what to think. These were interesting, sure. But maybe he'd paid too much.

Nagoski, then 30, returned to the box every week or so. He started to focus on seven or eight records made by a Greek immigrant who recorded in the 1920s. Her name was Marika Papagika, and her songs were nothing short of entrancing. She hit such sad notes, tones he'd never heard in all his years of listening to music. They seemed like "the sound of the very first cry from human beings." He eventually concluded that her tear-stained ballad "Smyrneiko Minore" was the best song he'd ever heard.

Papagika, he discovered, had been one of the most widely recorded artists in the United States in the 1920s. She'd made well over 225 records and had been successful enough to open up her own New York hotspot, called Marika's. But there wasn't much else he could find out. He could locate only two pictures of her. Her Wikipedia entry ran just three lines. He decided he had to rescue her from obscurity.

Papagika would just be the latest in a string of artists who'd been fuel for a Nagoski salvage operation, though none had seized him as thoroughly as she had. Over the years, he'd become a kind of flea-market scholar, excavating and celebrating vanished music and long-forgotten artists—from the earliest Afro-Cuban rumbas to the earliest Bollywood soundtracks—and had made a name for himself as an ethnomusicologist.

A life-long record fiend, he had found his calling in unearthing your great-grandmother's 78s collection—the songs immigrants made when they first reached America, the songs they craved most from back home. In 2007, he released a compilation of his archival work, *Black Mirror: Reflections in Global Musics*, which included "Smyrneiko Minore." The collection received glowing reviews on such taste-making music sites as Pitchfork and the Fader.

The Papagika song garnered more than 17,000 hits after being posted by a friend of Nagoski's on YouTube. Soon David Harrington, a Kronos Quartet violinist and the group's founder, took notice. The group has since included the song in its repertoire. "Nothing really could have prepared me for the entrance of Marika Papagika," Harrington says. "It just wiped me out—that first note. Even now, I listen to that at least once a week. That particular note raised the bar on what a musician could accomplish. I will always be grateful to Ian for uncovering that performance."

And Nagoski hasn't stopped uncovering lost treasures. In 2009, he released a second compilation, *A String of Pearls*, and helped reissue a collection of early Rembetika—Greek urban folk music popularized in the '30s. He recently began producing a radio show available as an Internet podcast dedicated to spinning and celebrating his 78s. Called "Fonotopia," it has played selections including a 1947 recording of a D.C. preacher and the earliest psychedelic music, recorded in Central Mexico in the 1940s. This month, Nagoski finally released an entire album of Papagika's work through the Portland-based label, Mississippi Records, and his own Canary Records.

"The more I discovered how little was known, the more I felt compelled, like, 'Okay, this is my job,'" Nagoski says. "That's me. That's what I contribute. I have to go learn this story and tell it. Part of it has to do not with her but with me, with my place in the world, with wanting to do something with my life, wanting to contribute something that I thought a force for good."

Growing up in Wilmington, Del., Nagoski didn't have to travel far to find songs worthy of obsession. He first heard the guitar at his father's knee, listening to him pluck out the house favorite, the gold-rush ballad "Sweet Betsy from Pike." His mother taught piano and voice. He can still remember her Bach and Beethoven, her cathartic renditions of '70s pop hits, and her deep tutorials on the Beatles' *Abbey Road*. He and his twin sisters were encouraged to play along. Thrift-store instruments hung on the walls—a banjo from 1865, an old Martin guitar, violins and recorders—museum pieces you could touch.

Listening to records or grabbing a guitar proved easier than real life. To make ends meet, Nagoski's parents, Joe and Marcelle, ran a photography business, taking portraits of baby ballerinas and shooting local recitals. The work was unsteady and a grind.

During the first eight years of his life, Nagoski had pneumonia three times, as well as a prolonged bout of tonsillitis. He spent his childhood on the couch, home-schooled by Jim Croce LPs and his father's art books. Although his illnesses eventually went away, his sense of isolation stayed with him. "I really didn't fit in when I went back [to school]," he says. "I was odd. I was not okay. Kids can sniff it out when another kid just doesn't know how to be."

But Nagoski did know how to get to the record store. The closest one was three blocks away: Bert's Tape Factory. In the fourth grade, he asked employees if they had any Ravi Shankar records in stock. His grandfather, who lived two doors down, introduced him to even older records and taught him to play drums. He'd watch the old man crank up Gene Krupa LPs and keep time in his garage on those exuberant breaks.

Nagoski introduced his mother to avant-garde composer John Cage and his sisters to the Velvet Underground. As a teenager, he'd show up for class in cowboy boots with a pair of headphones draped around his neck. "He was not popular in school," recalls Rich Pell, a friend from those days. "He was not thought of at school. Nobody knew what he was."

He started writing his own songs on an acoustic guitar; he named his first homemade tape *Pincher Martin*, after the William Golding novel. He sent letters to his favorite composers and artists. They all bore the same message: Please tell me how I can get out of Wilmington, Delaware. One artist sent him Christmas cards every year for a while.

Nagoski's therapist recommended to his parents that he drop out of high school—he was too depressed and wouldn't survive it. His parents agreed. "It was not smooth," his mother recalls. "But he knew that he could not just do what everybody else did. He couldn't settle down, get a job, get a grade. Everything just meant far too much or far more to him."

Nagoski enrolled in the University of Delaware's continuing education program and took a job at Bert's. He developed an almost spiritual love for free-jazz pioneer Ornette Coleman and Javanese gamelan music, and by then had delved headlong into New Zealand indie rock. But after two years in college, Nagoski still couldn't find his place. Too much experimentation with psychedelics, a bad breakup, and a lot of F's caused a breakdown. "So, I came home and sat around in my bathrobe for a couple months," he says.

He wanted to be a modern composer. He decided that if he couldn't go to college, he'd find his own teacher. At 21, he moved to New York to work for the pioneering modernist composer La Monte Young and to live in the artist's "Dream House," a loft space that had been converted into an experimental sound-and-light installation. But he spent most of his time attending to Young-ordered household chores ranging from the mundane (laundry and dish duty) to the ridiculous (shrine scrubbing).

"I was so lonely," Nagoski recalls. "I was living all alone in New York on $300 a month, and everyone around me was really stoned. And I wanted to, like, make something of myself. . . . I had to beg and plead finally in tears to get a music lesson." He lasted six months.

Nagoski moved to Philadelphia and took a job at a Borders bookstore. He later edited internal documents at a health-care company and then programmed databases for a small software firm. In his spare time, he began recording his own albums of dense electronic symphonies made with a CD burner, cassette tapes and a tone generator (an outmoded electronic device that produces single frequencies). For one song, he recorded a shower pouring over an upside down lobster pot. His pieces pulsed with menacing drones and dive bombs of piercing static, and he gave them titles such as "Feather," "Rain" and "A Joy Forever." They sounded like the most brutal New Age music—incredibly loud, incredibly slow—and reached very few people.

In 2000, Nagoski moved to Baltimore, lured by the city's receptive experimental music scene. He found friends, a community of likeminded, off-the-grid musicians, and steady shows. No venue was too obscure or too small. He introduced his noise experiments in the back room of a gay bar, and conducted a three-hour dronefest for 40 people in his living room.

With each show, Nagoski's expectations were always impossibly high. "He had this idea that sound could induce an ecstatic state in the listener," says Dan Conrad, a musician and collaborator. "That it didn't happen—sustained ecstasy—he would complain bitterly that the performance failed. It was an example of his desperate integrity."

For all his efforts, Nagoski's albums sold in the hundreds. "I've never really found an audience for my music," he admits. "There literally isn't one."

Nagoski found a far more receptive audience for his other love, championing old records, records that could be just as intense and foreign as his own, whether they were his prized prewar gospel sides or bagpipe novelties. "He has this way of talking about the actual item that is the 78 that makes it really important," says friend and guitarist Ben Chasny, who performs under the name Six Organs of Admittance. "It's almost in a mystical way. He's not just talking about: 'Here's this item I own.' When he talks about or writes about these items, they're discs that can really transport you."

That intense connection to old records soon became his route to an adult life. In 2004, a woman he'd been dating became pregnant with his daughter, June. Although the relationship didn't work out, Nagoski was determined to be a committed father. After being fired from another bookstore job, he decided to do what came most naturally: He opened True Vine in the Hampden neighborhood as its principal owner and day-to-day manager.

For the first year, Nagoski worked 80-to-100-hour weeks: running the store, scouring his favorite thrift store LP bins for fresh inventory, and in the evenings, turning his shop into a show space for out-of-town and local bands. A few nights a week, he even pulled out an old mattress and slept at the store. For his 30th birthday, he decided he needed a break and planned a three-city East Coast tour in which he'd perform at other record stores a piece he dubbed "The Baltimore Yowler" in which he simply got in front of a microphone and screamed. The shop owners were friendly enough to let him have his cathartic moment.

"My daughter had just been born," Nagoski says. "I was in a new business that didn't seem like it was going to particularly work out. I had no money. I was single and profoundly unhappy. . . . There's me screaming for 20 or 30 minutes in a record store. That was how I celebrated my 30th birthday. Obviously, I was freaking out."

Soon after he returned to Baltimore, the box of Papagikas came into the store.

Just as the Papagika song was becoming a mini-phenomenon on YouTube and beyond, Nagoski was conducting research for extensive liner notes to accompany an album of her recordings. He tracked down translations of her songs, interviewed the granddaughter of one of her contemporaries, rented reel-to-reel tapes of her performances, and even found a woman Papagika had babysat. He took a picture of her old club—now a jewelry store called Golden Paradise. The notes for the album are exhaustive but not overly academic.

Cornell professor Gail Holst-Warhaft, director of the school's Mediterranean Studies Initiative, assisted Nagoski's research and helped edit his notes on Papagika. She says that Nagoski may face criticism because he's not a traditional academic, and his notes can be "over the top."

Nagoski dedicated five years to his Papagika project. His liner notes ended up running 4,000 words long. He has chosen to begin with a mash note to his muse: "This is the nearly forgotten music of a great singer whose life spanned from the collapsing Ottoman Empire to the emerging American Empire. And it is the story of an early attempt to make a star out of an immigrant singer, an effort that nearly succeeded, but not quite. It is an introduction to what remains of one life, derived from magically speaking black discs which say as much about the eternal as the white stone of the Parthenon."

His notes may not be ready to be published in any university press, but Holst-Warhaft believes Nagoski has done Papagika justice. "Other people have recognized her great genius as a singer, but nobody thought to do an in-depth study of her as an all-around personality," she says. "There's very little known about her, and he's painstakingly gone about finding everything. I take my hat off to him."

Nagoski's domain is the yard sale, the thrift store, the eBay auction no one else is bidding on. "I like the smell of mold, because I associate it with the euphoria of discovery," he says.

Nagoski's "approach is great, because he has a DJ's ear and he's got this historian's perspective," explains Jace Clayton, a New York artist who performs under the name DJ/rupture. "He's looking at these songs as somewhere between a poem and an autobiography."

Nagoski says the true aim of his ethnomusicology is to simply add to the musical canon—to build on the efforts of older archivists, and uncover a bit more of our hidden history. This year, he hopes to have released another compilation, *Brass Pins and Match Heads*, a study of Armenian and Syrian immigrant music from New York, and a full-length study of an Indian virtuoso singer. He's constantly listening for his next great obsession.

"He's always on a project," says his wife, Amanda Vickers, a conservationist who remembers meeting him at one of his screaming performances, which she found uncomfortable but compelling. "There really isn't any Ian not on a project."

All of the work may not just add to the canon but correct it. African and other non-Western music used to be big business in the United States and England. In the '20s, record labels recorded countless Nigerian, Greek and Iraqi immigrants, selling these works as musical postcards from home. But the mid-century folk revival, which venerated such homegrown figures as Woody Guthrie and the Carter Family and whose version of history echoes throughout the annals of rock-and-roll, helped erase the non-Western material from the American playlist.

Nagoski is comfortable with his status as a DIY scholar-fan boy, a role that has led him all over the world, giving lectures on his 78s in a 100-year-old theater in Montpellier, France, an abandoned hotel-turned-legal-squat in Brussels, an art gallery in Milan and a warehouse space in Boston. "It's scholarship in the service of poetry," he says. "There [is] a part of me that likes being thought of seriously by serious people. But serious people take many, many forms. The academy is not entirely made up of serious people."

The first thing you notice about Nagoski's home is what you don't see. There aren't thousands of records lining the shelves. He will not be leaving behind a trove for any future treasure hunters. "I have virtually no records," he says. "I don't collect. I'm a conduit for records."

A few years ago, he exited True Vine (his partners reopened in a new space), only to end up in one low-wage job after another. Last year, he drove a city cab on the overnight shift for two months. Until recently, he had a job answering phones at a census office. Money is always tight.

In early spring, Nagoski took some records to the African music library in the basement of Voice of America's Washington headquarters. He had an appointment to see Leo Sarkisian, age 89. Sarkisian had spent decades crisscrossing Africa and the Middle East working as a field recorder, archivist and broadcaster for the Voice of America; he'd been hired by Edward R. Murrow. Sarkisian's family had immigrated to Lawrence, Mass., from Armenia at the start of the 20th century. He grew up engrossed in the music of his homeland and later became a fixture on the New York scene just after Papagika's time.

The library, whose walls are lined with dozens and dozens of his reel-to-reel recordings, is named after him. Nagoski hoped the ethnomusicologist could help him translate a batch of Turkish and Armenian records, assist him with research about the old immigrant music circuit in New York and maybe tell him about other recordings he should hunt down.

Nagoski played track after track for him, and Sarkisian started filling in the blanks. Every song came to life with a story, bits of translation, a flood of memories. These songs weren't mysteries or collector bait. They made up the soundtrack of his childhood. Nagoski had picked right. Soon Sarkisian took the hand of his wife, who had joined him for the meeting, and started to dance in a crowded aisle.

Toward the end of their two-hour meeting, Nagoski decided he had to put on his beloved Papagika song. Sarkisian said even he had never heard of the singer. He was curious.

When that first note struck the room, Sarkisian stopped fussing with the piles of old records and reminiscing with his wife about the old days. A big grin creased the man's face, his eyes brightened. And for the first time all day, he fell silent and let the music take hold.

The Curious Case of Nicki Minaj

Caryn Ganz

Nicki Minaj is a 25-year-old rapper from Queens, New York, with a wickedly clever flow and never-ending supply of pop culture punch lines. Except when she's Roman Zolanski, her gay male alter ego, who spits saucy verses at warp speed. Or the character Nicki Lewinsky, who cozies up to President Carter—better known as superstar rapper Lil Wayne—on a handful of salacious mix tape tracks. She raps about signing her fans' boobs in a bugged-out Valley girl accent. She's the first female hip-hop artist to hit No. 1 on *Billboard*'s top rap singles chart since 2003. She's stolen the spotlight on songs with pop heavyweights Mariah Carey and Usher. And she's done it all while playing hip-hop's most dangerous game: sexuality roulette.

Minaj may or may not be attracted to women (more on that later), but she draws a fierce gay following with her brazen lyrics and outsize persona. Beneath her blunt-cut bangs lies a cunning mind capable of weaving sports metaphors and references to '80s sitcoms into complex rhymes about scoring with girls and blowing guys' minds. Lady Gaga's audience was primed to accept her as a sexually adventurous nonconformist by artists like Madonna and David Bowie, but in hip-hop, Nicki Minaj is a real space oddity. Rap has never seen a mainstream rising star this eccentric and brave, yet for all Minaj's curious artistic choices (two-tone wigs, spontaneous British dialects, shout-outs to *Harry Potter*) she's also incredibly popular. She has nearly 1.1 million

Twitter followers and a cadre of famous fans like Kanye West, who recently proclaimed she could be the second-biggest rapper of all time, behind Eminem. When her first official album, *Pink Friday*, arrives in November, Minaj won't just be the "baddest bitch," as she calls herself—she'll be a bona fide phenomenon.

Three years ago, Minaj was an unknown from 50 Cent's neighborhood trying to get noticed on MySpace. Her mom had filled her childhood home with music ("I knew the whole Diana Ross collection before I was 8," she says), but her father introduced her to violence. On the 2008 track "Autobiography," she raps about how her drug-addicted dad tried to burn down the family's house with her mom still inside. Despite the turmoil—or perhaps because of it—young Nicki was passionately creative. She wrote her first rhyme before she turned 12 ("Cookie's the name, chocolate chip is the flavor / Suck up my style like a cherry Life Saver") and attended LaGuardia High School, the arts academy immortalized in *Fame*, where she studied drama and generated plenty of it.

"I was definitely one of those girls where you heard me before you saw me," Minaj recalls, kicking off a pair of velvety platform heels in a tidy Los Angeles hotel suite and stretching out her calves, which are tightly wrapped in black leather leggings. She pondered careers as a bus driver or lawyer and worked a day job at Red Lobster saving up money for studio time. When she started to get serious about music, her then-manager recommended she change her name to Minaj (she was born Onika Maraj). Though she now admits she hated it, she obliged, tarting up her image for her first mix tape, 2007's *Playtime Is Over*, which opens with a sex line call to 1-900-MS-MINAJ. After she skillfully remade the Notorious B.I.G.'s "Warning" for the DVD documentary *The Come Up*, she got a call from Lil Wayne. Over the course of two more mix tapes under his supervision, 2008's *Sucka Free* and 2009's *Beam Me Up Scotty*, she developed ferocious new identities, penned jaw-dropping explicit raps, and emerged as the first lady of Wayne's Young Money crew. She also started to fend off pervy guys stalking her online by playing to her female fans.

"I started making it my business to say things that would empower women, like, 'Where my bad bitches at?' to let them know, 'I'm here for you,'" she says. "Then, when I started going to the shows and it was nothing but girls, it was like, *Did I go too far with embracing my girls? Because now they want to kiss and hug me.*"

Minaj may have encouraged all the lady love with lyrics that imply she's sexually flexible—or at least curious. None of the famous female rappers rumored to be queer have dared utter the L word, but Minaj has used it repeatedly: "I only stop for pedestrians or a real, real bad lesbian," she raps on "Go Hard." On Usher's "Lil Freak" she trolls the club for a chick with "a real big ol' ghetto booty" for a ménage à trois, and in the song's video, which has been viewed more than four million times on YouTube, she spends more time rubbing up on a female conquest than she does with its star.

The rhymes brought attention, then rumors, then a denial in the July issue of *Black Men* magazine that reads remarkably like Bill Clinton's infamous "I did not have sexual relations with that woman" statement: "I don't date women and I don't have sex with women." Nicki Lewinsky laughs at the resemblance and adds almost tauntingly, "But I don't date men either." Her bottom line: No labels. "People who like me—they'll listen to my music, and they'll know who I am. I just don't like that people want you to say what you are, who you are. I just *am*. I do what the fuck I want to do." She likes to beckon ladies to the stage at her shows, brandishing a marker for sweaty boob-signing sessions, but 95% of her racy lyrics are about encounters with men. Adding that she'll grab her best friend's breasts for fun far from paparazzi cameras, she says, "The point is, everyone is not black and white. There are so many shades in the middle, and you've got to let people feel comfortable with saying what they want to say when they want to say it. I don't want to feel like I've got the gun pointed at my head and you're about to pull the trigger if I don't say what you want to hear. I just want to be me and do me."

Minaj definitely has a lot to say about the politics of being a woman in the 21st-century music biz. "Everybody knows I can go out and pick a dude and date him," she says. "But I want to do what people think I can't do, which is have the number 1 album in the country and be the first female rapper to sell records like dudes in this day and age." After taking some heat for identifying with one of the best-selling, and most disproportioned, toys in history—she ends phone calls with a screeched "It's Barbie, *bitch*!"—she was accused of being plastic. "It's interesting that people have more negative things to say about me saying 'I'm Barbie' than me saying 'I'm a bad bitch,'" she says, getting a bit heated. "So you can call yourself a female dog be-cause that's cool in our community. But if you call yourself a Barbie, that's fake." The criticism didn't just irk her; it inspired her. "Once I figure something is irritating people, I'm going to do it more," she says, smiling, "because I like to get on your nerves until you realize how fucking stupid you are."

If girls are attracted to Minaj's unapologetic feminism and appre-ciation for the female body (not to mention her own überhot photo shoots), gay guys can't get enough of her over-the-top wardrobe, neck-snapping put-downs, and theatrical play-acting. Hip-hop has always had a flair for the dramatic, from Flavor Flav's oversize clock to the comedic skits tucked between tracks on Wu-Tang Clan and Snoop Dogg albums. But Minaj has taken the art to the next level with her drag-queen-like outfits (she's rocked Wonder Woman span-dex and Freddy Krueger nails), wild-eyed rapping, and split person-alities. "Roman is so flamboyant, so outspoken, so open, and, you know, creative," she says of her inner gay boy Zolanski, which she pronounces "Zo-lan-sky" with a touch of an East End accent. The name is, of course, a play on director Roman Polanski, but she can't explain why she opted to identify with a white man known for being a deviant. Screwing with sexual conventions has become a Minaj trademark, though: In her guest spot on Mariah Carey's "Up Out My Face" she calls out a cheating boyfriend who wasn't just two-timing her with another girl—he was "sneakin' with the deacon."

As for her increasingly elaborate looks, Minaj insists, "No one would even have had the balls before to suggest things like my hair." She appears in Ludacris's "My Chick Bad" video with a pin stuck in her pink do, jet-black lipstick, and spikes on her shoulders. She sports a half-pink, half-blonde wig in the clip for Young Money's "Roger That" because her stylist "hadn't dyed one half of the wig yet, and I really wanted to wear it." Though she didn't realize it, these bold choices paired with her frank sex talk were making Minaj an underground gay heroine. She first learned of her gay male following when she spied fans' spot-on renditions of her verses on the Web. She was blown away by the replications of her voices and mannerisms. "If a gay guy impersonates you, you are a bad bitch. Period," she says, waving her bright-orange nails in the air. "There are no ifs, ands, or buts, because they only impersonate the best."

Hip-hop, however, has never been a hospitable place for gays, especially gay men. Female rappers including Lady Sovereign and Yo! Majesty's Shunda K have revealed they're queer to little fanfare, but the biggest names in the game wouldn't dare broach the subject. "I think there have been many gay rappers, they just haven't come out of the closet," Minaj says slyly. "Yup, lots of them. They're lurking around the industry now." While she believes we'll see a blockbuster gay rapper fess up soon, Minaj acknowledges it won't be an easy road. "Obviously, the majority of the men in hip-hop don't want you to think they're gay. That's just the reality of it," Minaj says. "I'm a woman, so I have a lot more flexibility. And I don't lose credibility in any way if I say I think girls are dope and sexy."

Saying girls are sexy and actually having sex with them are very different things, though, putting Minaj at risk of being labeled a "fauxmosexual"—someone who uses gay titillation to score pop culture points, like girl-kissing Katy Perry or muffin-bluffing Lady Gaga. While it's clear Minaj enjoys the attention she gets from both men and women for flirting with ladies—she licked her lips suggestively and batted her eyelashes when a female fan announced she wanted to kiss her on a recent Ustream webcast—because she's a hip-hop artist, she's gambling with her career, and the stakes are high.

"I still don't think hip-hop has any place for gay people," says New York City gay rapper Cazwell. Shunda K adds, "There are a lot of people in the industry fakin' it to make it. When you're not keeping it real, you can be any damn thing people want you to be." But Cazwell thinks Minaj could go to number 1 even if she had a sudden public revelation about her sexuality. "If she was butch and dressed like a guy, people would be turned off, but people like a pretty girl no matter who she sleeps with," he says. "It may even turn them on more!"

There may be no out MCs selling platinum records at the moment, but as rap has aged, it has moved further from the homophobic battleground where pink F bombs once reigned supreme. Nowadays, comments that could be perceived as gay in hip-hop songs are appended with the somewhat lighthearted phrase "no homo." Minaj used to say it, too, but traded it in for the less prejudicial "pause" after a gay male fan complained to her via Twitter.

"'Pause' means 'no sexual connotation intended,'" she explains, inadvertently demonstrating the proper usage when at one point she responds to a question about planning her upcoming tour with "I'm so freaking, like, anal about every single thing, pause. So it's going to be freaking crazy."

Minaj's craziness is a big part of her appeal, but as she makes the leap from street records to the mainstream, she risks losing some of the sharp edges that have become her hallmarks. She's toned down her most pornographic lyrics ("I feel like I've been there, done that"), and her chart-topping single "Your Love" is a gooey R&B ballad in which she sings, "You got spark, you, you got spunk, you / You got something all the girls want." Says Jayson Rodriguez, a hip-hop writer for MTV News, "'Your Love' is tame and muted, and she's anything but. Nicki Minaj is saucy, lyrical, animated, flirtatious, beautiful, smart—but she doesn't have a signature song that matches up to that yet. It feels like she'll explode once she gets that massive song that people identify with her on a mainstream level, but sometimes I fear she can't capture her persona on record."

But Minaj is already prepared to bring her gay fans with her to the next level. Musing about hitting the road with her mentor, Lil Wayne, once he's out of jail, she says, "Normally, Wayne probably wouldn't have gay guys coming to see his shows much, but they're definitely a big part of my movement, and I hope they'd still come out and see me." She reveals that Wayne loves discussing how much ladies love her, and that the crew jokes with him, "Nicki's gonna steal all your girls on tour this year!" She laughs and flashes one of her mischievous smiles that make the boys—and girls—swoon. "I think that will be really, really interesting, just to start bridging that gap. We'll see."

"Gasping, But Somehow Still Alive"

The Persistence of Meat Is Murder

Drew Daniel

On the subject of the twenty-fifth anniversary of *Meat Is Murder*, let's get the obvious part over: we have surely hugged "How Soon Is Now?" to death. From its shimmering Shondells-esque tremolo hook to its unforgettable miserabilist stanzas to its kitschy rebirth as a sampled loop in Soho's "Hippychick," the song enjoys the dubious distinction of being The Smiths' "Stairway to Heaven" (banister to purgatory?). All together now: "So you go and you stand on your own / and you leave on your own / and you go home, and you cry and you want to die." I first heard the song in eighth grade from a tall, bookish boy named Christian. His fierce love of The Smiths got me speculating. Was he? . . . He'd put on The Smiths and we'd listen and we'd look at each other. I knew what I wanted to know, but then a strange fear gripped me and I just couldn't ask. I still can't vouch for Christian, but I do know that back then listening a little too carefully to The Smiths was an adolescent rite of passage for lots of shy boys and girls my age. Sometimes you used their music to test the waters, and sometimes you used it to shield yourself and cover up.

By the time I was in college and out of the closet, the queers I hung out with engaged in bitter debates about the politics of Morrissey's, ahem, "celibacy." Radically political pals in ACT UP and Queer Nation decried what was seen as a corny case of the glass closet, a spineless switcheroo in which "celibacy" was a way of not having to stand up and be counted amongst the down and dirty perverts of the world. To such listeners, Morrissey's four-alarm faggotry was a fait accompli, which meant that his celibate posturing wasn't a radical form of straight-edge virtue but just a reactionary cop-out. I recall my friend Diet Popstitute listening to some such argument and harrumphing in disgust words to the effect that "worrying about Morrissey's sex life is about as interesting as debating the subtleties of acting technique in the career of Tom Selleck." Diet had a point. But if Morrissey upheld community-based models of belonging and togetherness and political solidarity then he wouldn't be Morrissey. Not fitting into any community was the point, and whether the "club" in "How Soon Is Now?" is a straight pick up joint or a gay bar doesn't really matter from this point of view. No matter what demographic you're in, sometimes you wind up alone. Diet died of AIDS and Morrissey has lived to (not) tell, a brutally indifferent outcome woven into the everyday which is surely of a piece with the business-like abattoir killings decried in the anti-animal cruelty anthem "Meat Is Murder." By the time I finished college minus Diet and many others, I didn't need The Smiths to tell me that in the midst of life we are in death. I didn't much feel like listening anymore.

Cut to twenty years after these early puppy-love imprintings and unresolvable resentments. From out of nowhere, just last month I was ambushed by a bite-size Proustian madeleine of keening nostalgia courtesy of this era of The Smiths. My band was setting up and getting ready to play in San Francisco at a big anniversary bash for the SFMOMA. We were dutifully booting up software, tuning oscillators on synths, and making sure that MaxMSP/Jitter patches were running smoothly on the video processing rig. I was testing a microphone when the DJ put on "Well I Wonder," the B-Side to "How Soon Is Now?," and I was instantly teleported back into my awkward, closeted teenage self. Then, bitterly stung by unrequited love for a straight bandmate in my high school hardcore band, I would play "Well I Wonder" over and over to myself while wallowing in hopeless ardor:

"Well I wonder / Do you hear me when you sleep? / I hoarsely cry . . . " at which point a wordless sighing croon erupts in the place of yet more useless demands. Within the contracted world of this song, it's a foregone conclusion that the answer to such human-doormat questions is a resounding No—and yet that knowledge doesn't extinguish the impossible desire for love, but only inflames it further. Like James Brown's "Prisoner of Love" or John Dowland's "In Darkness Let Me Dwell," it's the kind of song you can listen to until your tears distort the room.

Channeling my teenage self, years later the words poured out of my mouth and into the microphone as I lip-synced like a drag queen for a now kinda confused Matmos audience. They thought I was being snide and condescending; surely this electro-noise-improv-musique-concrete group has nothing but contempt for the heart-on-sleeve gush of The Smiths. Technology and abstraction killed the necessity for such vulgar displays of cheap sentiment, right? Embarrassingly enough, I remembered every one of Morrissey's words as they flooded through me: "Gasping / But somehow still alive / This is the fierce last stand of all I am . . . "

The words don't sound so out of place today—or do they? To be sure, there's plenty of hopelessness to go around in modern music: from the stark, gloomy anorexia of countless dubstep 12" singles to the suicidal smoke signals of Xasthur and Apathia on the depressive black metal scene to the Hobbesian brutality of Prurient on the noise scene, there are many hopeless musical worlds which are, paradoxically, deeply pleasurable in their effect and entirely current in their aesthetic. But there's nothing cool about the hopelessness of The Smiths: their hopelessness runs hot with desire, spilling over with basic, grubby, guts-on-the-floor emotional need. In this sense, it is not really hopeless at all, but rather over-full of a hope that is utopian, impossible, a painful burden which is going "Nowhere Fast" but which won't go away. People take the piss out of The Smiths for the relentless and mawkish self-pity of Morrissey's most over-the-top lyrics ("I Know It's Over," anyone?). In the case of "Well I Wonder," it is an excruciating listen—but that's because of a skinless vulnerability that skirts egotistical bathos and goes somewhere more interesting instead. The speaker never turns away from acknowledging the wider world of other people—on the contrary, he obstinately presses for a singular place within that wider world. Walter Benjamin wrote that "The only way of knowing someone is to love them without hope"; it is this stance that "Well I Wonder" (beautifully) refuses to achieve. The speaker of the song can't quite abandon longings for which he knows there is no hope in this world, and the music cradles its listeners from imminent proof of that fact for as long as it can. Letting indifferent nature have her say, in its final minute we gradually hear a field recording of steadily falling rain. Eventually, the song ends. It never gives up.

NASHVILLE SKYLINE: Searching for the Heart of Country

Chet Flippo

Where is the heart and the soul and the core of country music these days? Is it in Taylor Swift's on-the-road-around-the-world-empire dressing room? Is it in Garth Brooks' come-back Las Vegas dressing room? Is it in Miranda Lambert's glitzy dressing room at the Bridgestone Arena the night of the CMA Awards show, where she has a record nine CMA nominations?

Or is it in Dale Watson's lonely tour bus on the road in a midnight parking lot of a dark, bare-bones honky-tonk out in the boonies? Or in the hazy back of Jamey Johnson's tour bus sitting somewhere in lower Alabama? Or in the ghost-riders-in-the-sky tour bus that Willie Nelson will forever preside over?

Or is it in Robert's Western Wear or in Tootsie's Orchid Lounge on Lower Broad in Nashville where the pickers will eternally play for the tip jar? Is it at the Station Inn, which increasingly resembles Fort Apache, as Gulch chic-ness surrounds and overruns it?

Is it in the ghost-laden Ryman Auditorium? Or at the Grand Ole Opry? Or maybe at Billy Bob's Texas? Or in Gruene Hall? Maybe on George Strait's ranch? Is it maybe hiding at the end of a dirt road in some small town?

Is it in mega-mogul-manager Irving Azoff's back pocket as he shuttles from venue to venue and from act to act and from new country acquisition to new country acquisition? Or is it in a small, intimate club where a flower like Caitlin Rose blooms? Or in a rowdy Texas honky-tonk where the sassy Sunny Sweeney shows off her sugar-britches? Is it inside Zac Brown's cap?

Is it in some country star's Tweets, for God's sake?

Maybe, to lift a line from the Gatlin Brothers' song "All the Gold in California," the heart of country is actually "in a bank in the middle of Beverly Hills in somebody else's name."

Just where the hell is it?

I don't really know. No one does. And no one has even really known at any given time. And what's scary is that, these days, no one I know who has any sense knows either. The heart used to be at the center of the major Nashville record labels. And at the major recording studios. No more, no more. They're long ago eroding.

Country music is a wildly erratic radar screen these days. Random, unexpected blips are popping up all over the place and with no consistent patterns. May as well study tornado paths. The music is all over the map. So are the artists. And so is the audience.

But, if you sit back and reflect and study the music's recent and even ancient history, there's really no reason for panic.

It is ultimately in the listeners' hands. It's the fans, the true believers, who will choose their music. Each person's country is in the heart.

But it's also in marketing departments' hands. The breakdown of the sales pattern for Taylor Swift's first-week sales of more than 1 million copies of *Speak Now* is very revealing about present-day music marketing strategy. *Billboard* breaks the sales down thusly: Target, 350,000 units; iTunes, 220,000 units; Walmart, about 190,000 units; Amazon and Costco, each at about 40,000; Best Buy at about 35,000; and Starbucks at about 28,000. Starbucks was one of several nontraditional retailers pushing the album. Radio Shack will be another to be added.

Hot Topic stores, which mainly skew toward rock, moved about 5,000 copies. It has also been sold in Justice clothing stores for girls and in Rite Aid.

A Scholastic promo event also generated preorders and sales through schools. iTunes and Amazon also had preorder campaigns.

Big Machine set the CD's list price at $18.98, flying in the face of conventional wisdom that albums should list at $10. But it cut deals to get the pricing it needed for the physical CD.

Digital also heavily discounted the album—the media delivery company digital priced the *Speak Now* download at $4, and then Amazon lowered its download to $3.99. Amazon's price for the physical CD was $8. Walmart.com set the CD album price at $7.78. J&R Music World priced it in-store and online at $6.99.

To her credit, Swift insisted that *Speak Now* also be released as a vinyl record album.

But these million-plus sales numbers come after the world had decided that CDs and long, multi-song albums were quaint artifacts of the past. With Taylor Swift, it seems that all things are possible. Her fans voted with their wallets and purses. Heart and soul of country, though? The listeners will decide that.

The Honeymooners

Franklin Bruno

If you're drawn to musicians who salvage their art from tragic romance, addiction, and other personal wreckage, you may as well turn
elsewhere now. The lives and joint career of Felice and Boudleaux
Bryant, Nashville's first full-time, non-performing songwriters, offer
few attractions for the rubbernecker. By all accounts, their forty-
two-year marital and creative partnership was nearly idyllic, as
Boudleaux acknowledged when asked to explain the optimism of
many of their songs: "I suppose it's because we've had such a very
wonderful relationship." One song credited to Felice alone, the guile-
less "We Could," was written as a birthday surprise for her husband:

> *If anyone could find the joy*
> *That true love brings a girl and boy*
> *We could*
> *We could, you and I.*

The Bryants were consummate song-pitchers as well as lovebirds:
"We Could" was soon widely recorded, charting for Little Jimmy
Dickens in 1954—then for pop singer Al Martino in 1964, and for
Charley Pride a decade after that.

Of the several thousand songs they wrote—between three and
seven, depending on who's counting—many are perennials, from
"Take Me As I Am (or Let Me Go)" and "I Can Hear Kentucky Calling

Me" to several of the twenty-seven recorded by The Everly Brothers, including "All I Have to Do Is Dream," "Love Hurts," and "Sleepless Nights." Heartache and midnight longing not being the sole property of the self-destructive or professionally miserable, some of their songs convey these emotions as well as anyone's. Low-spirited or high-, however, the Bryants' work endures for its craft and concision as well as its depth of feeling. Felice called their style "basic black with a string of pearls," a not-very-countrified description of its economy of means and offhand elegance. Though versatile pop writers, they found their niche in country, bluegrass, and early rock & roll, genres about which some listeners (and too many critics) still cherish the illusion that words and melodies burst fully formed from performers' troubled souls. While rarely arty or showy in a way that would break the spell, the Bryants' songs also broke musical ground, especially harmonically. "The people who were around Nashville recording loved those chords," Felice once said, "and Boudleaux was able to put in even more for The Everlys because they were really good guitar players."

Diadorious Boudleaux Bryant was born in 1920; his father was a Georgia lawyer and also played trombone and violin at local hoedowns. Violin soon became the younger Bryant's main instrument as well. After spending a season with the Atlanta Symphony when he was eighteen, Boudleaux hitched his fiddle to the new jazz-hillbilly hybrid known as Western swing, joining banjo-playing bandleader Hank Penny in 1939. Penny, an Alabama native whose freewheeling shuffles were also shaped by a long stint in New Orleans, later made his mark in Nashville, Las Vegas, and especially Hollywood, where he opened the legendary Palomino Club and earned television fame as Spade Cooley's comic foil; during Bryant's tenure with Penny's Radio Cowboys, the band's bread-and-butter lay in barnstorming tours through the South—and beyond.

On a Milwaukee hotel booking in 1945, the violinist met elevator operator Matilda Genevieve Scaduto, five years his junior. Felice, to use the pet name she soon adopted, would later claim to have recognized the traveling musician—except for the absence of facial hair—as the lover that had appeared to her in dreams since she was eight. Boudleaux obligingly grew a beard, though presumably not in time for their wedding less than a week later.

Trading the touring life with Penny for radio work and the occasional appearance as a singing duo, the couple settled in Moultrie, Georgia, where they began to combine Boudleaux's tunes with Felice's poetry, though the roles of composer and lyricist quickly blurred. With Felice seemingly less inclined to buck the "good old boy world out there" than Cindy Walker (country's other important early female songwriter), early copyrights bore only Boudleaux's name, but they were collaborators from the start; only once established would the appearance of just one partner's name on a publishing credit—such as Felice's "We Could," or Boudleaux's mariachi-styled instrumental "Mexico," a 1961 hit for Bob Moore—be even a rough indication of a given song's sole authorship. Later, their son Dane reported that his father called Felice "the idea person," and, in the late 1970s, Boudleaux agreed that she was the more driven partner: "I can go for six months and not write anything more than a note: I've gone down to the lake and I'm fishing. . . . She writes constantly and puts it on paper." Boudleaux, the trained musician, often applied the final polish, codifying melodies and chord changes in the deft notations that fill the ledgers the couple used to collect finished and unfinished songs.

Peppering any publisher whose address they could find with lead sheets, the team sold a few early songs (such as Ernie Lee's long-buried "1-2-3-4-5-foot-6") to artists on regional labels. Their break came in 1949 when a friend passed their "Country Boy," a swinging, sharply rhymed statement of rural identity ("Epsom salts and i'dine" / "My s'penders out of plough-lines") to publisher Fred Rose.

It's worth pausing to note that a career of the kind the Bryants hoped for, and ultimately had, would not have been possible without Rose or someone like him. Early publishers of rural and hillbilly music paid recording artists a flat fee that included the eternal rights to their songs, effectively "strip-mining" their current repertoires with little thought for what they might produce in the future. (The vivid image is historian Richard Peterson's.) Later entrepreneurs wisely shared royalties with performers, encouraging them to generate new, if not always "original," songs. Victor Records' Ralph Peer drew a nominal one-dollar salary from his employers, but became rich from his personal share of The Carter Family's and Jimmie Rodgers's copyrights. In 1942, Rose, a Tin Pan Alley veteran who had written for Sophie Tucker and Gene Autry, joined forces with Roy Acuff to distribute the Opry star's song folios. Refining Peer's model, Acuff-Rose became Nashville's first publishing giant, midwifing the crossover smash "Tennessee Waltz," providing advances to contract writers like Hank Williams, and matching singers who didn't write with writers who didn't sing.

Rose wired the Bryants money to pull their trailer into Nashville; if he knew that "Country Boy" was the handiwork of a former symphony violinist and his Wisconsin-born Italian-American bride, he didn't care. Authentic or not, the song was perfect for Little Jimmy Dickens, whose recording initiated a string of hits written or co-written by Boudleaux ("I'm Little But I'm Loud," "Out Behind the Barn") that fit Dickens's 4' 11" stature and "banty rooster" persona as comfortably as his kiddie-cut Nudie suits. (Another of their hits for Dickens, the rocking "[I Got] a Hole in My Pocket," was revived by Ricky Van Shelton in 2008.) Writing bespoke songs was fine practice for what the Bryants would achieve with The Everlys; just as importantly, Dickens's fondness for minor chords encouraged Boudleaux's harmonic flights.

In 1953, the Bryants scored their first No. 1 with Carl Smith's "Hey Joe" (predating by several years the blues-rock standard of the same name, popularized by Jimi Hendrix), an I'm-gonna-steal-your-girl number with long, syncopated lines, quilted with nearly senseless internal rhymes:

> *Come on let's be buddy-duddies*
> *Show me you're my palsy-walsy*
> *Introduce that pretty little chick to me.*

(Like it or not, here is the germ of "Achy Breaky Heart.") Its success led to a pop cover by Frankie Laine, a Sinatra rival with a penchant for quasi-folk material. Other crossovers followed: Laine's "Hawkeye," Tony Bennett's "Have a Good Time," and, in England, Alma Cogan's "Willie Can," an oddly poetic inversion of "Can She Bake a Cherry Pie, Billy Boy?" Throughout the mid-1950s, the Bryants—sometimes sharing credit with early supporter Chet Atkins—also scored country hits for Ernest Tubb and Red Foley, and several for Eddy Arnold, whose way with the word "world" inspired "How's the World Treating You" and "The Richest Man (in the World)."

Fred Rose never signed the Bryants to an exclusive contract, but after his death in 1954, his son, Wesley Rose, did exactly that, agreeing to a then-unheard-of "reversion clause" that provided for full ownership of the songs to return to their writers after ten years. In 1957, the publisher also brought them together with the artists who would make their songs mainstays of early rock & roll. Don and Phil Everly had recently split off from their family's singing act, with which they had honed their voices on Iowa and Tennessee radio. Since then, Columbia Records had taken a flyer on one flop single, and Don's original "Thou Shalt Not Steal" had charted for Kitty Wells. The duo, now twenty and eighteen, respectively, was treading water in Nashville until an audition for Wesley Rose, who in turn brought them to the attention of Cadence Records, a pop-oriented independent looking for a way into the country market. Cadence chief Archie Bleyer, formerly Arthur Godfrey's orchestral director, had passed on the brothers before, but an improved demo tape and Rose's enthusiasm made him reconsider.

The Everlys learned "Bye Bye Love" for their first Cadence session the day before they recorded it, probably from Boudleaux himself. The song, developed from a chorus idea of Boudleaux's on a car trip, had been kicking around for the better part of a year. Conceived as a duet ("[Boudleaux] was a harmony freak," according to Felice), it had been turned down by thirty acts, solo and otherwise; it was dropped from a Chet Atkins–produced Porter Wagoner session when the guitarist insisted on a chord alteration Boudleaux disliked. ("If I'd had a song that was a little doubtful, or had a small chord change that didn't matter, I'd have been very amenable.") The Everlys cut it to stay in the business and collect the sixty-four-dollar session fee. "I was probably more interested in doing my own material, but I didn't say that," Don admitted later. "It isn't the kinda thing you pipe up and say when you're twenty years old." None of their diffidence can be heard in the spirited performance The Everlys and an Atkins-led studio group laid down on March 4, 1957.

Everyone knows how this story ends: "Bye Bye Love" topped the country charts, outperforming Webb Pierce's hastily released cover, and, thanks to Bleyer's clout with disc jockeys and a hunger for sounds that had something of Elvis's verve without his sexual threat, rose to No. 2 on the pop charts. Within weeks, The Everlys went from playing tent shows to fielding calls from Ed Sullivan. It's impossible to say whether other artists could have landed a similarly scaled hit with this material: While "Bye Bye Love" is a professionally crafted song, with tight eight-bar sections and an exciting melodic lift on the third line of each verse ("That I'm so *free*"), it isn't an especially distinctive one. What makes The Everlys' version remarkable is The Everlys—not just their close mountain harmonies, but also the spring-loaded acoustic guitar introduction, imported into the arrangement from Don's unreleased "Give Me a Future."

Follow-up singles would be expressly tailored to The Everlys' strengths. "Wake Up, Little Susie," their first pop No. 1, reinforced their clean but lively teen image—especially after Felice toned down Boudleaux's original idea to make clear that the protagonists were out until 4 a.m. merely because they fell asleep. (Still, the implications of the "ooh-la las" got it banned in Boston and elsewhere.) This time, those tough acoustic figures were entwined with the title hook, and the song as a whole is formally ambitious by both country and rock & roll norms, with four distinct melodic sections, artfully placed triple rhymes ("hot" / "plot" / "our reputation is shot"), and a surprising dip into the boys' lower registers for the anxious realization "we gotta go home."

"Bird Dog" and "Problems" successfully mined the same vein, but not every conceit stuck. "Poor Jenny," in which a party-turned-melee ends with the narrator's girl in jail, stalled at No. 22 in spring 1959, The Everlys' worst chart performance up to that point. In their mid-thirties, with two sons of their own, the Bryants' youth-oriented songs were hardly drawn from life, but this is the one where their technical sophistication gives the game away. Its thirty-two-bar AABA form is as inventively filled out as any Gershwin standard, with multiple key changes and chordal turnarounds within each verse. (It says volumes about the "Nashville Sound" players on the session that they zip through these complexities as though running down a twelve-bar blues.) A delight to students of pure songwriting, "Poor Jenny" proved less so to its intended audience of actual high-school students, who may have sensed the distance in the lyrics' light satire on "JD" alarmism: "According to the story in the paper this morning / Jenny is leader of a teenage gang!"

At the same time, The Everlys excelled at realizing what Boudleaux called "vanilla love songs that had no age direction at all." Or hardly any: "All I Have to Do Is Dream," so unerringly commercial that Phil Everly believed Boudleaux's demo acetate could have charted, locates a generic romantic lyric ("lips of wine," the musty "arms" / "charms" rhyme) in teendom with a single colloquial turn ("only trouble is / *gee whizz!* / I'm dreaming my life away"). Its author chalked up this touch to "a lucky rhyme fall," but also knew what he had, refusing to rewrite the bridge for more adult artists. Ballads with no comparable lyric hook were tailored to The Everlys in other ways. For "Devoted to You," Phil Everly learned the harmony line note-for-note from Boudleaux; the singer later said, "I didn't know fifths from a hole in the ground," but the open sound of the combined vocal lines produces a madrigal-like effect distinct from the close, country-styled thirds of their rockers.

Though The Everlys recorded another dozen Bryant songs after their move to Warner Bros. in 1960, their biggest singles of the period were the originals "So Sad (to Watch Good Love Go Bad)" and "Cathy's Clown" (on which Don used the "Bye Bye Love" / "Susie" trick of placing the chorus first). This was fine with Wesley Rose, who was the brothers' personal manager, and their publisher, as well as the Bryants'. What *wasn't* fine was the act's increasing attraction to non–Acuff-Rose material. In the wake of a prolonged battle over releasing Don's arrangement of "Temptation," a 1933 Arthur Freed/Nacio Herb Brown semi-standard, The Everlys fired Rose as manager in early 1961. In retaliation, Rose denied them access to his stable of writers, including the Bryants and John D. Loudermilk ("Ebony Eyes"), for three crucial years. "I went to Wesley once with eight songs that I had written for The Everlys and he just refused to let me show them to Don and Phil. They wanted the songs but Acuff-Rose just wouldn't license them," Boudleaux later recalled.

A glance at The Everlys' recording chronology shows the strain. Much of 1961 and 1962 found the brothers struggling to adapt their style to such ill-chosen novelties as "Mention My Name in Sheboygan" and "When It's Nighttime in Italy, It's Wednesday Over Here." Matters improved, artistically if not always commercially, as The Everlys essayed Brill Building material ("Crying in the Rain") and blues and r&b warhorses ("Step It up and Go") as well as their own songs. Though both brothers were strong writers, touring commitments inevitably kept them from being as prolific or consistent as the husband-and-wife team enduring Rose's freeze-out back in Nashville. (On the personal side, you could add simmering sibling rivalry and Don's dependency on Dr. Max Jacobson's hypodermic cocktails.) Phil later admitted, "Leaving Wesley was no problem for us, but missing the Bryant songs was a tremendous problem. . . . It's like a Rolls-Royce compared to a Chevy. Now, you might have a great Chevy, but a Rolls-Royce is something else, and Boudleaux's songs will be mostly Rolls-Royce songs."

Even before the Rose affair, The Everlys' renditions of some enduring Bryant songs were not released as singles. Recorded at their first studio session for Warners, "Sleepless Nights" slipped out on the 1960 LP *It's Everly Time*, though the harmonically striking ballad is anything but filler. This is difficult to explain non-technically: suffice to say that each verse leaves its home key at the fifth measure ("and wondered *who*"), and veers even farther from what the ear anticipates on the very next phrase ("is kissing you"), before inching back to a familiar resolution. The bridge, flickering between major and minor, is just as artful. The air of instability these changes bring to the lyrics' elemental yearning ("Why did you go?") is an impressive trick, though it is hardly heard as one in The Everlys' limpid delivery. Don Everly taught the song to Gram Parsons in 1969, and Parsons's posthumously released duet with Emmylou Harris brought the song wider attention. Since then, "Sleepless Nights" has coursed through the punk-country underground (The Mekons' bleak 1987 reading) and back into the pop-country mainstream, most recently in a 2008 version by Patty Loveless and Vince Gill.

The other Everlys/Bryant hit-that-wasn't was "Love Hurts." Credited to Boudleaux alone (though one can never be sure), the song is a master class in pop structure, with the stoic regularity of its verses' two-and-five-note motifs giving way to a soaring, insistently rhymed bridge:

> *Some fools dream of happiness*
> *blissfulness*
> *togetherness*
> *Some fools fool themselves, I guess.*

Though later a highlight of The Everlys' 1984 reunion concert, their first recording was again relegated to a 1960 album release. Perfectly suited for Roy Orbison's brand of fatalism, his 1961 cover brushed the charts as the flip side of "Running Scared." (Don Everly later charged that Wesley Rose fed the song to Orbison to undercut the brothers' own version.) It's mildly shocking to learn that "Love Hurts" reached the U.S. Top 10 only in a 1975 version by Scottish hard-rock journeymen Nazareth, in which the distance between Dan McCafferty's piercing, post-Plant wail and the sludgy undertow of chords beneath the vocal hook reveals the song for what it may have been all along: rock's first great power ballad. (Unlike later recordings by Jim Capaldi and Cher, Nazareth alters "love is like a stove / burns you when it's hot" to "love is like a *flame*," losing the phonetic link between "love" and "stove," and introducing a solecism—when, exactly, is fire *not* hot?)

Released after fence-mending with Rose, The Everlys' 1965 album *Gone, Gone, Gone* included five Bryant cuts, joining top-flight pop-rockers ("Radio and TV" and the previously released "Donna, Donna") and the tropical contrivance "Lonely Island," all recorded and shelved before the split, with two newer compositions. But the British Invasion had altered the landscape, and neither these songs nor the singles "You're the One I Love" and "Don't Forget to Cry" checked the act's decline in the U.S. The interruption did little long-term damage to the Bryants, who even during The Everlys' peak years had continued to write for artists like Jim Reeves ("Blue Boy") and Buddy Holly ("Raining in My Heart," his final chart appearance). In 1967, the Bryants founded their own publishing company, House of Bryant, and refocused on the country market. Dissatisfied with their own demo recordings ("we just don't want to send them out, they're so lousy"), their favored practice in later years was to invite artists for an evening at their home in the Smokies, where they would play and sing unrecorded material, some of it written much earlier, from their accumulated ledgers.

While their '70s and '80s successes, such as Roy Clark's "Come Live With Me" (which also went pop for Ray Charles) and Eddy Arnold's "(I Need You) All the Time," were often for legacy artists to whom the country audience and industry were often kinder than their pop and rock equivalents, the Bryants still took a hand in breaking new acts. Long before her exclusive concentration on devotional songs, Christy Lane recorded their "Sweet Deceiver" and "Tryin' to Forget About You" before scoring a major hit in 1978 with the ragtime oddity "Penny Arcade." Boudleaux astutely noted, "It's a so-called country song now, but there was a time when that type of song would not have been accepted. . . . It would have been a pop novelty."

Boudleaux Bryant passed away in 1987; Felice's name occasionally surfaced on newly published songs until her death in 2003. By any measure, the signature song of their later years is "Rocky Top," conceived and completed in fifteen minutes (by the authors' account) during a working vacation in 1967. As an official state song of Tennessee and the (technically) unofficial fight song of the U of T football team and marching band, it's become standard for name country artists (Keith Urban, Brad Paisley) touring the Knoxville region to lead the crowd in at least one verse and chorus. Though Lynn Anderson's 1970 cover charted higher, The Osborne Brothers' 1968 recording is definitive. Active since the '50s, The Osbornes irked bluegrass purists by backing Sonny's banjo and Bobby's mandolin with drums and electric bass—and by soliciting material from commercial-country tunesmiths. Like all the Bryants' best work, the tune's unorthodox moments sound inevitable: The bold modulation at "home sweet home" cries out for The Osbornes' parented parallel harmonies.

The lyrics are equally suited to an act that combined tradition with innovation. The first verse evokes a time before rural electrification ("ain't no telephone bills") before switching to lost love. The second celebrates Prohibition-era lawlessness: corn-liquor bootleg-ging and the disappearance of "strangers . . . looking for a moonshine still," most likely federal revenuers. These memories are framed from the point of view of one who no longer enjoys the simple mountain life, as the very first line makes clear: "Wish that I was back on Rocky Top." (There is also some question as to just which mountain the Bryants had in mind. Though the middle peak of the Thunderheads, not far from Gatlinburg, is known by that name, it is a barren place, "too rocky by far" to support settlement.)

When The Osbornes rerecorded the song for the all-Bryant double-LP *From Rocky Top to Muddy Bottom*, its theme was extended in "Georgia Mules and Country Boys," which casts an eye over the van-ishing ways described in the Bryants' "Country Boy" nearly thirty years earlier: "Who have you seen lately churning butter? Who do you even know that might know how?" Mixing recent material with bluegrass reworkings of "Hey Joe" and "Love Hurts," the 1977 release meditates on the cultural and musical changes the Bryants saw—and in some cases, helped to popularize—over the course of their career. Curiously, The Osbornes' album is a more compellingly per-sonal retrospective than *A Touch of Bryant*, a 1979 victory-lap album of pleasant duets sung by the now-venerable songwriters them-selves—perhaps a mark of how accustomed they had become to hear-ing their sentiments realized by other voices.

If the melancholy side of "Rocky Top" is not evident on an October afternoon at Knoxville's Neyland Stadium, it may be because the sing-alongs don't make it to the final half-verse:

> *I've had years of cramped up city life*
> *Trapped like a duck in a pen*
> *All I know is, it's a pity life*
> *Can't be simple again.*

The song offers no comforting suggestion that life can or will be simple again, but what's most revealing is the way that the finely wrought mid-line rhyme between "city life" and "pity life" conveys the narrator's nostalgia and his urbanity in equal measure. The syntactic shift between the two occurrences of "life" is woven into the phrasing of the melody so seamlessly that most listeners may never register the subtlety. The moment also suggests that the writers were amusing themselves (and each other) by indulging in a touch of Sondheim-grade sophistication not normally associated with regionalist anthems. But after twenty years in the field they helped create, and with twenty more to go, the Bryants could wear Felice's "string of pearls" with style, and pride.

The Long War

Sasha Frere-Jones

It sounds implausible now, but there was a time when soft jazz was almost radical. This brief moment should be credited largely to the English. In the early eighties, groups like Everything but the Girl and the Style Council developed a hybrid kind of pop that drew from the more plangent side of soul and jazz—think of an area triangulated by the Delfonics, Dave Brubeck, and Chet Baker. Their style was a marked departure from the dominant sounds of the charts: Madonna's blocky drum machines and the noisy guitar bands of the third or fourth wave after punk. In this overheated context, playing mellifluous, unthreatening versions of soul and jazz could surprise, maybe even shock. It was several years before the release of David Lynch's *Blue Velvet,* and years further from cabaret retro becoming a calcified style. One act in particular understood the potential of going quiet, and eventually made its lead singer the most successful female solo artist in British history, with more than fifty million albums sold.

Sade was born Helen Folasade Adu in Nigeria, to a Nigerian academic and an English nurse, in 1959. When she was four, her parents split and she moved to England with her mother, spending most of her childhood in the seaside resort of Clacton-on-Sea. After college, at St. Martins School of Art, in London, Adu joined a band called Pride, which played Latin soul and various iterations of a genre that would later be called acid jazz, though it was anything but acerbic. Several musicians in Pride became her backing band, and together they went by the name she used for herself—Sade, pronounced "sha-DAY," to the consternation of radio DJs across the world. Signed to Epic Records on the strength of the appropriately titled song "Smooth Operator," Sade and her band became the benchmark for smoothness. With her group—the saxophonist Stuart Matthewman, the keyboardist Andrew Hale, and the bassist Paul Denman—Sade has created one of the most profitable catalogues in pop, while appearing in public so rarely that her friends have nicknamed her Howie, after Howard Hughes.

Exactly how much do people want the Sade sound? The new Sade album, *Soldier of Love*, separated from the group's last studio release by ten years (in pop years, many generations), spent three weeks at No. 1 on the *Billboard* chart. In this commercially unstable moment, when a popular album is lucky to spend one week at the top, that's no minor feat, especially for a fifty-one-year-old woman who is entirely absent from the gossip centrifuge. What is the formula for her success?

Discussing the looks of a female pop star always feels a bit reactionary; even the most evenhanded, politically committed critic probably doesn't do it as often for male pop stars. Sade's beauty, though, is not simply a matter for the gawkers and the sales department; there are very few faces like hers. She has pellucid, pale-cocoa skin, a large, gently curved forehead, and wide-set eyes, which, in 1983, made her look as close to a global citizen as anyone we'd seen. With nothing to go on but her light English accent, it was difficult to tell where she was from, making her a candidate to represent populations who usually didn't get their own global pop stars. Sade, the band, could have sneaked a Situationist manifesto into its material while everyone sat still, hypnotized by the mystery of Sade, the person.

Sade's delightfully glittery début album, *Diamond Life*, was a bit like the perfect night of dress-up, everyone playing at jazz and secret-agent cool, an image that the videos did their best to establish over and over. That devilish smooth operator was playing with girls' hearts, moving "in space with minimum waste and maximum joy." A similar rake was also to be found over on the boat in Duran Duran's "Rio" video. So what made Sade different? For starters, the pretty woman up front didn't seem to give a damn about this Lothario, and was obviously twice the catch he was. We could already hear the graphite core in Sade's voice, a grainy contralto full of air that betrays a slight ache but no agony, and values even imperfect dignity over a show of pain. (It is this quality, deeply English, that drives soul purists crazy when trying to categorize Sade.) Though her style wasn't going to knock over anyone's gimlet, it wasn't necessarily dedicated to soothing, happy stories. The album closed with a cover of a minor soul classic, Timmy Thomas's "Why Can't We Live Together?," a direct plea for racial harmony that hinted at a political sensibility, easier to hear in later songs about immigrant workers and slaves. And, as easy as the band's sound has always been, Sade's songs have tended toward exploring the heavier lifting inside love: commitment, consistency, friendship.

The success of Sade and her anodyne band highlights one of the maddening aspects of popular music: no matter what musicians intend, music can often be a background element in a moment, in a way that books and movies can't. Sculpture and painting, by virtue of never turning off, can pierce the familiarity of their surroundings. Albums end, and even when they were on they might simply have been part of the mood, whatever that was.

You can hear the downside of all this on Sade's 2002 live album, *Lovers Live*, where the background singers and horns keep things under control. Nothing, not even the chance to solo in front of thousands of screaming fans, can sway the band from its flatlining hum of reason and gentility. Never has a talented group of musicians been in such need of a few bursts of noise or gaps of painful silence.

But the band is fantastic at setting up a bed of coals for its singer, and, when the song matches Sade's voice, there is an intensity to the work that sears through all the good manners. My favorite of Sade's six albums, *Lovers Rock* (2000), was the first to largely ditch the jazz trappings and use more acoustic guitars. There are also flecks of the reggae implied by the title ("lovers rock" is a reggae subgenre that sounds exactly like what the name implies), in an emotionally resonant set of songs attached to murmuring beats.

The lead single on *Lovers Rock*, "By Your Side," is a basic pledge of loyalty that, here, sounds like a blood pact. There's nothing necessarily dark about it, and in the wrong hands it could turn into "Don't Worry, Be Happy." The band does its work, though, gesture by gesture, note by note. The song begins in the middle of doubt: "You think I'd leave your side, baby? / You know me better than that. / Think I'd leave you down when you're down on your knees? / I wouldn't do that." Sade sings as if there are plenty of reasons to leave, and as if this conversation has happened before, maybe many times. She restrains her voice, as if she's not calming anyone as much as herself. When she drops down into the dependable lower part of her register—now slightly more ragged than in 1983—to reassure her lover, it blocks the easygoing gait of the band and holds you in place: "Oh when you're cold, I'll be there / Hold you tight to me." These words are the basic Legos of pop songs, nothing but overly familiar shapes until they're built into something. Sade's fans seem to trust that she doesn't build something until something's happened to make it necessary. She may not provide an explosion of raw expression, but she also won't saddle you with any hammy set pieces. Sincerity is one of pop's weirdest phantoms—can we ever really be sure we've detected it?— and yet it is central to Sade's popularity. Listeners get the impression that her care and her gentle pacing aren't about being your audio bubble bath; they're about making good on a promise to be as clear as possible and not futz around.

This mission doesn't always succeed. Wallpaper is as wallpaper does, and if I could wipe ninety-five per cent of the saxophone work off Sade albums I would. For the moment, at least, the band seems to agree. *Soldier of Love* is so bereft of saxophone and leans so heavily on acoustic guitar that it's almost an ambient version of country music, which suits the singer's strengths just fine. The title track is Sade's best single in ages, a combination of gently martial snare tattoo, tense strings, and dirtier drum sounds than the band usually allows. (Skip the video, which makes it seem as if Sade and the director, Sophie Muller, have not had access to a television since 1991.) This is our Sade, more serious than we expect her to be and unconcerned if we find her a little solemn. Hell, the first line of the song is "I've lost the use of my heart, but I'm still alive." Welcome back! *Soldier of Love* is slightly too dour for its own good, though the band is getting better at framing Sade's voice, which is hard to tire of. One nice thing about *Lovers Rock* was the lilt that kept our heroine's bleaker side moving. Here, her sincerity is perhaps too easy to detect. But I still trust that voice, and I want to see that face just once. It won't be easy. She hasn't appeared live since 2001, and no future tour dates have been announced.

The "Thriller" Diaries

Nancy Griffin

October 13, 1983; 8 p.m.
Downtown Los Angeles.

On a chilly autumn night, gaffers rig motion-picture lights around the entrance to the Palace Theatre, which bears the title "Thriller" on its marquee. A cascade of shrieks—"Michael! Michael!"—drifts on the breeze from a few blocks away, where hundreds of fans strain against police barricades for a glimpse of their idol. Although everyone involved in the production has been sworn to secrecy, word of tonight's shoot has leaked and been broadcast on local radio. Security guards patrol the set.

Michael Jackson, a shy pixie in a red leather jacket and jeans, stands in shadow in the theater's entryway, talking with actress Ola Ray and director John Landis. The camera crew is making final preparations for a crane shot that will pan down from the marquee as Jackson and Ray, playing a couple on a date, emerge from the theater. Judging from the saucy looks she is sending his way, Ray is clearly besotted by her leading man, who responds by casually throwing an arm around her shoulders.

I am on set covering the shoot for Life *magazine. Landis says that he needs a "ticket girl" in the background and orders me to sit in the booth—a prime spot from which to watch the performances.*

Just before calling "Action," Landis fortifies his actors with boisterous encouragement.

"How are you going to be in this shot?" he shouts.

"Wonderful," Jackson chirps, barely audibly.

Seconds later Jackson steps into his nimbus of light, and it is as if he flips on an internal switch: he smiles, he glows, he mesmerizes. Landis executes the long crane shot, then moves in for close-ups and dialogue. "It's only a movie," Jackson reassures his date. "You were scared, weren't you?"

Landis calls for another take and coaxes: "Make it sexy this time."

"How?" asks Jackson.

"You know, as if you want to fuck her."

The star flinches and licks his lips uncomfortably, then gazes earnestly into Ray's eyes. Landis gets the shot he wants and calls for the next setup, satisfied. He whispers to me, "I bet it will be sexy."

The world certainly thought so, and apparently still does. The campy horror-fest with dancing zombies that is "Michael Jackson's Thriller," originally conceived as a 14-minute short film, is the most popular and influential music video of all time. In January of this year it was designated a national treasure by the Library of Congress, the first music video to be inducted into the National Film Registry.

Unlike forgotten favorites from MTV's heyday (Duran Duran's "Hungry Like the Wolf," anyone?), "Thriller" is thriving on YouTube, where one can view, along with the original, scores of "Thriller" dance tutorials and re-enactments by Bollywood actors and Bar Mitzvah celebrants. The dance has become an annual tribal ritual in major cities around the world, with initiates in ghoul makeup aping Michael's moves en masse; the current record for largest dance of the undead is 12,937, held by Mexico City. A YouTube 41-million-hit sensation features more than 1,500 inmates in a Philippines prison yard executing the funky footwork as part of a rehab program designed to "turn dregs into human beings"; the prison, in the city of Cebu, has become a T-shirt-selling tourist attraction.

None of this was imaginable back at the Palace Theatre 27 years ago. Jackson then was a naïve, preternaturally gifted 25-year-old "who wanted to be turned into a monster, just for fun," as Landis recently told me—and had the money to make it happen. "Thriller" marked the most incandescent moment in Jackson's life, his apex creatively as well as commercially. He would spend the rest of his career trying to surpass it. "In the *Off the Wall/Thriller* era, Michael was in a constant state of becoming," says Glen Brunman, then Jackson's publicist at his record company Epic. "It was all about the music, until it also became about the sales and the awards, and something changed forever."

It was the "Thriller" video that pushed Jackson over the top, consolidating his position as the King of Pop, a royal title he encouraged and Elizabeth Taylor helped popularize. "Thriller" was the seventh and last single and third video (after "Billie Jean" and "Beat It") to be released from the album of the same name, which had already been on the charts for almost a year since its release, in November 1982. The video's frenzied reception, whipped up by round-the-clock showings on MTV, would more than double album sales, driving *Thriller* into the record books as the No. 1 LP of all time, a distinction it maintains today. But, for anyone paying close attention during the making of the "Thriller" video—and Jackson's collaborators were—the outlines of subsequent tragedies were already painfully visible.

Jackson would dominate pop culture for the remainder of the decade, owning the '80s as Elvis had owned the '50s and the Beatles the '60s. To rule the entertainment universe had been his dream since he belted out "I Want You Back" on *The Ed Sullivan Show* in 1969 as the precocious lead singer of the Jackson 5. Under the strict, physically and psychologically abusive tutelage of his father, Joseph, he had sacrificed his childhood to make money for the family and Motown Records. He would later describe his boyhood as a blur of tour buses and tutors, and rehearsals that his father supervised with a belt in his hand, ready to whip any son who stepped out of line. Joe reserved especially harsh treatment for his most gifted and defiant son; although extremely sensitive by nature, Michael was also quietly stubborn and frequently clashed with his father. The brief moments Michael spent onstage were when he felt happiest. "I remember singing at the top of my voice and dancing with real joy and working too hard for a child," he recalled in his autobiography, *Moonwalk*.

His mother, Katherine, whom he adored, called him "the special one." A musical savant, young Michael hungrily devoured show-business knowledge and studied favorite entertainers from Fred Astaire to James Brown to the Beatles. Ron Weisner, hired by Joe Jackson in '76 to co-manage the Jacksons, recalls that on tour Michael— exhibiting the insomnia that plagued him throughout his life (and would be a factor in the drug overdose that killed him)—stayed up late after each show. "We'd be on the bus and we had a little TV and VHS player. He would watch tapes of James Brown and Jackie Wilson over and over until his brothers were screaming and cursing him and throwing things at the TV. The next day they would hide the tape, and Michael would be crying. He would never, never, never stop."

As he grew older he pulled away from his family to venture into solo projects, notably the 1979 funk-disco smash *Off the Wall*, which he layered with lush grooves and falsetto vocals with the help of producing partner Quincy Jones. The pair teamed up again three years later for *Thriller*. This time Jackson's aim was nothing less than a Beatles-like domination of the charts that would lay waste to the divisions between rock, soul, and pop. The strategy was to compile a succession of hit singles that would offer something for everyone: the first release was the ballad "The Girl Is Mine," a duet with Paul McCartney. Second up was the funky anthem "Billie Jean." Third was the rocker "Beat It," which featured a blistering Eddie Van Halen guitar solo. Executives at Epic pushed the LP tirelessly, pressuring a range of radio formats to play it and marketing it as a mainstream disc.

Most serendipitously, Jackson was the ideal video star. Not only did he radiate an epicene glamour that was at once innocent and intensely erotic, but he was also conceptually inventive, a great dancer, and a sartorial trendsetter. He judged the quality of what the fledgling rock network MTV was airing to be poor, and felt he could do better. He hired the best directors and choreographers and applied everything he had soaked up from watching Gene Kelly and Astaire movies. In a black jacket and pink shirt he slid and spun his way down a surreal city street in the "Billie Jean" video—an electrifying, transformative performance. Although the song's thumping bass line and synthesizers excluded it from MTV's definition of a rock song, the network knew a hit when it saw one and put the clip into heavy rotation. The "Beat It" video was grittier, an homage to *West Side Story*, with Jackson strutting and spinning in a red-orange leather jacket in the midst of 20 dancers and recruited gang members.

More than any other artist, Jackson ushered in the heyday of the music video, demonstrating its promotional power, raising the bar creatively, and paving the way for greater acceptance of black musicians on MTV. But the *Thriller* campaign, concocted by the album's brain trust—Jackson; his lawyer and closest adviser, John Branca; CBS Records chief Walter Yetnikoff; and Epic head of promotion Frank DiLeo—did not include plans for a third video, and certainly not a video of the title track, which wasn't even going to be released as a single. "Who wants a single about monsters?" says Yetnikoff, summing up how the group felt at the time about the song's potential.

But in June of 1983 the album, after four months as No. 1 on the *Billboard* 200 chart, was bumped from the top slot by the *Flashdance* soundtrack. It briefly regained the top position in July, then was toppled again, this time by *Synchronicity*, by the Police. The three remaining planned singles—"Wanna Be Startin' Somethin'," just released in May, "Human Nature," scheduled for July, and "P.Y.T." for

September—were not expected to drive album sales as "Billie Jean" and "Beat It" had, nor were they suitable for videos.

Jackson was upset. Obsessive about tracking his sales figures, he compared them constantly with those of his competitors in the top echelon, including Prince and Madonna. "He enjoyed being on top," says Larry Stessel, Epic's West Coast marketing executive, who worked closely with the star. "He reveled in it. He didn't like it when it ended." With his own album making history, Jackson yearned to shatter records held by the Fab Four. "It was all about the Beatles," says Stessel. "He knew in his heart of hearts that he would never be bigger than the Beatles, but he had such tremendous respect for them, and he certainly wanted to come as close as he could."

In the summer of '83, Yetnikoff and Stessel answered calls at all hours of the night from Jackson. "Walter, the record isn't No. 1 anymore," Yetnikoff remembers Jackson saying. "What are we going to do about it?" "We're going to go to sleep and deal with it tomorrow," Yetnikoff told him. It was DiLeo who first mentioned the idea of making a third video, and pressed Jackson to consider the album's title track. "It's simple—all you've got to do is dance, sing, and make it scary," DiLeo recalls telling Jackson.

In some ways "Thriller," written by Rod Temperton, is the album's sore thumb, a semi-novelty song with sound effects of creaking doors and eerie footsteps and bwah-ha-ha narration by Vincent Price. Horror was a genre with which Jackson had an ambivalent relationship. As a child, he had known episodes of real-life terror. Michael's biographer J. Randy Taraborrelli recounted that Joe Jackson had once put on a fright mask and crawled into Michael's bedroom through a window at night, screaming; Joe Jackson said his purpose was to teach his son to keep the window closed when he slept. For years afterward Michael suffered nightmares about being kidnapped from his room, and said that whenever he saw his father he felt nauseated.

Jackson had reason to be fascinated by scary disguises and things that go bump in the night, but he didn't want them to seem too real.

His tastes generally ran to benign Disney-esque fantasies where people were nice and children were safe. "I never was a horror fan," he said. "I was too scared." He would make sure that the tone of his "Thriller" film was creepy-comical, not genuinely terrifying.

In early August, John Landis, whose most successful films had been *National Lampoon's Animal House* and *Trading Places*, picked up the phone and heard Jackson's wee voice on the line. The star told Landis how much he had enjoyed the director's horror spoof *An American Werewolf in London*. Would he be willing to direct Jackson in a music video with a spooky story line that had him transform into a werewolf? At the time, making music videos was not something feature directors did. But Landis was intrigued enough by Jackson's entreaty to take a meeting.

On the afternoon of August 20, Landis and his producing partner, George Folsey Jr., drove through the gates of Hayvenhurst, the high-walled mock-Tudor estate in Encino where the family had moved when Jackson was 13, and where he still lived with his parents and sisters LaToya and Janet. In 1981, Jackson had purchased the house from his parents and rebuilt it, installing such diversions as an exotic animal farm stocked with llamas, a Snow White and the Seven Dwarfs diorama, and a 32-seat screening room with a popcorn machine. In the corner of his second-story bedroom suite stood his "friends," five lifesize, fully dressed female mannequins.

At the time, Jackson was a practicing Jehovah's Witness who obeyed his religion's mandate to spread the faith by knocking on doors in his neighborhood, wearing a crude disguise of mustache and glasses. He attended services at the local Kingdom Hall and abstained from drinking, swearing, sex before marriage, and, supposedly, R-rated movies. The gregarious Landis teased Jackson about having watched the R-rated *An American Werewolf in London*. "I said, 'Michael, what about the sex?' He said, 'I closed my eyes.'"

Landis told Jackson that he would not direct "Thriller" as a music video, proposing instead that they collaborate on a short narrative film that could be released in theaters—reviving that endangered species, the short subject—before it went to video. Landis would write a story line, inspired by the song, about a cute young guy on a date who turns into a monster. The short would be shot on 35-mm. film with feature-film production values, including great locations and an impressive dance number. Landis would call in a favor from Rick Baker, the Oscar-winning makeup wizard who had created the title creature for *An American Werewolf in London*, and get him to design Jackson's transformation makeup. Jackson was enthusiastic about Landis's vision and immediately said, "Let's do it."

Although CBS/Epic had ponied up $250,000 for the "Billie Jean" video, Yetnikoff had refused to underwrite "Beat It," so Jackson had paid $150,000 out of his own pocket. When Folsey and Landis worked up the budget for "Thriller," they put it at an estimated $900,000. Landis and Jackson placed a call to "Uncle Walter," as Jackson referred to him, to explain the "Thriller" concept and what it would cost. Landis says that Yetnikoff screamed so loudly that the director had to hold the phone away from his ear. "I've only heard three or four people swear like that in my life," he says. When Landis hung up the phone, Jackson said calmly, "It's O.K. I'll pay for it." Eventually Yetnikoff agreed that the record company would contribute $100,000 to pay for the video, but that left a long way to go and Jackson's collaborators didn't want the star to be on the hook.

It was Folsey and John Branca, Jackson's lawyer, who put their heads together to solve the budget shortfall. Although cable TV was a new phenomenon and the home-video market had yet to explode, they decided to film behind the scenes on 16-mm. for a nearly 45-minute documentary, *Making Michael Jackson's Thriller*, which, bundled with the "Thriller" video, could be sold to cable. MTV agreed to pay $250,000 and Showtime $300,000 for the one-hour package; Jackson would cover some upfront production costs and be reimbursed. Then Vestron came in and offered to distribute *Making*

Michael Jackson's Thriller as a $29.95 "sell-through" video on VHS and Betamax, a pioneering deal of its kind. (Most videos were then sold for far higher prices to rental stores, rather than directly to consumers.) "You have to remember, back in those days none of us realized quite what home video was going to become," says Folsey. "The studios treated it pretty much the way they treated television in the '50s and '60s, with total disdain. They had no idea that the home-video business was going to save Hollywood—it never crossed their minds."

With the financing in place and only six weeks before the first shooting day, October 11, the team moved swiftly into an accelerated pre-production. Landis hired his director of photography from *Trading Places*, Robert Paynter, and drafted his own wife, Deborah Nadoolman Landis, best known for putting Harrison Ford in a fedora and leather jacket for *Raiders of the Lost Ark*, as costume designer. "Beat It" choreographer Michael Peters was brought in and began auditioning dancers and developing streethip dance phrases for the zombie choreography. Folsey crewed up, securing locations and equipment.

Jackson was driven by the pop star's occupational affliction: the desire to be a movie star. He had met and befriended Steven Spielberg when he narrated the soundtrack album and audiobook for *E.T.: The Extra-Terrestrial*. (Jackson cried when recording the part where E.T. dies.) He and Spielberg were in discussions about Jackson's playing the lead in a filmed musical version of J. M. Barrie's *Peter Pan*.

But Landis had precisely the opposite of "I won't grow up" in mind: he wanted Jackson to satisfy his young female fans by showing some virility. He wrote a script that loosely spoofed *I Was a Teenage Werewolf*. Michael would go on a date with a sexy girl in two separate time periods, the '50s and '80s. There would be dialogue interspersed with music. As the '50s guy, Michael would ask his girl to go steady, tell her, "I'm not like other guys," then transform into a werewolf and terrorize her. As the '80s guy, he would woo her with seductive dance moves before turning into a ghoul. "The big thing was to give him a girl," says Landis, pointing out that Jackson hadn't interacted with females in the videos for "Billie Jean" or "Beat It." "That was the big breakthrough."

After Jennifer Beals of *Flashdance* turned down an offer to co-star, Landis cast an unknown 23-year-old former *Playboy* Playmate named Ola Ray. "I auditioned a lot of girls and this girl Ola Ray—first of all, she was crazy for Michael," Landis says. "She had such a great smile. I didn't know she was a Playmate." Jackson signed off on Ray, then reconsidered the seemliness of cavorting with an ex-Playmate and came close to derailing the casting. According to Landis, "I said, 'Michael, she's a Playmate, but so what? She's not a Playmate in this.' He went, 'O.K., whatever you want.' I have to tell you, I got along great with Michael."

It was Deborah Landis's job to play up Jackson's masculinity while dressing him in hip, casual clothes that were comfortable for dancing. Since the video would be shot at night in a mostly somber palette, she says, "I felt that red would really pop in front of the ghouls." She chose the same color for both his jacket and jeans to emphasize a vertical line, making his five-foot-seven-inch, 100-pound frame appear taller. "The socks and the shoes were his own," she says. "He took that directly from Fred Astaire, who always wore soft leather loafers to dance in, and socks. And Michael was elegant. I worked with David Bowie, who was also that same body frame, again very, very slim. Fred Astaire was a 36 regular; Michael was a 36 regular. David and Michael and Fred Astaire—you could literally put them in anything, and they would carry themselves with a distinction and with confidence and with sexuality."

October 13, 1983; 10:30 p.m.
Downtown Los Angeles.
On a desolate city street, Jackson lipsynchs to a playback of "Thriller" as he dances and skitters playfully around Ray. Landis has barely re-

hearsed the scene because he is hoping for some spontaneous sexual energy between his actors and has asked Jackson to improvise. Ray, who looks deliriously smitten, is supposed to keep the beat with each footstep. Landis puts his hand over his eyes and quietly shakes his head as she repeatedly messes up the tempo, necessitating many takes. Jackson remains charmingly frisky in every one, hugging her as he sings, "Now is the time for you and I to cuddle close together . . . "

Ray has made it clear to Jackson and everyone else that she wants the cuddling to continue after the "Cut!" "Michael is very special, not like any other guy I've met," she says, kicking off her high heels and settling into her set chair after the scene wraps. "Since we've been working together we've been getting closer. He was a very shy person, but he's opened up. I think he's lived a sheltered life. He knows a lot of entertainers, but he needs friends that he can go out and relax and enjoy himself with, instead of talking to his mannequins in his room."

The congenial atmosphere on "Thriller" seemed to have a salutary effect on Jackson. He delighted the crew by hanging out on the set between shots, and although he didn't say much, he responded graciously to anyone who approached. Landis frequently got him giggling with horseplay, once lifting him up by the ankles and shaking him upside down while Jackson shrieked, "Put me down, you punk!"

He would also enjoy a secret interlude with Ola Ray. The actress had her makeup done each day at a studio where Jane Fonda happened to be shooting a workout video. Ray engaged in girl talk with Fonda, a friend of Jackson's, and solicited tips on how to pique Jackson's romantic interest. As Ray remembers, "Miss Fonda said, 'Be yourself—just be sweet and talk to him about things he might be interested in or like to do. He's a Jehovah's Witness, so you should talk to him about religion. Maybe he will want you to go to church with him one day.'"

Arriving at the set, Ray would sit outside her trailer and finish touching up her makeup. "Every day Michael came and sat and watched me," she says. "He was in awe of me. He was always in my face trying to learn to do things with makeup like I did." When he asked her to come give pointers to his own makeup person, saying, "I have a shine on my nose that I can't get off," she agreed. "So I'm seriously talking to his makeup artist, trying to explain what to do, and she looked at me and said, 'Girl, don't you know that no matter how much powder I put on his nose it's going to shine? Do you know how many nose jobs he's had?' Then Michael started laughing, because I didn't know he had had nose jobs! I guess the whole world knew."

The flirtation progressed. "I had some intimate moments with him in his trailer," says Ray. How intimate? "Let me see how I can say this without, you know, being too . . . " She pauses. "I won't say that I have seen him in his birthday suit but close enough," she says, laughing. Because he was shy, she tried not to scare him by coming on too strong. "What we had was such like a little kindergarten thing going on. I thought it was important for him to be around someone who would make him feel comfortable, and that was my main objective." Did they make out? "Kissing and puppy-love makeout sessions," she confirms, "and a little more than that." That is all she cares to divulge. "I've already told you more than I've ever told anyone!"

Ray watched Jackson switch seamlessly from silly to sober for business meetings. When Jacqueline Onassis's white limousine pulled up, he greeted the Doubleday Books editor, who had flown out from New York to discuss publishing Jackson's memoir (which eventually became *Moonwalk*), with courtly professionalism. Landis says that he barged unknowingly into Jackson's trailer, and the star coolly said, "John, have you met Mrs. Onassis?"

An eclectic assortment of luminaries appeared on the set to see Jackson. Fred Astaire and Rock Hudson both dropped by. Quincy Jones, watching the filming of the zombie dance, mused about Jackson's ability to maintain his child-like quality: "It takes a lot of maturity to control all that innocence." Perhaps the most unlikely visitor to appear was Marlon Brando, who, Landis learned, was slipping acting advice to Jackson. One day when Landis admonished him for not knowing his lines, Jackson said, "Marlon told me to always go for the truth, not the words." When MTV executive Les Garland arrived for a scheduled visit, he waited in the living room of Jackson's trailer, chatting with a couple of female assistants. Then "a pair of socks came bouncing out from the bedroom and landed by me," says Garland. "One of the ladies said, 'That means Michael is up and ready to see you now.' I said, 'Oh, that's unique.'"

If his spirit on the set seemed carefree, behind the scenes Jackson was emotionally stressed by long-simmering family and business pressures. As he grew to trust some of his "Thriller" collaborators, including Landis, Baker, and Stessel, he opened up about his loneliness, his perception that he had been robbed of his childhood, and his troubled relationship with his father.

Jackson faced a critical moment in his personal development: would his new mega-success and wealth spur him to grow, becoming more confident and independent, or to withdraw further into his gilded fantasy world? His "Thriller" friends marveled at his paradoxical qualities: simultaneously sophisticated as an artist, canny to the point of ruthlessness in business dealings, and breathtakingly immature about relationships. "I dealt with Michael as I would have a really gifted child," says Landis, "because that's what he was at that moment. He was emotionally damaged, but so sweet and so talented."

More than once Landis found himself caught up in the twisted dynamics of the Jackson family. One night when Joseph and Katherine Jackson visited the set, the director recalls, "Michael asked me to have Joe removed. He said, 'Would you please ask my father to leave?' So I go over to Mr. Jackson. 'Mr. Jackson, I'm sorry, but can you please? . . .' 'Who are you?' 'I'm John Landis. I'm directing this.' 'Well, I'm Joe Jackson. I do what I please.' I said, 'I'll have to ask security to remove you if you don't leave now.'" Landis says he had a policeman escort Joe Jackson off the set, which Jackson, through his lawyer, denies.

Distancing himself from his father was a theme in Michael Jackson's life. He had to approve the reams of promotional materials that Epic generated to support "Thriller," and one day he called the record label's art department and asked an art director if she could retouch his nose on a famous photo of him as a child. "I want you to slim the wings of my nose," Jackson told her. "O.K., but why, Michael?" she asked, and tried to reassure him that his face looked fine just the way it was. "I don't want to look like my father," Jackson replied. "Every time I look at that photograph I think I look like my father."

Although he was no longer Michael's manager, Joe Jackson remained an intimidating and powerful presence in his life. In the summer of '83, Jackson relied on his close adviser John Branca to communicate with his father about business matters, avoiding direct confrontation with Joe whenever possible. "Michael was scared to death of Joseph," says Larry Stessel, who vividly recalls an evening when Joe walked into the room at the Encino house and Michael literally moved behind Stessel to hide, cowering. (Not until a 1993 interview with Oprah Winfrey would Michael publicly acknowledge how his father had brutalized him as a child.)

Michael was the Jackson family's golden goose, and ever since he emancipated himself, at the age of 21, Joe had been hostile to his solo endeavors. Now, with millions of *Thriller* dollars flowing in Michael's direction, Joe and Katherine and the brothers—all of whom needed money, thanks partly to extravagant spending habits—felt entitled to cash in. They set about organizing a Jacksons "Victory" reunion tour to take place the following summer, railroading Michael into serving as the star attraction. Joseph sent his secret weapon, Katherine, to implore her "special one" to do right by the family, knowing that Michael could not say no to his mother. "Michael did not want to tour," says Stessel. "He said to them, 'I will do this for you this once, but don't come and ask me for money again. After this I have to do my own projects.'"

At Hayvenhurst, Jackson led a strange, cocooned existence. A round-the-clock security team kept the ever increasing swarms of fans outside from breaching the walls. Inside, the family's interactions were gothic and tense. While Katherine had filed for divorce the previous year following revelations of her husband's infidelity (he had fathered an out-of-wedlock daughter, Joh'Vonnie, whom he visited regularly), Joe had simply moved into a bedroom down the hall rather than move out. Michael tried to make his mother's life more pleasant and avoid colliding with his father. "Michael would lock his bedroom door," remembers Branca, "and Joe would threaten to bang it in." (Joe Jackson, through his lawyer, denies this account.)

Michael transcended the oppressive atmosphere with bursts of musical creativity. He once described his songwriting process as "a gestation, almost like a pregnancy or something. It's an explosion of something so beautiful, you go, Wow!" When a song was ready to be birthed, he drafted siblings to help him record demos in his home studio; Janet sang backup on the first version of "Billie Jean." The night before his now legendary appearance on the Motown 25th-anniversary TV special on NBC, where he introduced the Moonwalk, he had choreographed and rehearsed his performance in the kitchen.

On Sundays, Jackson observed the Sabbath with fasting and hours of cathartic ritual dancing. "It was the most sacred way I could spend my time: developing the talents that God gave me," he later said. Sometimes he invited young street dancers to come show him the latest moves; that was how he learned the Moonwalk.

Jackson also reveled in the company of children at Hayvenhurst, which was like a warm-up for Neverland, a kids' paradise, which he loved sharing. He had struck up a friendship with the four-foot-three-inch television star Emmanuel Lewis, 12, with whom he would invent games and roll around on the grass, laughing. When George Folsey's son, Ryan, 13, accompanied his father to meetings at the Jackson home, Michael behaved like a kid who was bored hanging out with the adults, jumping up to show Ryan around. They would feed the llamas, play the video game *Frogger*, and drive toy Model T's around the grounds. "Michael was 25, but I'd say that he was 13," says Ryan. "Mentally, he was 12 to 15 years behind. He could relate to me because he was my age."

Ryan hung out with Michael in his bedroom, which had a mattress on the floor, toys everywhere, and illustrations of Peter Pan on the walls. They talked about music—"I was amazed that Michael didn't

know who U2 was"—and the girls they had crushes on. Jackson revealed how discombobulated he had been by Ola Ray's sexual allure
after a dance rehearsal with her. "He started getting all nervous and
stuff," says Ryan. "He said, 'She's adorable, she's adorable. She's so
hot!' It was just so funny seeing him that way."

No one knew if Jackson, who told Landis he was a virgin, was practicing abstinence for religious reasons, or because he had gotten spooked
about women by the obsessed fan who accused him of fathering her
child (inspiring "Billie Jean," according to some reports), or because
he was simply too shy to date. Vince Paterson, who helped with the
choreography in "Thriller," says that Jackson would ask him startlingly
ignorant questions about sex—"simple, biological, stupid 12-year-old
questions." He adds, "I never saw Michael as a sexual creature. He
was always sort of asexual to me—some people are like that. I never
had one vibe, as dynamic and electric and powerful as he was. He
was like nobody I had ever met in my life. On the one hand he was so
socially retarded, and on the other hand he was a creative genius."

Paterson remembers Jackson asked him once after a dance rehearsal, "'Where are you going?' I said, 'I'm just going to a party with
some friends. Do you want to come?' 'No, I've never been to a party.
If I ever went to a party I would just want to go stand behind the cur-
tain and be able to peek out and watch what people do.'"

"Friendship is a thing I am just beginning to learn about," Jackson
told *Ebony* magazine in 1982. "I was raised on the stage and that is
where I am comfortable. And everything else is, like, foreign to me."
Jackson had high-profile showbiz buddies such as Brooke Shields,
Elizabeth Taylor, and Diana Ross, whom he could gossip with on the
phone or invite to be his date for a public function. But when
"Thriller" colleagues invited him for dinner and suggested that he
bring a friend, he showed up alone. He frequently hung out at John
and Deborah Landis's house. "I liked Mike," says John. "He used to
come over to our house all the time and just stay there. I think he
was so lonely. He and I got along fine, watching television until three

or four in the morning, or looking at books. Deborah [called me into] the kitchen once, and she said to me, 'John, the most famous human being on the planet is in the library, and I want you to get him the fuck out. Tell him he has to go home!'"

October 23, 1983; 9:45 a.m.
Rick Baker's studio, North Hollywood.
"He's completely unreliable," sputters Landis, fuming and pacing as Baker, the makeup creator, arranges werewolf ears, paws, and teeth on his worktable. (Actually, given Jackson's delicate features, Baker has created a look that is more along the lines of a werecat.) Jackson was scheduled to arrive 45 minutes ago to be made up for his grisly metamorphosis sequence. Finally the star's black Rolls pulls up outside. Jackson trots in and plunks himself down in the chair. He is wearing a yellow T-shirt, black pants short enough to show his argyle socks, and black loafers with one sole flapping loose. He is carrying the book How to Be a Jewish Mother *with a copy of the Jehovah's Witnesses magazine,* The Watchtower, *inside.*

As Baker hovers over him, working meticulously, Jackson sits silently with his hands folded in his lap. An assistant arrives carrying a yellow pillowcase with something lumpy inside and puts it down in the outer room. "Say Say Say" comes on the radio, the latest Jackson hit single, another duet with Paul McCartney, this one appearing on McCartney's album Pipes of Peace. *Jackson yawns. "I have to tinkle," he says, and gets up for a bathroom break.*

He returns carrying an eight-foot boa constrictor—retrieved from that yellow pillowcase—which he has named Muscles. He wraps the snake around my neck. "Don't be afraid—Muscles won't hurt you," he says in a feathery voice.

When shooting was finished, Landis and Folsey worked every night in an editing room on the Universal Studios lot; after the original editor departed for another project, Folsey took over cutting. Jackson liked to hang out with Landis and Folsey while they worked, driving himself and arriving in the editing room at about 9 p.m. They'd bring in his preferred dinner of salad and brown rice and vegetables. "We'd look at cut footage and talk about things, and it was always fun," says Folsey. "He was very appreciative and had good ideas." All three were pleased with the way the short film was shaping up, and looked forward to the premiere at the Crest Theatre, in Westwood, on November 14. When Jackson departed at one or two in the morning, he'd find mash notes on the windshield of his Rolls.

About two weeks before the premiere, Jackson called Branca and, hyperventilating and speaking in a halting voice, ordered him to destroy the negative of "Thriller." After much cajoling he revealed the reason for his decision. "He said the Jehovah's Witnesses heard he was doing a werewolf video," Branca recalls. "They told him that it promoted demonology and they were going to excommunicate him." Branca conferred with Folsey and Landis, and all agreed that the "Thriller" negative had to be safeguarded. Landis immediately removed the film canisters from the lab and delivered them to Branca's office, where they were locked up.

Next, according to Landis, he got a call from Jackson's security chief, Bill Bray, who reported that the singer had been in his room with the door locked for three days, refusing to come out. Landis drove to the Encino estate. "Bill and I kicked in the door, knocked it down, and Michael was lying there. He said, 'I feel so bad.' I said, 'Michael, have you eaten?' He hadn't eaten. It was weird. I just said, 'Look, I want you to see a doctor right now.'"

Landis returned to see Jackson the next day and found him at Frank DiLeo's house, a few blocks from the Encino estate, in a more cheerful state. He apologized for issuing the order to destroy "Thriller": "I'm sorry, John. I'm embarrassed." Landis then informed the star that his directive had been ignored. "I said, 'Michael, I wouldn't let it be destroyed.' He went, 'Really? Because I think it's really good.' I go, 'Michael, it's great and you're great.'"

Still, Jackson was concerned about the video's content. Branca, desperate to mollify his client, invented a ruse. "I said, 'Mike, did you ever watch Bela Lugosi in *Dracula*?' He goes, 'Why?' I said, 'Do you know that he was a devout Christian?' I was just making it up. And I said, 'Did you ever notice there were, like, disclaimers on those movies?' He goes, 'No.' 'So, Michael, before we destroy this film, let's put a disclaimer on it saying that this does not reflect the personal convictions of Michael Jackson.' 'Oh!' He liked it." Problem solved. Says Landis, "You know, what's wonderful about Michael—this is where genius comes in. No matter how wacky something was, it always had some amazing benefit. That disclaimer caused a lot of talk, and it generated a lot of interest."

The A-list turned out for the premiere at the 500-seat historic Crest Theatre: Diana Ross, Warren Beatty, Prince, Eddie Murphy. "I've been to the Oscars, the BAFTAs, the Emmys, and the Golden Globes, and I had never seen anything like this," remembers Landis. Ola Ray looked for Jackson before the lights went down and found him in the projection booth. He told her that she looked beautiful, but refused her entreaty to come sit in the audience. "This is your night," he told her. "You go enjoy yourself." Landis warmed up the audience with a new print of the Mickey Mouse cartoon "The Band Concert." Then came "Thriller," with its sound mix cranked up to top volume. Fourteen minutes later the crowd was on its feet, applauding and crying, "Encore! Encore!" Eddie Murphy shouted, "Show the goddamn thing again!" And they did.

As the December 2 MTV debut of "Thriller" approached, there was massive audience anticipation. Former MTV executive Les Garland says the network settled on a saturation strategy he describes as "'Every time we play "Thriller," let's tell them when we are going to play it again.' We played it three to five times a day. We were getting audience ratings 10 times the usual when we popped 'Thriller.'"

Showtime aired *Making Michael Jackson's Thriller* six times in February. Within months the Vestron release had sold a million copies, making it at the time the biggest selling home-video release ever.

Landis's dream for "Thriller" to have an international theatrical run, like the short films from Hollywood's golden age, would not be fulfilled. In a sense, he became a victim of his own success: Yetnikoff and DiLeo killed any chance of that when they realized that the video was a spectacular marketing tool. "Epic gave away the video free all over the world, to every television station that wanted it," says Landis. "There was a month when you couldn't turn the television on and not see 'Thriller.'" Since Landis and Folsey together owned 50 per cent of both "Thriller" and *Making Michael Jackson's Thriller*, they had the legal right to be consulted. "I don't think it was very kosher," says Landis, "but it was the right thing for CBS Records to do."

Having transformed a fun but marginal song into a heroic and historic video, Michael Jackson rode "Thriller" to the mountaintop. The video sent the album's sales back into the stratosphere, with Epic shipping a million copies a week; by the end of 1984, the album had sold 33 million copies in the U.S. Since then, *Thriller* has remained unchallenged as the No. 1 album of all time (current sales worldwide: an estimated 110 million).

Jackson grew accustomed to shattering records, collecting spoils and statuettes. On February 28, 1984, he dressed like American royalty in a spangled military jacket to escort Brooke Shields to the Grammy Awards at the Shrine Auditorium, where he picked up an unprecedented eight trophies for *Thriller*. By this time he was a fabulously wealthy man, thanks to the industry's highest royalty rate, more than $2 per record, which Branca had negotiated for him.

Thriller had profound consequences for Jackson's life and subsequent career: it was both a source of his greatest pride, and his curse. Like most entertainers, he was happiest during the heady days of the upward trajectory, and hated the downward journey; his story became uniquely tragic because he viewed everything that came afterward as a failure, and the satisfactions of his private life were not sufficient to compensate. "Michael didn't see *Thriller* as a phenomenon," says

Brunman. "He saw it as a stepping-stone to even greater things. We were ecstatic when [his next album] *Bad* shot past the 20 million mark. Michael was disappointed."

"To me what happened with Michael is he felt like he needed to top himself," says Branca, who represented Jackson on and off for the rest of the star's life and has been named a co-executor of his estate. "That was a lot of pressure. I remember we were in Hong Kong on vacation after *Thriller*, and I said to him, 'Mike, you should think about doing an album of the songs that inspired you.' He said, 'Why would I do that?' 'Well, it would take the pressure off you. Nobody would expect you to have to top *Thriller*.' And he looked at me like I was from Mars. And he said, 'Branca, the next album is going to sell 100 million.'"

In January 2009, six months before the star's death, John Landis and George Folsey filed suit against Michael Jackson and his company Optimum Productions for breach of contract, alleging that they had not been paid their 50 percent of royalties in many years, and accusing Jackson of "fraudulent, malicious and oppressive conduct." Landis says that over the years he had spoken with Jackson many times to complain that he, Landis, was not receiving the royalties due him, and that Jackson promised to correct the matter. But the entertainer's financial affairs were chaotic for the last decade of his life as he continually shuffled his business managers. Branca and his own attorney Howard Weitzman report that the "Thriller" video's accounting records are currently being audited as part of the executor's obligation to settle the Jackson estate's debts. "From our perspective Landis and Folsey are priorities," says Weitzman. "They will definitely get paid what they are owed."

Ola Ray also sued Jackson, on May 5, 2009, for nonpayment of royalties. "I got the fame" from "Thriller," she says, "but I didn't get the fortune." (The suit is ongoing.) In 1998 she fled Los Angeles and the casting-couch syndrome she says plagued her during the years following

"Thriller." "There were so many big-name directors who told me that if I wanted to do films I had to sleep with them," she says. She moved to Sacramento to be closer to her family, and is today a stay-at-home mom to her 15-year-old daughter. Ray enjoys hearing from Michael Jackson fans on Facebook and Twitter. "I can't walk down the street without people recognizing me," she says.

Ray thinks about Jackson every day, with considerable regret. "I just wish I would have had the opportunity to be a little bit more in his life. I bet he would have been happy with me. It would have taken someone like me who would not put pressure on him or play him for his money or anything other than that I wanted to be with him for who he was," she says. "I had no other agenda than that."

Ola Ray and I strongly agree on one thing: we both like to remember Michael Jackson the way he was on the night of October 13, 1983. I can't forget the way he looked as I peered at him through the glass of the ticket booth at the Palace Theatre: elfin, radiant, ascendant. To me, *Thriller* seems like the last time that everyone on the planet got excited at the same time by the same thing: no matter where you went in the world, they were playing those songs, and you could dance to them. Since then, the fragmentation of pop culture has destroyed our sense of collective exhilaration, and I miss that.

For Ray, the scene with Jackson later that evening, as he scampered adoringly around her, was a defining experience. "That walk with Michael, when he was dancing around me and singing, I felt like I was the most, I don't know, blessed girl in the world. Being able to do that and being able to play with Michael, and having him play around me. I felt so in love that night. You can see it in my eyes. You can see it for sure."

The Runaways
Wild Thing

Evelyn McDonnell

On a summer day in 1975, a 16-year-old girl carrying a Silvertone guitar took four public buses from Canoga Park to a two-story house in Huntington Beach. At the door, she was greeted by another 16-year-old, a surfing beauty with piercing blue eyes, feathered blond hair and muscled arms. The two strangers climbed to the above-garage rec room, which doubled as Sandy Pesavento's bedroom. Sandy sat down at her red Pearl drum set. Joan Larkin plugged in her guitar.

"We just clicked; we locked in right away," says the guitarist. "She was so friendly and outgoing. She was like me: She was a tomboy, she loved sports, she was a roughhouser. I couldn't believe how she played. She was such a solid, strong, powerful, really good drummer. I don't even want to say for being 16—for being anything. She had this shit down and it was powerful."

That suburban rec room was ground zero for the Runaways, the all-girl teenage band that busted down rock barriers and took an unbelievable amount of shit. Sandy West and Joan Jett, as they would soon become known to the world, formed the nucleus of the group that is now the subject of a much-hyped feature film, *The Runaways*, directed by Floria Sigismondi and starring Kristen Stewart and Dakota Fanning as Jett and singer Cherie Currie.

Declaring themselves the queens of noise, Jett, West, Currie, guitarist Lita Ford and bassist Jackie Fox were pre-punk bandits fostering
revolution girl-style, decades before that became a riot grrrl catch-
phrase. West, played in the film by Stella Maeve, was a powerhouse
who proved that girls could play just as hard as boys. The band's
breakup affected her more than any other Runaway, and during the
following decades, as she created great, little-heard music with other
players but fell into horrific, sometimes violent, drug-fueled episodes,
she continued to advocate for the band's reunion—or at least their
due critical appreciation.

Yet West is the one band member who is not around to see the
Runaways get the kind of attention that eluded them when they were
treated as a jailbait novelty act. On October 21, 2006, the strong,
charismatic, bighearted woman succumbed to the lung cancer that
first struck her while she was in prison on a drug charge. It was a
tragic end for a bon vivant whose very entrance filled a room with
energy, a drummer who beat a path for girl musicians, a tomboy
whose skills and search for thrills included a facility with guns, a California dreamer who created, and was passed up by, musical history.

Sandy wasn't supposed to be there. She told her parents that she was
going to Disneyland, but actually, she was at a happier place on Earth
that Saturday night during the summer of 1975—the parking lot of
the Rainbow Bar and Grill. Sandy knew this Sunset Strip spot was
the place to hang out if you wanted to meet rock stars and/or their
handlers.

"She was with her friends from Huntington Beach," says Kim Fowley, the pop-industry veteran who would become both the Runaways'
manager and, to some at least, their villain. "They were up there
standing around like everybody did that didn't have ID to get into
the Rainbow or the Roxy. They were up there as tourists, weekend
warriors coming to Hollywood."

Fowley speaks derisively of young suburbanites, but they were the
demographic key to the Runaways, whose homes ranged from the

San Fernando Valley to Orange County. On weekends, teenagers from all over L.A. converged on West Hollywood, first at Rodney Bingenheimer's English Disco, then at places like the Sugar Shack (teens only) and the infamous Starwood. There, they discovered the music of David Bowie, the New York Dolls, Sweet and Suzi Quatro (Jett's hero), and could even rub elbows with stars like Led Zeppelin.

"There's Sandy standing there looking like [Beach Boy] Dennis Wilson's sister," says Fowley. "She was with a bunch of musicians in a musician's stance. One of those, 'Hi, I bet everybody here should know I'm a musician.' Like Billy the Kid coming to town ready to have a gunfight. So I said, 'Are you a musician?'"

Sandy's timing was dead-on. Just that afternoon, Fowley had auditioned Jett. He gave her phone number to West and, not long after, Jett took that long bus ride to Huntington Beach, where the girls played basic rock progressions—Chuck Berry and Rolling Stones riffs—and "bonded over the straight, pure thing of rhythm guitar and drums locking up," says Jett. They played over the phone for Fowley, who was having lunch with a writer from *Billboard*. Fowley held the phone up, and the writer smiled at what he heard. "At that moment, I knew it would work," he says.

They auditioned musicians. One day, a sexy guitarist from Long Beach with long, blond hair came to the rehearsal studio on Sunset and Vine.

"I walked in and Sandy and I hit it off right away," says Ford. "I started playing this old Deep Purple song, 'Highway Star.' She knew the entire song; I couldn't believe it. We just jammed it out. As soon as we did that, we were like, 'I love you.'"

Fowley and Jett found Currie at the Sugar Shack. After trying out a few bassists, they settled on Jackie Fuchs, redubbed Fox. Once set, the Runaways were promptly signed to Mercury Records. For most of them, it was their first band. None of them was older than 17.

Until tragedy struck the Pesaventos, Sandy was an active, happy child from prosperous, middle-class suburban L.A. Maybe because he realized he was never going to have a son, father Gene bonded with the youngest of his four daughters, fixing cars and playing ball together. "They were close," says Teri Miranti, the second-oldest daughter. "She related to him and he related to her."

Second-wave feminism and Title IX were opening doors for women, and the youngest Pesavento eagerly rushed through them. That challenge to do whatever the guys did was both Sandy's lifelong drive and part of her downfall. She played tennis and basketball, swam competitively, ran track, surfed, waterskied and rode horses. "She was incredibly energetic, hysterical, very funny, athletic," says Lori, the third daughter.

Sandy was smart, but she struggled in school. Lori attributes her difficulties to conditions with which she was diagnosed decades later: "Early on, she had a lot of challenges with academic performances primarily because she had a lot of learning disabilities, which later on in life we learned that she had ADHD. She had challenges that were around things like mood disorders, bipolar disorders."

In fourth grade, Sandy made it clear that she was not going to follow in the classical path paved by her sisters. Ellen played violin, Lori viola, Teri cello. The family wanted Sandy to be a violinist, so the daughters could form a string quartet. Sandy lasted about two weeks. "She said, 'No way,'" her mother, Jeri, says. "'You know what: I can be the first girl drummer in Prisk Elementary School.' That's how it began."

On January 25, 1971, Sandy had just returned from school when Gene Pesavento had a massive heart attack at home, and died. "It was very traumatic for my family," says Lori. "It was off the Richter scale."

Sandy, 11, took it especially hard. "When I first met her, she talked a lot about her dad, how much she missed him," says Pam Apostolou, who befriended West in 1980. "Her dad got her."

In 1972, Jeri married Dick Williams, a former colleague of Gene's, whose wife had also recently died—and who, oddly enough, had three daughters, including a Sandy. The new, blended family moved to Huntington Beach, a place where they could start over on equal ground, not surrounded by memories of lost loved ones. Some of the daughters were in college or lived elsewhere. Still, the Huntington Beach house held five girls, three cats and two dogs who were trying to navigate deep hurt, massive change, puberty and one another's spaces. This was no *Brady Bunch* story.

"We were struggling at first, getting to know each other," says Jeri.

Sandy was outgoing, fun, easy to get along with, popular enough to be elected governor of her seventh grade. But Lori recalls her transition into puberty as bumpy. "She was very androgynous. She was one of those girls who didn't develop very early. People used to call her a boy. That upset her."

Around this time, Lori and Sandy were realizing they had something in common: They both liked girls. During her lifetime, Sandy also had boyfriends, but her primary relationships were with women. "Early on," says Lori, "she was very clear with me about her orientation. I don't sense she ever really struggled with it."

Music and sports were Sandy's outlets. By the mid-'70s, she was listening to hard rock and playing in a local band. Her drumming heroes were Led Zeppelin's John Bonham and Queen's Roger Taylor. Sandy poured her athleticism into pounding those skins.

"Sandy early on was pretty determined that she wanted to play rock music," Lori says. "It was a way for her to translate the grief. And she was a phenomenal natural drummer. I don't think the boys in the business ever even saw that coming."

By 1975, pop music had a noble history of female-vocal groups, but not of bands made up of women playing the instruments. Such acts as Goldie and the Gingerbreads and Fanny broke ground culturally but did not have much impact commercially. And they weren't composed of five hot teenagers, three of whom, at least—Lita, Sandy and Joan—could seriously play. Another, Currie, was a Promethean ingenue, a rape victim who strutted in a corset like it was armor and sang like she was going to draw blood. The Runaways created a West

Coast version of glam rock that was part metal, part bubblegum and proto-punk.

The five strangers got to know one another fast. Shoved into a van and sent touring across the U.S., and then England, they eventually made it to Japan, where they were greeted with something like mass hysteria. The Runaways were like a girl gang, or a deranged sorority. "Being on the road was like taking a small child and a few of her friends to the zoo for the first time," says Currie. "There was wonderment of everything we were experiencing, good or bad. We were a family."

They were forging and experiencing something woefully rare in American society: the power of females working, creating, living and loving together. Occasionally, the love was physical. Currie got intimate with both Jett and West. "Back then in the mid-'70s, that was just what happened," Currie says. "At that time—David Bowie and Elton John—everybody was coming out. We experimented together. We had fun. We loved each other."

The Runaways had to become one another's support, because by choice and by circumstance, they were separated from their families. Currie's parents had recently divorced. Jett's father had left. Perhaps caught up in their own sorrows, the others didn't even realize West had issues. Sandy's parents loved her, but they didn't care for the music—and they certainly didn't care for Fowley.

"When he walked in the door, I was not happy," says Jeri. "He was not good news."

The Williams' understandable parental concern could have felt to West like lack of support. The band's name was a gimmick, but maybe, in a sense, she was running away from a relatively conservative upbringing. In order to be closer to the band and the action, West was living in West L.A. with her sister Teri, who was in college and had her own life to live.

"I think that [her] family didn't know what to do with her need to be a drummer, her need to kick ass, her need to dominate the world of rock & roll and be a crusader," Fowley says. "I think that was her burning need to get out there. She escaped the golden ghetto."

West saw the Runaways as a team. While other band members were taking shots at each other, she was quick to punch out anyone who threatened or insulted her bandmates. She told her friend Jerry Venemann about an incident when the band was hanging out with the Sex Pistols in London. On a houseboat on the Thames, Sid Vicious kept pawing at Jett, who was in no mood, or condition, for love. West told him to quit. Vicious kept harassing Jett, so West picked up the skinny bassist and dropped him into the river.

And then it began to seem that the people the Runaways most needed protection from were the people with whom they were working.

In Sigismondi's cinematic version of *The Runaways*, which opens March 19, Michael Shannon's Fowley steals the film—as any good villain should. There's no doubt Fowley, who was 36 at the band's inception, was the Runaways' evil genius, picking their name and accompanying bad-girl image, priming and primping—and pimping?—them for rock stardom.

The girls went along with this to a degree, dressing and posing provocatively. But sometimes, the sexploitation went too far. An English ad for *Queens of Noise*, for example, featured disembodied crotch shots of the teenagers in fetishistic gear. In article after article, male journalists slobbered over the Runaways, asking them for their body measurements, passing over their musical talents.

West's family blames Fowley for exposing her to the chemical lifestyle that ultimately derailed her. West herself spoke bitterly of the manager, and most of the people who know her say she stayed angry with him for much of her life. There were serious money issues. Bun E. Carlos, the drummer for Cheap Trick, remembers when his band and Tom Petty and the Heartbreakers opened for the Runaways in Detroit in 1977. The girls were driving a rental car they hadn't returned and were "living off nothing, no advances, peanuts. The gild was off the lily for the band. We knew they were being taken advantage of." Still, Carlos says, "Without Kim, they wouldn't have been there at all."

Jett, who remains friendly with Fowley, firmly rejects the charge that the girls were his victims: "This whole abuse thing is maddening to me. I think in hindsight people have to create monsters, but they should look at their own shit and responsibility in not making it happen. If you feel abused, get the fuck out. Nobody was forced to stay."

Fox and Currie did get out of what by 1977 had become an overheated pressure cooker of underage sex, ready drugs and kick-ass rock & roll. In Japan, Fox cut herself with a broken glass and left the band, replaced by Victory Tischler, aka Vicki Blue. Currie quit a few months later, when the Runaways were in the middle of recording their third studio album, *Waitin' for the Night.* The final straw for the singer: a *Crawdaddy!* article in which Fowley said that the best thing Currie could do would be to hang herself.

Fowley admits he was in over his head as the Runaways' manager, denying either knowledge or memory of many of the charges against him. He was not on the road with the band and puts much of the blame for unhealthy high jinks on the tour manager, Scotty Anderson (who got Currie pregnant, according to her book).

"Their age group was rebelling against parents, teachers, Sunday school," Fowley says. "The feminist movement started in the early '70s, here we were in '75. Suddenly I have five warriors, cheerleaders with atomic weapons, ready to kick ass."

In the end, it was Fowley's ass the girls kicked, firing him in '77. The band was a trio by '78: West, Jett (who also sang lead) and Ford (on lead guitar and bass). They hired a new manager, Toby Mamis, and a new producer, John Alcock, a Brit who had worked with Thin Lizzy. "They had a sense of frustration that they were previously not really allowed to develop as musicians," says Alcock. "They wanted to focus more on the music and less on the image."

But by the time they recorded their fourth studio album, *And Now . . . the Runaways*, their musical tastes were splitting. While West and Ford cut their teeth on metal, glam fan Jett was getting more and more into punk. "We all had dark stuff going on toward the end of the band, after Cherie left," Jett says. "I just sensed it was going to slowly die. . . . Look at any picture of us as a four-piece; you won't find one picture of us smiling. . . . We decided that New Year's Eve 1978 would be our last gig."

One song in the Runaways' live set focused on West's showmanship and singing: a cover of the Troggs' 1960s garage-rock classic, "Wild Thing," captured in a video moment in Japan. The instruments stop on the verses and West raises one of those long, sinewy arms—she had arms like Tina Turner has legs—and sings: "Wild thing, I think I love you." Then she smashes the sticks down for two beats. "I want to know for sure." She's pointing at the audience. "C'mon and hold me tight." Her hand is in the sky now, twirling the stick like a Wild West gunman. "You move me."

"Wild Thing" was West's signature. After the Runaways broke up, it became a way of life.

The Runaways introduced West to a lifestyle she never figured out how to move beyond. At the age when she should have been learning practical life skills, she was shooting heroin with Keith Moon (according to a story she told her sister Ellen). Careers and lives lost to drug abuse are unfortunately a dime a dozen in rock & roll, but West took an especially crazy turn. She freebased coke and took crystal meth. She became a drug runner and dealer's bodyguard. She carried a gun. She was involved in scary, violent scenes that she told only a select few friends about, memories of which probably only deepened her depressive states. She was arrested and jailed repeatedly.

Initially, West was excited to start a new, mixed-gender band with Ford, working with Alcock. But after a few months, when that failed to get off the ground and Ford moved on, she began to realize the enormity of what she had lost.

West saw the success Jett and Ford had as solo artists and was determined to compete. She formed her own group, the Sandy West

Band. The music was good, but if labels thought the Runaways were dead without Currie, they certainly weren't interested in a band fronted by a drummer.

"She had a very healthy ego," says her sister Ellen. "She became delusional about how great she was. She had visions of being a really big star getting an enormous amount of attention. Meanwhile there was the deterioration of the addiction, all that going downward. It's such a Greek tragedy."

Family remained important to West. But she didn't see her parents and sisters that often. She seemed to feel alienated by how different her life had become. Instead, she built an alternative family. Often, West turned to fans for friendships. Some of those people were vital links in her support network, but there were also hangers-on who took advantage of her, who just wanted to party with a rock star.

"Because Sandy's life didn't move forward as well as the others', it was easier for her to fall back on drinking and drugs," says Alcock. "She started doing some fairly heavy partying with people I didn't know, somewhere down in the beach communities. Those were not great people."

She would disappear with these people, into black holes of drug-fueled behavior. Family and friends staged interventions; West went into rehab a few times. But she always fell off the wagon.

At one point, says Currie, "she came over to the house and she was freebasing cocaine, which I tried desperately to get her to stop. It was extremely difficult to watch her do it. Having been in her position, I knew all the begging in the world wouldn't stop her."

The thing that was destroying West, says Ellen, was "the evil drug . . . crystal meth. One time I drove her home. I just remember trying to relate to her. I looked at her and saw her teeth getting black. I saw the tremors. She was disconnected, couldn't have a coherent conversation."

Sometimes, when West disappeared from friends' and families' lives, it turned out she was in jail. Her life of crime had begun harmlessly enough: On a Runaways tour in Europe, she, Currie and Jett were arrested for stealing hotel keys. Her stateside arrest record starts in 1988, when she was picked up in Orange County for driving under the influence. There were at least six arrests after that, in multiple counties: more DUIs, possession of controlled substances, possession of illegal substances, driving with a suspended license. She was able to serve some of her sentences concurrently. Friends say she took her jail time in stride, that perhaps it was easier for her to be institutionalized.

"She told me that in some ways being in prison reminded her of being in a band," says Lauren Varga, who befriended and played guitar with West in the '90s. "She said, 'I was living in such a bad way that when I went away, that was the only stability I had for a year. When I got back out, it was back into the chaos.'"

In fact, West was lucky to get put away for minor charges when she was doing much worse things. "Sandy got involved with mob-type figures," says Tischler-Blue: "Because she had this all-American-girl look, people wouldn't red-flag her. She started running drugs into the recording studios. Sandy loved coke. That was this turn that took her down a very different road. That road led to the underbelly of the Hollywood music scene. At that time, there were some really bad characters moving around. Heavy-duty drug people. Gunrunning people."

Looking tough but emotional, West talks about "the dangerous adventures of me" in Tischler-Blue's 2004 documentary about the band, *Edgeplay*. "Maybe that was the self-destructive side of me. Maybe I was out to push it. I was fearless. You go down and break somebody's door down. They've got guns all over you, you've got guns all over them. You don't know who's going to get killed. . . . I had to break somebody's arm once. I had to shove a gun down somebody's throat once and watch them shit their pants. And then you look around and say, 'I just wanted to be a drummer in a rock band.'"

Near the end of her life, West lived in circumstances demeaning to a former rock star: in a trailer in San Dimas. She appeared to be getting her life together. She released a four-song EP that shows her multiple talents: singer, songwriter, guitarist, pianist, drummer. She shared the trailer with Jan Miller, a quiet widow nine years older than West with an adult son. They signed a domestic-partnership agreement, and with Miller's insurance, West was able to get a needed hysterectomy. She was playing with Venemann and had formed a band with guitarist Varga and others, which they jokingly called Blue Fox after the Runaways' bassists. She was also working different jobs—handyman, vet's assistant, drum teacher. She had a dog, CJ, her surrogate child. "I just want to settle down and have a family," she told Miller.

But then she was arrested again, for possession of drugs and paraphernalia. In the era of three strikes, this was one offense too many. This time, West was sent not to the relatively tame county jail for a short stint, but to state prison in Chowchilla for 18 months. She found herself surrounded by hard-core criminals.

Before she went in, she did rehab one more time, this time at a facility specifically for musicians. Friends say this stint may have succeeded better than others. "She really was a different person," says Varga. "She said, 'It's taken me almost 30 years to get over this band. I really just have to let it go.'"

But West didn't have time to find out if she was cleaned up for good. Not long after arriving at Chowchilla, she developed a bad cough. It was small-cell lung cancer—the deadly, aggressive kind.

West underwent chemotherapy while still in prison. When finally released, she returned to Miller's care, and they moved to a house in West Covina. By this point, West's family was back in her life, helping to take care of her. Currie, Blue and other friends were there often. Jett visited her. She and Ford talked on the phone.

West's last months of life were full of pain, as the cancer, which moved to her brain, ate away at her. She lost some of the things that defined her: her golden hair and the strength to drum. She gained religion and a determination to do good. When she recovered, she said, she planned to speak to young people about the perils of drug use. "Through her suffering, and she really did suffer a lot, she became closer to her faith and wrote quite a few songs that were spiritual," says Jeri.

West was moved to a hospice. On October 21, 2006, Ellen had the feeling she had to get there right away, so she drove like crazy from San Francisco. Half an hour after her arrival, Sandy "West" Pesavento died. She's buried at Forest Lawn cemetery in Cypress, next to her father.

West had two dying wishes, Miller says: to have her autobiography published and the music she was working on released. Varga is working on both, though West's family is not eager to have her secrets exposed. The family donates West's royalties to the hospice and to a scholarship fund at the Rock 'n' Roll Camp for Girls in Portland. So West is not only still inspiring other women to rock, she's helping to pay their way.

West did live long enough to sell her life rights to the producers of *The Runaways* and to know that the band might be immortalized on film. But Sigismondi's movie focuses on the relationship between Currie and Jett. Sandy West has only a bit part.

The Fun Stuff

James Wood

My life as Keith Moon

I had a traditional musical education, in a provincial English cathedral town. I was sent off to an ancient piano teacher with the requisite halitosis, who lashed with a ruler at my knuckles as if they were wasps; I added the trumpet a few years later, and had lessons with a younger, cheerier man, who told me that the best way to make the instrument "sound" was to imagine spitting paper pellets down the mouthpiece at the school bully. I sang daily in the cathedral choir, an excellent grounding in sight-reading and performance.

But what I really wanted to do, as a little boy, was play the drums, and, of those different ways of making music, only playing the drums still makes me feel like a little boy. A friend's older brother had a drum kit, and as a twelve-year-old I gawped at the spangled shells of wood and skin, and plotted how I might get to hit them, and make a lot of noise. It wouldn't be easy. My parents had no time for "all that thumping about," and the prim world of ecclesiastical and classical music, which meant so much to me, detested rock. But I waited until the drums' owner was off at school, and sneaked into the attic where they gleamed, fabulously inert, and over the next few years I taught myself how to play them. Sitting behind the drums was like the fantasy of driving (the other great prepubescent ambition), with my feet established on two pedals, bass drum and high hat, and the willing dials staring back at me like a blank dashboard.

Noise, speed, rebellion: everyone secretly wants to play the drums, because hitting things, like yelling, returns us to the innocent violence of childhood. Music makes us want to dance, to register rhythm on and with our bodies. The drummer and the conductor are the luckiest of all musicians, because they are closest to dancing. And in drumming how childishly close the connection is between the dancer and the dance! When you blow down an oboe, or pull a bow across a string, an infinitesimal hesitation—the hesitation of vibration—separates the act and the sound; for trumpeters, the simple voicing of a quiet middle C is more fraught than very complex passages, because that brass tube can be sluggish in its obedience. But when a drummer needs to make a drum sound he just . . . hits it. The stick or the hand comes down, and the skin bellows. The narrator in Thomas Bernhard's novel *The Loser*, a pianist crazed with dreams of genius and obsessed with Glenn Gould, expresses the impossible longing to become the piano, to be at one with it. When you play the drums, you are the drums. "Tom-tom, c'est moi," as Wallace Stevens put it.

The drummer who was the drums, when I was a boy, was Keith Moon, though he was dead by the time I first heard him. He was the drums not because he was the most technically accomplished of drummers but because his joyous, semaphoring lunacy suggested a man possessed by the antic spirit of drumming. He was pure, irresponsible, restless childishness. At the end of early Who concerts, as Pete Townshend smashed his guitar, Moon would kick his drums and stand on them and hurl them around the stage, and this seems a logical extension not only of the basic premise of drumming, which is to hit things, but of Moon's drumming, which was to hit things exuberantly. "For Christ's sake, play quieter," the manager of a club once told Moon. To which Moon replied, "I can't play quiet, I'm a rock drummer."

The Who had extraordinary rhythmic vitality, and it died when Keith Moon died, thirty-two years ago. I had hardly ever heard any rock music when I first listened to albums like *Quadrophenia* and *Who's Next*. My notion of musical volume and power was inevitably

circumscribed by my fairly sheltered, austerely Christian upbringing—I got off on classical or churchy things like the brassy last bars
of William Walton's First Symphony, or the densely chromatic last
movement of the "Hammerklavier" Sonata, or the way the choir
bursts in at the start of Handel's anthem "Zadok the Priest," or the
thundering thirty-two-foot bass pipes of Durham Cathedral's organ,
and the way the echo, at the end of a piece, took seven seconds to
dissolve in that huge building. Those things are not to be despised,
but nothing had prepared me for the ferocious energy of The Who.
The music enacted the mod rebellion of its lyrics: "Hope I die before
I get old"; "Meet the new boss, same as the old boss"; "Dressed right,
for a beach fight"; "There's a millionaire above you, / And you're
under his suspicion." Pete Townshend's hard, tense suspended chords
seemed to scour the air around them; Roger Daltrey's singing was a
young man's fighting swagger, an incitement to some kind of crime;
John Entwistle's incessantly mobile bass playing was like someone
running away from the scene of the crime; and Keith Moon's drumming, in its inspired vandalism, was the crime itself.

Most rock drummers, even very good and inventive ones, are
timekeepers. There is a space for a fill or a roll at the end of a musical
phrase, but the beat has primacy over the curlicues. In a regular 4/4
bar, the bass drum sounds the first beat, the snare the second, the
bass drum again hits the third (often with two eighth notes at this
point), and then the snare hits the bar's final beat. This results in the
familiar "boom-DA, boom-boom-DA" sound of most rock drumming.
A standard-issue drummer, playing along, say, to the Beatles' "Carry
That Weight," would keep his 4/4 beat steady through the line "Boy,
you're gonna carry that weight, carry that weight, a long time," until
the natural break, which comes at the end of the phrase, where, just
after the word "time," a wordless, two-beat half-bar readies itself for
the repeated chorus. In that half-bar, there might be space for a quick
roll, or a roll and a triplet, or something fancy with snare and high
hat—really, any variety of filler. The filler is the fun stuff, and it could
be said, without much exaggeration, that nearly all the fun stuff in

drumming takes place in those two empty beats between the end of one phrase and the start of another. Ringo Starr, who interpreted his role modestly, does nothing much in that two-beat space: mostly, he provides eight even, straightforward sixteenth notes (da-da-da-da / da-da-da-da). In a good cover version of the song, Phil Collins, a sophisticated drummer who was never a modest performer with Genesis, does a tight roll that begins with featherlight delicacy on a tomtom and ends more firmly on his snare, before going back to the beat. But the modest and the sophisticated drummer, whatever their stylistic differences, share an understanding that there is a proper space for keeping the beat, and a much smaller space for departing from it, like a time-out area in a classroom. The difference is just that the sophisticated drummer is much more often in time-out, and is always busily showing off to the rest of the class while he is there.

Keith Moon ripped all this up. There is no time-out in his drumming, because there is no time-in. It is all fun stuff. The first principle of Moon's drumming was that drummers do not exist to keep the beat. He did keep the beat, and very well, but he did it by every method except the traditional one. Drumming is repetition, as is rock music generally, and Moon clearly found repetition dull. So he played the drums like no one else—and not even like himself. No two bars of Moon's playing ever sound the same; he is in revolt against consistency. Everyone else in the band gets to improvise, so why should the drummer be nothing more than a condemned metronome? He saw himself as a soloist playing with an ensemble of other soloists. It follows from this that the drummer will be playing a line of music, just as, say, the guitarist does, with undulations and crescendos and leaps. It further follows that the snare drum and the bass drum, traditionally the ball-and-chain of rhythmic imprisonment, are no more interesting than any of the other drums in the kit; and that you will need lots of those other drums. By the mid-nineteen-seventies, when Moon's kit was "the biggest in the world," he had two bass drums and at least twelve tomtoms, arrayed in stacks like squadrons of spotlights; he looked like a cheerful boy who had built elaborate fortifications for the sole purpose of destroying them. But he needed all those drums, as a flute needs all its stops or a harp its strings, so that his tremendous bubbling cascades, his liquid journeys, could be voiced: he needed not to run out of drums as he ran around them.

Average musical performance, like athletics and viticulture, has probably improved in the last century. Nowadays, more pianists can brilliantly run off some Chopin or Rachmaninoff in a concert hall, and the guy at the local drum shop is probably technically more adept than Keith Moon was. YouTube, which is a kind of Special Olympics for showoffs, is full of young men wreaking double-jointed virtuosity on fabulously complex drum kits rigged up like artillery ranges. But so what? They can also backflip into their jeans from great heights and parkour across Paris.

Moon disliked drum solos, and did not really perform them; the only one I have seen is atrociously bad, a piece of anti-performance art—Moon sloppy and mindless, apparently drunk or stoned or both, and almost collapsing into the drums while he pounds them like pillows. He may have lacked the control necessary to sustain a long, complex solo; more likely, he needed the kinetic adventures of The Who to provoke him into his own. His merry way of conceding this was his now-famous remark "I'm the best Keith Moon–style drummer in the world."

Keith Moon–style drumming is a lucky combination of the artful and the artless. To begin at the beginning: his drums always sounded good. He hit them nice and hard, and tuned the bigger tomtoms low. (Not for him the little eunuch toms of Kenney Jones, who palely succeeded Moon in The Who, after his death.) He kept his snare pretty "dry." This isn't a small thing. The three-piece jazz combo at your local hotel ballroom almost certainly features a "drummer" whose sticks are used so lightly that they barely embarrass the skins, and whose wet, buzzy snare sounds like a repeated sneeze. A good dry snare, properly struck, is a bark, a crack, a report. How a drummer hits the snare, and how it sounds, can determine a band's entire dynamic. Groups like Supertramp and the Eagles seem soft, in large part, because the snare is so drippy and mildly used (and not just because elves are apparently squeezing the singers' testicles).

There are three great albums by The Who, and these are also the three greatest Moon records: *Live at Leeds* (1970), a recording of an explosive concert at the University of Leeds on February 14, 1970, and generally considered one of the greatest live albums in rock; *Who's Next* (1971), the most famous Who album; and *Quadrophenia* (1973), a kind of successor to *Tommy*, a rock opera that nostalgically celebrates the sixties mod culture that had provoked and nourished the band in its earlier days. On these are such songs as "Substitute," "My Generation," "Won't Get Fooled Again," "Baba O'Riley," "Bargain," "The Song Is Over," "The Real Me," "5:15," "Sea and Sand," and "Love Reign O'er Me." There is no great difference between the live concert recordings and the studio songs: all of them are full of improvisation and structured anarchy, fluffs and misses; all of them seem to have the rushed gratitude of something achieved only once. From this exuberance emerges the second great principle of Moon's drumming; namely, that one is always performing, not recording, and that making mistakes is simply part of the locomotion of vitality. In the wonderful song "The Dirty Jobs," on *Quadrophenia*, you can hear Moon accidentally knock his sticks together three separate times while travelling around the kit. Most drummers would be horrified to be caught out on tape like this.

This vitality allowed Moon to try to shape himself to the changing dynamics of the music, listening as much to the percussive deviations of the bass line as to the steady, obvious line of the lead singer. As a result, it is impossible to separate him from the music that The Who made. The story goes that, in 1968, Jimmy Page wanted John Entwistle on bass and Keith Moon on drums when he formed Led Zeppelin; and, as sensational as this group might have been, it would not have sounded either like Led Zeppelin or like The Who. If Led Zeppelin's drummer, John Bonham, were substituted for Moon on "Won't Get Fooled Again," the song would lose its passionate propulsion, its wild excess; if Moon sat in for Bonham on "Good Times Bad Times," the tight stability of that piece would instantly evaporate.

Bonham's drumming sounds as if he'd thought about phrasing; he never overreaches, because he seems to have so perfectly measured the relationship between rhythmic order and rhythmic deviation. His superb but tightly limited breaks on the snare and his famously rapid double strokes on the bass drum are constantly played against the unvarying solidity of his high hat, which keeps a steady single beat throughout the bars. (In a standard 4/4 bar, the high hat sounds the four whole beats, or perhaps sounds eight beats in eighth notes.) That is "the Bonham sound," heard in the celebrated long solo—one of devilish intricacy—in "Moby Dick," on the live album *The Song Remains the Same*. Everything is judged, and rightly placed: astonishing order. Moon's drumming, by contrast, is about putting things in the wrong place: the appearance of astonishing disorder. You can copy Bonham exactly; but to copy Moon would be to bottle his energy, which is much harder.

The third great Moon principle, of packing as much as possible into a single bar of music, produces the extraordinary variety of his playing. He seems to be hungrily reaching for everything at once. Take, for instance, the bass drum and the cymbal. Generally speaking, drummers strike these with respectable monotony. You hit the crash cymbal at the end of a fill, as a flourish, but also as a kind of announcement that time-out has, boringly enough, ended, and that the beat must go back to work. Moon does something strange with both instruments. He tends to "ride" his bass drum: he keeps his foot hovering over the bass-drum pedal as a nervous driver might keep a foot on the brake, and strikes the drum often, sometimes continuously, throughout a bar. When he breaks to do a roll around the toms, he will keep the bass drum going simultaneously, so that the effect is of two drummers playing together. Meanwhile, he delights in hitting his cymbals as often as possible, and off the beat, rather as jazz and big-band drummers do. The effect, of all these cymbals being struck, is of someone shouting out at unexpected moments while waiting in line—a yammer of exclamation marks. (Whereas his habit of entering a song by first crashing a cymbal and then ripping around the kit is like someone bursting into a quiet room and shouting, "I'm here!")

So alive and free is this drumming that one tends to emphasize its exuberance at the expense of its complexity. But the playing on songs like "Won't Get Fooled Again" and "Bargain" and "Love Reign O'er Me" and "The Song Is Over" is extremely complex. In addition to demonstrating intricate cymbal work, Moon is constantly flicking off little triplets (sometimes on the toms, but sometimes with his feet, by playing the two bass drums together), and doing double-stroke rolls (a method by which, essentially, you bounce the sticks on the drum to get them to strike faster notes) and irregular flams on the snare drum (a flam involves hitting the drum with the two sticks not simultaneously but slightly staggered, and results in a sound more like "blat" than "that").

New technology allows listeners to isolate a song's individual players, and the isolated drum tracks from "Won't Get Fooled Again" and "Behind Blue Eyes" can be found on YouTube. On "Won't Get Fooled Again," the drumming is staggeringly vital, with Moon at once rhythmically tight and massively spontaneous. On both that song and "Behind Blue Eyes," you can hear him do something that was instinctive, probably, but which is hardly ever done in ordinary rock drumming: breaking for a fill, Moon fails to stop at the obvious end of the musical phrase and continues with his rolling break, over the line and into the start of the next phrase. In poetry, this failure to stop at the end of the line, this challenge to metrical closure, this desire to get more in, is called enjambment. Moon is the drummer of enjambment.

For me, this playing is like an ideal sentence, a sentence I have always wanted to write and never quite had the confidence to do: a long, passionate onrush, formally controlled and joyously messy, propulsive but digressively self-interrupted, attired but dishevelled, careful and lawless, right and wrong. Such a sentence would be a breaking out, an escape. And drumming has always represented for me that dream of escape, when the body surrenders its awful self-consciousness. I taught myself the drums, but for years I was so busy being a good boy that I lacked the courage to own any drums. At school, I played in a rock band, but I kept the fact very quiet. The kids I played rock music with did not overlap with the world of classical music. Drumming was a notional add-on, a supplement to the playing of "proper" instruments. The classical-music path was the scholastic path. Choir school was like being at conservatory—daily rehearsal and performance. And then, later, as a teenager, to work hard at the piano, to sing in the choir, to play the trumpet in a youth orchestra, to pass exams in music theory, to study sonata form in Beethoven, to sit for a music scholarship, to talk to one's parents about Bach (or, daringly, the Beatles!), to see the London Symphony Orchestra at the Albert Hall, even just to fall asleep during *Aida*—all this was approved, was part of being a good student. Nowadays, I see schoolkids bustling along the sidewalk, their large instrument cases strapped to them like coffins, and I know their weight of obedience. Happy obedience, too: that cello or French horn brings lasting joy, and a repertoire more demanding and subtle than rock music's. But fuck the laudable ideologies, as Roth's Mickey Sabbath puts it: subtlety is not rebellion, and subtlety is not freedom, and it is rebellious freedom that one wants, and, most of the time, only rock music can deliver it. And sometimes one despises oneself, in near-middle age, for being so good.

Georges Bataille has some haunting words about how the workplace is the scene of our domestication and repression: it is where we are forced to put away our Dionysianism. The crazy sex from the night before is as if forgotten; the drunken marital argument of the weekend is erased; the antic children have disappeared; all the passionate music of life is turned off, and a false bourgeois order clothes you, with the sack and quick penury waiting if you don't obey. But Bataille might also have emphasized school, for school is work, too—work before the adult workplace—and school tutors the adolescent in repression and the rectitude of the bourgeois order, at the very moment in life when, temperamentally and biologically, one is most Dionysiac and most enraged by the hypocritical ordinances of the parental league.

So adolescents quickly get split in two, with an inner and an outer self, a lawless sprite inside and a lawful ambassador outside: rock music, or your first sexual relationship, or reading, or writing poetry, or probably all four at once—why not?—represent the possibilities for inward escape. And playing rock is different again from playing classical music, or from writing poetry, or from painting. In all these other arts, though there may be trancelike moments and even stages of wildness and excess, the pressure of creating lasting forms demands discipline and silence; mindful of Pascal's severe aphorism about the importance of staying quietly in one's own room, one does just that, and stares at the sheet of paper, even if the words are not coming. Writing and reading still carry with them the faintest odor of the exam room. (It is exam-silent in the room where I write these words, and how terrible, in a way, is this disjunction between literary expression and the violence of its content.) Rock music, though, is noise, improvisation, collaboration, theatre, showing off, truancy, pantomime, aggression, bliss, tranced collectivity. It is not concentration so much as fission.

Imagine, then, the allure of The Who, whose battering velocity was such an incitement to the adolescent's demon sprite. "I'm wet and I'm cold, / But thank God I ain't old," young Roger Daltrey sang on *Quadrophenia*, in a track about a mod teenager (named Jimmy, no less) who gets thrown out of home:

> *Here by the sea and sand*
> *Nothing ever goes as planned*
> *I just couldn't face going home.*
> *It was just a drag on my own.*
> *They finally threw me out.*
> *My mum got drunk on stout.*
> *My dad couldn't stand on two feet*
> *As he lectured about morality.*

It is no accident that punk rock got a fair amount of its inspiration from The Who (the Sex Pistols often performed "Substitute"), or that, a generation later, a band like Pearl Jam devotedly covered "Love Reign O'er Me." Here was a band that, in one obvious way, embodied success, but that, in a less obvious way, dared failure—the large amount of improvisation in their songs, the risky, sometimes loose excess of their concert performances, the flailing earnestness of so many of the lyrics. And the epicenter of this successful failure, this man who wanted to pack as much of the fun stuff into his playing as humanly possible, was Keith Moon.

The Who was a kind of performance-art band: there was plenty of calculation amid the carelessness. Pete Townshend attended Ealing Art College (whose other musical students from the nineteen-sixties included Freddie Mercury and Ronnie Wood), and has sometimes claimed that the idea of smashing his guitar onstage was partly inspired by Gustav Metzger's auto-destructive-art movement. That high tone is quite Townshendian. But it is hard not to think of Keith Moon's life as a perpetual "happening"; a gaudy, precarious, self-destructing art installation, whose gallery placard reads "The Rock and Roll Life, Late Twentieth Century." In a manner that is also true of his drumming, he seemed to live at once naïvely and self-consciously: spontaneous in his scandalous misbehavior and yet also aware that this is how one should live if one is a famous and rich rock musician. His parody is very hard to separate from his originality; his parody is his originality. This is one of the most charming elements of his posture behind the drum kit: he is always clowning around—standing up sometimes, at other times puffing out his cheeks like Dizzy Gillespie, grimacing and grinning like a fool in some opera buffa, twirling his sticks, doing silly phantom rolls just above the skins of the drums. A child might think that Moon was a circus performer. His drumming, like his life, was a serious joke.

Nowadays, Moon would probably be classed as both ADHD. and bipolar; fortunately for the rest of us, he grew up in non-therapeutic Britain, and medicated himself with booze, illegal drugs, and illegal drumming. Tony Fletcher's entertaining biography *Moon: The Life and Death of a Rock Legend* (1999) is one of the most reliable sources for all the famous "Moon the Loon" stories. Born into a modest, working-class household, in north London, in 1946, Moon had a paltry education. He was restless and hyperactive, and often played to the gallery. An art teacher described him as "retarded artistically, idiotic in other respects," and the authorities were doubtless relieved when he left school at the age of fourteen. "You never felt, 'One day he is going to be famous,'" a friend tells Fletcher. "You felt more likely that he was going to end up in prison."

He had little formal training on the drums. As Gogol's brilliant prose or Richard Burton's swaggering acting embodies the temperamental exhibitionism of their creators, so Moon's playing is an extension of his theatrical hyperactivity. His mother noticed that he got bored easily, and quickly lost interest in his train set or Meccano. Throughout his short life, he was seemingly addicted to practical jokes: he set off cherry bombs in hotels, dressed up as Adolf Hitler or Noël Coward, rode a wheelchair down an airport staircase, smashed up hotel rooms, drove a car into a pond, got arrested for breaching the peace. On planes, Moon might do his "chicken soup" routine, which involved carrying a can of Campbell's chicken soup on board, emptying it, unseen, into a sick bag, and then pretending to retch violently. At which point he "would raise it, and pour the sicklike soup back into his mouth, offering up a hearty sigh of relief while innocently inquiring of fellow passengers what they found so disgusting." Fletcher captures the patient relentlessness of this theatricalism, which often needed preparation and forethought, and certainly demanded a kind of addicted commitment: "Keith wore the Nazi uniform like something of a second skin, donning it intermittently for the next six or seven years." His boozing and coke-snorting were certainly addictions, but perhaps they were merely the solvents needed to maintain the larger, primal addiction to joking and playacting.

Performance is a way of sublimely losing oneself, and there is a sense in which Moon as drummer was another role, alongside Moon as Hitler, Moon as Noël Coward, Moon as arsonist, Moon as sick-bag buffoon, and Moon as crazy rock star. ("I don't give a damn about a Holiday Inn room," he grandly said, after some act of vandalism. "There's ten million of them exactly the same.") But "role" suggests choice, freedom, calculation, whereas these roles don't seem to have been chosen so much as depended on. Or put it another way: despite all the gaiety and partying, the only performance that seems to have truly liberated Moon was the one he enacted behind the drum kit.

I often think of Moon and Glenn Gould together, notwithstanding their great differences. Both started performing very young (Moon was seventeen when he began playing with The Who, Gould twenty-two when he made his first great recording of the Goldberg Variations); both were idiosyncratic, revolutionary performers, for whom spontaneity was an important element (for instance, both enjoyed singing and shouting while playing); both had exuberant, pantomimic fantasy lives (Gould wrote about Petula Clark's "Downtown," and appeared on Canadian television in the guise of invented comic personae like Karlheinz Klopweisser and Sir Nigel Twitt-Thornwaite, "the dean of British conductors"); both were gregarious yet essentially solitary; neither man practiced much (at least, Gould claimed not to practice, and it is impossible to imagine Moon having the patience or the sobriety to do so); and all their performance tics (Gould's hand-washing and coat-wearing and pill-popping hypochondria) have the slightly desperate quality of mania. The performance behind the instrument, however, has the joyous freedom of true escape and self-dissolution: Gould becomes the piano, Moon becomes the drums.

For both Moon and Gould, the performer's life was short: Gould abandoned concert performance at the age of thirty-one; Moon was dead by the age of thirty-two, and had not played well for a long time. He had perhaps five or six really great drumming years, between 1970 and 1976. Throughout this period, Moon was ingesting ludicrous volumes of drink and drugs. There are stories of him swallowing twenty or thirty pills at once. In San Francisco, in 1973, he took so many (perhaps to come down from a high, or to deal with pre-concert nerves) that, after slopping his way through several songs, he collapsed and had to be taken to hospital. When his stomach was pumped, it was found to contain quantities of PCP, described by Fletcher as "a drug used to put agitated monkeys and gorillas to sleep." What magically happened onstage, while Moon was being carted away, was incised on my teenage cerebellum. Pete Townshend asked the crowd if anyone could come up and play the drums. Scot Halpin, a nineteen-year-old, and presumably soon to be the most envied teenager in America, got onto the stage, and performed in Moon's place. "Everything was locked into place," Halpin later said of the gargantuan drum kit; "anyplace you could hit there would be something there. All the cymbals overlapped."

Both Moon and Gould were rather delicate, even handsome young men who coarsened with age, and developed a thickness of feature, an almost simian rind. At twenty, Moon was slight and sweet, with a bowl of black hair upended on his head, and dark, dopey eyes, and the arched eyebrows of a clown. By the end of his life, he was puffy, heavy, his features no longer sweetly clownish but slightly villainous—Bill Sikes, played by Moon's old drinking friend Oliver Reed—the arched eyebrows now thicker and darker, seemingly painted on, as if he had become a caricature of himself. Friends were shocked by his appearance. He was slower and less inventive, less vital, on the drums; the album *Who Are You*, his last record, attests to the decline. Perhaps no one was very surprised when he died, from a massive overdose of the drug Heminevrin, a sedative prescribed for alcohol-withdrawal symptoms. "He's gone and done it," Townshend told Roger Daltrey. Thirty-two pills were in his stomach, and the equivalent of a pint of beer in his blood. His girlfriend, who found him, told a coroner's court that she had often seen him pushing pills down his throat, without liquid. Two years later, John Bonham died from asphyxiation, after hours of drinking vodka. And then English drumming went quiet.

There are two famous Glenn Gould recordings of "The Goldberg Variations": the one he made at the age of twenty-three, and the one he made at the age of fifty-one, just before he died. The opening Aria of that piece, the lucid, ornate melody that Gould made his own, sounds very different in each recording. In the young man's version, the Aria is fast, sweet, running clear like water. In the middle-aged man's recording, the Aria is half as fast, the notes so magnetically separated that they seem almost unrelated to one other. The first Aria is cocky, exuberant, optimistic, vital, fun, sound-filled; the second Aria is reflective, seasoned, wintry, grieving, silence-haunted. These two Arias stand facing each other, separated by almost thirty years, as the gates of a life. I prefer the second version; but when I listen to the second, how I want it to *be* the first!

Direction Nowhere

Nate Chinen

In the loosely related fields of planetary science and apocalyptic fiction, the phrase "minimum orbit intersection distance," or MOID, describes the closest point of contact between the paths of two orbiting objects. Most vividly invoked whenever an asteroid encroaches on our corner of the solar system, that bit of jargon also has its aesthetic uses. Consider the coordinates of Neil Young and Miles Davis on the evenings of March 6 and 7, 1970, at the juncture of East Sixth Street and Second Avenue in Manhattan.

That setting, cosmic only in culturally suggestive terms, was the Fillmore East, a New York outpost of Bill Graham's hippie empire. Young was the headliner, and Davis the opener. As far as we know, there was no particular spark of friction or connection between the two. But the musical evidence, even 40 years later, attests to the mysterious gravity of that moment. For all their differences—what you might inadvisably call their intersection distance—Young and Davis were both in the thrall of reinvention, pushing a distinctly contemporary, shrewdly cooperative agenda. It also happened that they were each in the midst of creative transition as they took the Fillmore stage.

Few musicians of any era have outdone Davis or Young when it comes to catalog savvy. For Davis, that development has been posthumous: the trumpeter died in 1991, just as the compact-disc reissue boom was getting under way. His music has since been endlessly repackaged and repurposed, and in some instances—like *Live at the Fillmore East (March 7, 1970): It's About That Time*, released by Sony Legacy in 2001—made commercially available for the first time. Last year Legacy put out what would seem to be a culminating gesture: *The Complete Columbia Album Collection*, spanning 70 discs.

Young's camp released a fetish object of their own in 2009: *Neil Young Archives Volume 1 (1963–1972)*, a 10-DVD or Blu-Ray set consisting of obscurities, rarities and assorted other flotsam from a roughly half-century career. Among its bounty is the concert recording that was also released, in more standard form, as *Live at the Fillmore East* on Reprise in 2006. The material was assembled with active participation from Young, who had ample reason to reflect fondly on the Fillmore shows.

At that time, he was on tour with Crazy Horse: Danny Whitten on guitar, Billy Talbot on bass and Ralph Molina on drums. Not quite a year earlier they had released their first album, *Everybody Knows This Is Nowhere*. Young had spent much of his time since toiling as the final consonant in CSNY: Crosby, Stills, Nash and Young, the supergroup whose album *Déjà Vu* would be issued within a week of Young's Fillmore East shows, delivering what *Billboard* hailed as "a skill and sensitivity bound to be the measure of excellence in rock for 1970."

Whatever he thought of such proclamations, Young felt the call to work with musicians who upheld what you might call different aesthetic aspirations than CSN. Their raggedness was not entirely planned. Young himself has said: "With Crazy Horse it's such a special thing, because none of us can really play. We know we aren't any good. Fuck, we'd get it in the first take every time, and it was never right—but we could never do it better." That's overstating the case a bit, as his own solos at the Fillmore would demonstrate. But there *is* something to his assertion of anti-virtuosity. Long before Crazy Horse, he was a skinny kid with a nervous voice, the embodiment of vulnerability. After a session with his Winnipeg high school band, the Squires, the engineer complimented his guitar playing but said he'd never make it as a singer.

Which somewhat implausibly brings us to Miles Davis, a trumpeter long appraised in jazz circles more in terms of resourcefulness than proficiency. Gary Giddins has credited him with "a thoroughly original style built on the acknowledgement of technical limitations." The conservative orthodoxy often compares Davis unfavorably to Dizzy Gillespie or Clifford Brown, which is not unlike saying Neil Young was no Stephen Stills.

In a 1993 essay, musicologist Robert Walser analyzed the most notoriously flawed performance of the Miles Davis canon, a 1964 rendition of "My Funny Valentine," and argues that Davis had mastered the process of signifyin' famously articulated by Henry Louis Gates. To really hear what he's saying, you have to dislodge standard notions of legitimacy, or spike them with the awareness of an alternative technique. To that end, perhaps the most striking analogue between Miles Davis and Neil Young, or just the most obvious, is the fact that both artists make expressive and powerful use of an instrument regarded in some circles, even now, as imperfect.

Listen to the sprawling version of "Down by the River" that anchors *Live at the Fillmore East*, and you'll hear that voice, along with that of a partner, Danny Whitten. The ringleader of Crazy Horse before it was Crazy Horse—that is, when it was the Rockets—Whitten *was* a good singer, in the conventional sense. He was also an excellent guitarist, especially in this context. Young once pegged him this way:

> A really great second guitar player, the perfect counterpoint to everything else that was happening. So sympathetic. So unthoughtful. And just so natural. That's really what made "Cowgirl in the Sand" and "Down by the River" happen—Danny's guitar parts. Nobody played guitar with me like that—that rhythm.

The Fillmore tapes represent the only known live document of Whitten with Crazy Horse. Soon after this tour, heroin addiction ended his tenure in the band and, within a couple of years, his life.

This drama played out famously in song: first, "Come on Baby Let's Go Downtown," a set opener at the Fillmore East featuring Whitten's soulful lead vocal. Then Young singing "The Needle and the Damage Done," never more nakedly than in the acoustic solo version caught on the recently released 1971 Massey Hall concert.

Young's description of Whitten is telling. Sympathetic. Natural. These are the attributes of a certain kind of intuitive virtuoso, an "unthoughtful" one. You often hear similar descriptions of jazz musicians. Young locates Whitten's ability as a component force, "the perfect counterpoint." His artistry, in other words, functioned best as a catalyst. In the same interview, Young goes on to say, "When I played these long guitar solos, it seemed like they weren't all that long, that I was making all these changes, when in reality what was changing was not one thing, but the whole band. Danny was the key."

Jazz discourse is full of theorizing about the expression of the self within a collective: Ralph Ellison put it succinctly in his famous formulation about "an art of individual assertion within and against the group." For his part, Young has recalled that it was during a 1970 CSNY tour that he grew obsessed with the John Coltrane Quartet, hiding in his hotel room with cassettes of *Equinox* and *My Favorite Things*. "I used to listen to that shit all the time," he said, adding: "The bass player was really good." The fact that Young's appreciation includes a special nod to Steve Davis may help explain why he isn't often lumped together with the other rockers who valorized Coltrane at this time. Unlike Carlos Santana or Duane Allman, he didn't fixate on the heroic and suggestively spiritual solo voice, but the cohesive and hypnotic properties of the group.

Speaking of which, Davis also came to the Fillmore East with a working cohort: saxophonist Wayne Shorter, keyboardist Chick Corea, bassist Dave Holland, drummer Jack DeJohnette. Also on hand was percussionist Airto Moreira, who had been present the previous year for the recording of *Bitches Brew*. That album was issued in April, one month after the Fillmore stand. So Miles was not yet the hero that he would become to this crowd; *Cashbox* reported that most of the kids waited out his set in the lobby. This was the trumpeter's first-ever performance explicitly for a rock audience. He had been cajoled into playing there by Clive Davis, his label head at CBS. (The cajoling probably had a lot to do with the opening slot.)

Jazz-rock was not a brand-new development, and Miles was no naïf. A year and a half earlier he had recorded "Mademoiselle Mabry," an adaptation of "The Wind Cries Mary," by Jimi Hendrix. That song was dedicated to a mutual acquaintance, Betty Mabry, who married Miles six days after the tune was recorded, and graced the cover of the album on which it appeared. (She has enjoyed a recent reissue revival of her own.)

Almost 20 years Davis's junior, Mabry led him by the hand into a new social circle, one that included Hendrix and Sly Stone. Abruptly, he abandoned Brooks Brothers for bell-bottoms, opening the door to what Robin Kelly has called "the pimp aesthetic." Musically, the shift was more methodical, as a trove of Legacy reissues has underscored.

His most recent album at this time was *In a Silent Way*, a bated-breath sound collage that has about as much in common with rock as it does with jazz. (Not much, in other words.) The composer of that album's title track also wrote "Directions," the song that opened every set at the Fillmore East. His name was Joe Zawinul, and together with Wayne Shorter, he would lead Weather Report. That '70s fusion flagship was just preparing to sail: the Fillmore East marked Shorter's last gig as a member of Davis's band. (You can hear him in incipient Weather Report mode on "Spanish Key.")

Personnel-wise, it was becoming a difficult stretch for Davis. His 1960s quartet, one of the finest-ever jazz ensembles, had splintered. Its slipstream post-bop had matured past its prime, as Davis had been forced to admit. So where to go next? He had no great regard for the avant-garde scramble of the era, which Corea and Holland would soon explore vigorously in a band called Circle. (Those interests crept into the Fillmore sets; check their conspiratorial glee on "Directions," from 6:30 on.)

Quite the contrary: in his memoir, Miles recalls yearning for the sound of the Muddy Waters band, because his own music had grown so "abstracted." This jibes with Greg Tate's suggestion that the trumpeter "left post-bop modernism for the funk because he was bored fiddling with quantum mechanics and just wanted to play the blues again."

The blues proposed a complicated racial dynamic for Davis. "Let the white folks have the blues," he had told Herbie Hancock as the end of the '60s loomed. "They got 'em, so they can keep 'em." In 1969 he told *Rolling Stone*: "All the white groups have got a lot of hair and funny clothes. They got to have on that shit to get it across."

"But," he added in the same interview, "Jimi Hendrix can take two white guys and make them play their asses off. You got to have a mixed group: one has one thing, and the other has another. For me, a group has to be mixed." One can only imagine how Davis might have vibed with Jack Nitzsche, who played keyboards with Crazy Horse at the Fillmore East, and later made the assertion that Danny Whitten "gave Neil the blackness he lacks." Race was rarely far from Miles's mind during this era, but it probably loomed larger on this night than most. He had lately been fretting about how to reach young black audiences, and only one of those adjectives applied broadly to this Fillmore crowd.

And he was probably still seething from a fresh indignation. On March 3, a few days before this concert, Miles was sitting in his red Ferrari in a no-standing zone on Central Park South. Reportedly he was with a young woman, and he was dressed in a turban, a sheepskin coat and cobra-skin pants. An officer approached and asked for his registration. Somehow a pair of brass knuckles was discovered, and Miles, booked on a weapons violation, spent the night in jail. Later he told *Newsweek*: "It wouldn't have happened if I hadn't been a black man driving a red car."

What, then, to make of Davis opening for Young? Would he have been upset about playing an opening set for one of those all-white rock bands? There's always danger in ascribing intentions to art, but the trumpet playing on *It's About That Time* is slashing and aggressive, almost confrontationally virile. (The album *Jack Johnson*, when it landed, would echo this quality.) And yet it's more than possible that Davis heard something appealing in Young's music. Three months earlier, he had recorded a group hallucination on David Crosby's

"Guinevere," which would go unreleased until 1979. And if Miles heard something redeeming in CSNY, he might have done the same with just the Y, despite—or maybe because of—the rugged musical vocabulary of the accompaniment.

And what did Neil get from Miles? It's just as hard to say. His method of recording in the next few years would come to resemble Davis's in its shambling, say-nothing, capture-everything intensity. He even had his Teo Macero in the producer David Briggs. But if Young was taken with Davis, he didn't say much about it. He had plenty else on his mind, including an increasingly unmanageable Whitten, whose strong delivery at the Fillmore East—notwithstanding a few bum chords in "Wonderin'"—was deceptive.

Whitten would soon be cast out of Young's performing entourage, as Shorter would decamp from Davis's. Within a month, *Bitches Brew* would appear as if out of a haze, with a sound much cooler and more alluring than what was heard at the Fillmore East. Miles would usher in the album's release at the Fillmore West, sharing a bill with the Grateful Dead. (That gig would yield its own catalog release, in 1997.)

That was April; in May the Kent State shootings would prompt Young to write "Ohio." CSNY would perform it on each of their shows the following month, back at the Fillmore East. August comes. Miles performs at the Isle of Wight Festival. September: Neil releases *After the Gold Rush*. Their sounds had both changed more than once already, and would change again. Along the way there would be obsolescence and resurgence, and finally something like permanence. (When Davis was inducted into the Rock and Roll Hall of Fame in 2006, he once again joined the company of Young, a member since '95.)

It's almost strange to think that Neil Young and Miles Davis are icons of our culture, one stubborn and rumpled and the other truculent and proud. It's strange because each is a study in restless motion, fumbling forward with steady purpose. Which is perhaps the singular recommendation for this Fillmore testimony: It captures both artists at a pinpoint moment, spinning hard on their separate trajectories, each on his way to someplace else.

I Wish I Knew How It Would Feel to Be Free

The Secret Diary of Nina Simone

Joe Hagan

DISCUSSED: "Mississippi Goddam," Bertolt Brecht, Kurt Weill, Valium, Barack Obama's iPod, Juilliard, The Apollo Theater, The Ed Sullivan Show, Threatening Notes in Magic Marker, Private Hell

DON'T LET ME BE MISUNDERSTOOD

The door swung open and there she was: Nina Simone, alone in her dressing room, sweat cascading down her shaved head, a wig thrown to the floor and two glittering fake eyelashes mashed unceremoniously against the mirror.

It was after midnight and the compact and muscular woman radiated anger following a performance at the smoke-filled Village Gate in New York City. "She was scary, for sure," recounts playwright Sam Shepard, who during the summer of 1964 was a twenty-one-year-old busboy tasked with delivering ice to chill Simone's champagne.

Only moments before, her long fingers arched over a black Steinway, Simone held the audience rapt, even terrified. "Mississippi Goddam," her first bona fide protest song, had caused ripples across the country, especially in the South, which was roiling with racial unrest. And in her version of "Pirate Jenny," the Bertolt Brecht–Kurt Weill song about a beleaguered hotel maid who vows revenge when a pirate ship returns to liberate her, Simone added a biting pathos all her own.

> *And they're chainin' up people*
> *And they're bring'em to me*
> *Askin' me, "Kill them now, or later?"*
> *Askin' me!*
> *"Kill them now, or later?"*
> *[. . .]*
> *And in that quiet of death*
> *I'll say, "Right now . . . RIGHT NOW!"*

"It was absolutely devastating to watch," says Shepard. "It was a real performance as well as just being something heard."

During the riveting and historic concerts Shepard witnessed that summer, Simone was herself devastated, descending into a terrible darkness. "Must take sleeping pills to sleep + yellow pills to go on-stage," she wrote in July 1964, referring to Valium. "Terribly tired and realize *no one* can help me—I am utterly miserable, completely, miserably, frighteningly *alone*."

Every night after her shows that summer, Simone drove home to Mount Vernon, New York, a leafy suburb of Manhattan where prominent blacks were living at the time, including Malcolm X. There, unknown to anyone save her husband, she kept a small, leather-bound diary, inscribed, "This book belongs to Eunice Waymon," Simone's given name growing up in rural North Carolina. While she electrified audiences in Greenwich Village that night, a musical icon in the making, she struggled privately with mental illness, likely bipolar disorder. In the 1960s, that diagnosis didn't exist, so Simone was left to manage her erratic moods in any way she could: psychoanalysis, hypnosis, drugs, sex, and, ultimately, writing.

"Now we have names for that shit," says Shepard. "Back then nobody had names for it, nobody was categorizing it. It was part and parcel of what it meant to be an artist."

By turns luridly raw and heartbreaking, Simone's diary and letters illuminate her defining years as an artist, before she left the U.S. in 1972 for an itinerant life overseas, a single mother and divorcee, broke and wildly unstable. It's the period when she first embraced protest music against a backdrop of crushing self-doubt and ambiguous sexual identity. For every step she took toward personal freedom, drawn to the liberation ideologies of the 1960s, her dream of wider acceptance slipped further from reach.

"*I can't be white* and I'm the kind of colored girl who looks like everything white people despise or have been taught to despise," she wrote in an undated note to herself. "If I were a boy, it wouldn't matter so much, but I'm a girl and in front of the public all the time wide open for them to jeer and approve of or disapprove of."

Simone's music has survived the decades precisely because of how strange and impossible to categorize it seemed forty years ago. The oddly masculine register of her voice, its raw quaver, was and is an acquired taste. Years later, it's more obvious how, in the absorbing melancholy and pained beauty of her early songs, she was channeling the sexual and racial searching of the era, which is why she's since become both a gay and black icon. In 2008, Barack Obama named Simone's "Sinnerman" among the top ten tracks on his iPod, prompting Sony to quickly release the boxed set *To Be Free: The Nina Simone Story*. Contemporary artists like M.I.A. and Antony Hegarty, breakers of ethnic and sexual barriers, have cited her as a crucial inspiration. The first authoritative biography of Simone, Nadine Cohodas's *Princess Noire: The Tumultuous Reign of Nina Simone*, appeared in 2010. And a biopic called *Nina* is being made with Mary J. Blige cast in the title role.

Simone's ex-husband Andrew Stroud, a cantankerous man of eighty-four living in the Bronx, has rarely spoken about his nine-year marriage to the famed songstress in the '60s, and never before given access to his cache of Simone's writings. He refused to talk to Simone's biographer. But after a year of cajoling, Stroud agreed to open up for this story, if only to help sell a small catalog of CDs and DVDs he's packaged from home movies and leftover recordings. He has kept Simone's papers in pristine condition, though loosely organized. Many notes had to be dated from the content of the material; some could be pegged only to a general period. But what is immediately striking is how lucid and candid Nina Simone could be, how easily she could tap her emotions in writing, and how, occasionally, she seemed to take great solace in getting thoughts on paper, often in her most desperate hours. Having studied at an all-girls boarding school as a teenager, she had flawless grammar and spelling. And at her most self-aware moments, her language is informed by psychiatry, a result of time spent in therapy in the late '50s and early '60s.

But the tumult of her life just as often leaves her scratching for the barest clarity, entering raw fragments and ideas, drugs she consumed, the sex she had the night before. When she's happy, her writing is in a lovely, flowing cursive; when depressed, a sloppy chicken-scratch. And when her mania has reached a critical mass, she defaults to large printed letters, virtual billboards that scream from the page.

I LOVES YOU, PORGY

"Did you come in here to hear me sing or come here to talk?" seethed Nina Simone, halting midway through a song at Abart's Lounge, a jazz club in Washington, D.C. It was the late 1950s and the mixed-race crowd watching her on a stage behind the bar went stone silent. "I want it quiet when I sing, goddammit!"

In the crowd was a young Vernon Jordan, future head of the National Urban League and Bill Clinton's lawyer in the 1990s. "When she was performing, it really pissed her off if somebody was having a conversation," he recalls. "I was a great fan. I loved it when she would say, 'Shut the fuck up!'"

It was a shocking display of impropriety from a female entertainer, especially a black woman, but this was Simone's reputation from the start. She was considered eccentric. A 1960 profile in *Rogue* magazine noted that she was "painfully fragile . . . sliding back and forth between a sulkiness bordering on the moribund and frenetic, fleeting ecstasies of happiness."

What inspired her outbursts was less overt racial anger than a desire for the decorum and dignity she associated with classical music. It had been her escape from poverty in Tryon, North Carolina, where she was born in 1933, her mother a stern country minister, her father a handyman who played guitar. At fourteen, Simone began piano lessons with a white British teacher in town whose neighbor had discovered her while Simone's mother cleaned the neighbor's house. Simone, who had played only church hymns to that point, immediately fell in love with Bach. Her white benefactors raised money to send her to the Juilliard School in New York in the summer of 1950. After one semester, however, Simone's money ran out and she moved to Philadelphia, where her family had relocated, to try entering the prestigious Curtis Institute of Music for more piano studies.

To her dismay, she was rejected. For years, she would believe it was because of her skin color, though she later learned that other black students were accepted. But it was a fortuitous rejection: Forced to give music lessons to earn a living, she met college students who encouraged her to play pop music in nightclubs, starting with the Midtown Bar in Atlantic City. It was there she first tried interpreting jazz standards as "Nina Simone," the made-up name she used to avoid her mother discovering her alternative life.

"All my life I've felt the terrible pressure of having to survive," she told *Rogue*. "Now I've got to get rich . . . very, very rich so I can buy my freedom from fear and know I'll have enough to make it."

Typical of Simone was a 1961 show at New York's Apollo Theater, when she refused to perform to a packed house until she was paid in cash. When told the money was in an envelope on the piano, Simone walked onstage to wild cheers, only to sit down and count the money out, bill by bill. Satisfied, she got up to take it backstage but fell backward over her piano bench, eliciting roars of laughter and applause.

"Don't applaud! Don't applaud!" she screamed. Al Schackman, Simone's main guitar player for forty-four years, recounts that when some in the audience replied, "We love you, Nina!" Simone shrieked, "No, you don't! You don't love me!" and scrambled offstage. She returned minutes later as if nothing had happened and played a full set.

Simone first gained notoriety in 1959 with her take on George Gershwin's "I Loves You, Porgy," singing the song as if it were her own private confession. She told interviewers she meant it to be about the man she'd just married, a white beatnik named Don Ross whom she met in New York but would divorce after a year. The success of that hit led to appearances on *The Ed Sullivan Show* and won her prominent fans like James Baldwin and Langston Hughes, the latter calling her "strange" and "far out" in a paean published in the *Chicago Defender*.

At age twenty-eight, when her diary begins, Simone had an apartment on Central Park West, furnished with a baby-grand Steinway, and drove a steel-gray convertible Mercedes Benz 220 SE with a red leather interior and matching suitcases in the trunk. She had her crooked teeth capped in gleaming white. (She never smiled in her early publicity shots.) On sunny afternoons she drove to Greenwich Village to go shopping with her best friend, Kevin, a black female prostitute who had educated Simone in the ways of fashion and men. Simone's nights were now spent in clubs, especially the Village Gate, an upscale jazz and folk venue fast becoming a hub for a cultural renaissance: Richard Pryor, Bill Cosby, and Woody Allen all performed there, opening for Nina Simone.

By 1961, however, with no new hits and her career sagging, Simone was having more trouble convincing club owners to book her, because of her confrontational style. What happened next would define her life and art in the 1960s: a chance meeting with an unlikely suitor named Andrew Stroud, a swaggering police detective from Harlem.

Stroud was about as powerful a black man as one could find in New York at the time. Having risen in the force after cracking a major jewel-theft case in 1954, he was notorious for taking bribes, beating up petty criminals, and consorting with the Mafia figures who ran the nightclubs. He cut a handsome, if roguish, profile. Light-skinned and barrel-chested, he had a pencil-thin mustache, wore tailored suits, and carried a .38 pistol, which he was not shy about brandishing.

In March 1961, at a New York supper club called the Roundtable, a mutual friend introduced Stroud to the lanky, exotic chanteuse, who slyly pinched a french fry from his dinner plate as they talked. Stroud drove her uptown to the Lenox Lounge, a hub for Harlem's elite, and bought her drinks. A love affair ensued. Stroud recounts the first time he sat down next to Simone at her piano, hip to hip, shoulder to shoulder, in her apartment. She began playing "When I Fall in Love," a hit made famous by Nat King Cole.

"It felt like I was sitting next to a furnace," he remembers. "There was all this energy and quivering, and [when] she sang and got into the song, all this feeling came out, the heat and whatnot—I've never experienced anything like that before."

For Stroud, a frustrated musician who had played jazz trumpet in the navy, Simone was a mysterious creature, his first introduction to the Greenwich Village renaissance, where racial and sexual barriers were fast melting away. Simone took him to her regular hangout, Trude Heller's, a jazz club frequented by women Stroud describes as having short hair, large muscles, and wearing men's pants.

Even as she dated men, Simone had an obvious affinity for assertive women and was also greatly beloved by gay men. Coming from a traditional Southern upbringing, she was ambivalent about gay identity her whole life, even though her greatest friends, like Baldwin and Hughes, were homosexual, as was her first devoted fan in Philadelphia, Ted Axelrod, a college student and clubgoer who introduced her to Billie Holiday and "I Loves You, Porgy." Simone's sexuality seems to have been fluid, and some former associates, like Al Schackman, insist Simone had female lovers, pointing to her relationship with Kevin. (Stroud says Simone supported Kevin with a fifty-dollar weekly allowance.)

The strange men and women who streamed in and out of Simone's life threatened Stroud's ego, even while he hid from her that he himself was married and had two sons (his wife had tried to scald him with a bucket of lye when she found Simone's lipstick on a shirt). That summer, while dancing at the Palladium, Stroud, drunk on rum, accused Simone of sneaking away for a tryst and began beating her on the drive home. The beating continued on the street after they parked uptown. When Simone ran for a passing policeman, the man saw the higher-ranking Stroud and backed off. "I can't help you, lady," he said. The beating continued in her apartment, where Stroud aimed his gun at Simone's face and threatened her life. (He claims there were no bullets in it.)

Some accounts have claimed Stroud raped Simone that night, but he denies it. In any case, Simone escaped to Schackman's apartment, her face beaten and her eye swollen shut. "He hurt me bad," she cried. "He hurt me bad."

When Stroud saw Simone's face several days later, he claimed not to remember what had happened, blaming the rum. But even as he asked for forgiveness, he also demanded Simone stop consorting with people he deemed intent on manipulating her (including her psychiatrist). "I got rid of the gay crowd and the hangabouts," he says. "I made that part of the deal: you want to be serious, you want to be steady, you've got to be straight."

From her letters, it's clear she was deeply in love with Stroud, perhaps because he brought an iron-willed order to her mercurial emotional life and drifting career. In the summer of 1961, Simone was scheduled to play club dates in Philadelphia when she came down with an unspecified illness, thought to be meningitis. Stroud proposed marriage while she lay in the hospital bed. After saying yes, Simone spent the rest of her month-long stay writing love letters. "Maybe it's your eyes, Andy," she wrote in July 1961. "I don't know what it is, but I like giving to you. . . . I feel like you are a bottomless well that I can pour water into endlessly and it would never be all you needed or wanted . . . and you're so gentle—you're my gentle lion, my saint Bernard and sometimes my stud bull! (And sometimes bully.)"

In another letter, she wrote, "I pray we'll be together till death."

MISSISSIPPI GODDAM

A psychiatrist told Nina Simone to make lists of all the good things in her life as a way of warding off depression. And so her diary opens with a description of the three-story house she and Stroud bought after getting married, in December 1961.

"The trees, green grass, all the little flowers, apple tree, cherry trees, the vacant spot where greens should be growing," she wrote. "How about that, Nina! $50,000 worth of house. That's really something. So much I'll have to get used to—so many good things! I even got fountains in the yard that just need hooking up. Two cars: 1 nigger, 1 classy (paid for, too). My own room that's big enough for all my stuff and neat beside. And I don't have to feel guilty about it and I don't have to share it."

From the start, Stroud saw Simone as his ticket to a better life. And Simone, though she hated performing every night, believed in his vision for her. If they had had money, she wrote in December 1962, "I'd be *twice* as free as I am now—And you know what that means, Daddy!: Pancakes in the morning, diet food in the P.M. and loving at night."

That year, Stroud decided to retire early from the police force, firing Simone's lawyer and taking over as her manager. A quick study, Stroud had learned the music business from famed jazz writer and record producer Nat Shapiro, whom he'd befriended while Simone played the Village Gate. Stroud drew up a new contract with nightclub owners promising Simone would forfeit her pay if she attacked the audience, which helped expand her bookings. But Simone wanted to escape the clubs altogether for classier venues. So to prove himself, Stroud promised to fulfill her childhood fantasy of starring at

Carnegie Hall, ostensibly as the first black classical piano player to appear there. (They didn't realize that Hazel Scott had already beaten her to it, in the 1940s.)

To pay for it, Stroud cashed out his police pension of six thousand dollars and used it to promote a performance at Carnegie Hall on April 12, 1963. It was recorded by Colpix, Simone's record label, and released that same year. Though the album didn't yield any hits, it shored up Simone's optimism. On July 5, 1963, Simone wrote to Stroud: "Today (as I was playing the piano) it occurred to me how thankful I should be for all that I have—all of a sudden, I could see just over the hill and I knew that all my alleged big problems were going to be solved so soon now."

But there was still the issue of Stroud's regular beatings. "Those I can't take," she wrote in the same letter. "For some reason they destroy everything within me—my confidence, my warmth and my spirit! And when that happens I just feel that I must kill or be killed—you know how I just about lost my mind the last time."

In late 1962, Simone had given birth to her only child, a daughter named Lisa Celeste. Stroud wouldn't allow Simone to breastfeed the baby, telling her he was jealous. Perhaps inevitably, Simone began spending more time with a woman who would alter her worldview: Lorraine Hansberry, the activist and playwright who wrote *A Raisin in the Sun* and who authored "The Movement," the handbook for the Student Nonviolent Coordinating Committee (SNCC). The two spent weekends together at Hansberry's country home in Westchester County, outside Manhattan, talking for hours about black identity and revolutionary politics, which had held little interest for Simone in the past. "Lorraine carried her over into high gear, put her on fire," Stroud says. After meeting Hansberry one afternoon, Simone asked him to help locate the basin that fed water to New York City. "Why?" he asked. Because, she declared, "We've got to go poison the reservoir!"

At the time, Stroud never suspected Simone of sleeping with Hansberry, and there's no proof the two were lovers (Simone never records anything about gay affairs in her writings). Nikki Giovanni, the gay black poet and a close friend of Simone's in the late '60s, says, "What is important is that she loved her and she was loved in return. She never had to watch her back. With Andy, she watches her back."

Her passion for politics was fully catalyzed by the murder of civil rights activist Medgar Evers on June 12, 1963, followed by the Mississippi church bombing that killed four black schoolgirls two months later. Ablaze with anger, she sat at her piano and wrote "Mississippi Goddam" in an afternoon. She recorded it in the spring of 1964, her first single on her new record label, Philips. The song was an immediate sensation with students and activists, but riled her traditional audience. A crate of records was mailed back to the label, each one broken in half.

Thus began Simone's struggle to reconcile her musical career and her conscience as an activist. She immediately saw her audience divide after "Mississippi Goddam," between upper-club regulars and the new crowd emerging on college campuses. The choice seemed literally to hurt Simone.

"I wish I could *really* consider it work and just do a job and not care," she wrote in her diary in August 1964. "The truth is *I'm not* on the *same* circuit as the typical American audience. I *can't* reach them unless I turn myself inside out! And sometimes it takes too much energy. And then I *feel so hurt* that they don't get me. Maybe if I thought of myself as Lenny Bruce, it wouldn't hurt so much."

She concludes, "Maybe I'll have to get so hard that I don't care at all. Then there'll be NO hope for me. And I don't want to reach that point."

That same month, after weeks of depression following the Village Gate shows that Shepard witnessed, Simone found a spark of determination to forge ahead. "I mustn't stop," she wrote. "There's Dinah [Washington] + Billie [Holiday] who died without the world knowing what they said. Can the world know what I'm *saying* while I *live*? Maybe not the whole world, Nina, but most of it—I believe it. The world knows what the Beatles are saying—the kids do—I must save the older ones.

"And I must not start regretting what has passed," she ends, after switching from pencil to blue pen. "Everything must be new."

The music was both her wound and her salve. She complained constantly of being overbooked by Stroud, even while craving a radio hit and the money to maintain an upper-class lifestyle. A pragmatist, Stroud saw the "message" music as the problem, not the solution. Songs like "Pirate Jenny," performed as harrowing threats and sometimes punctuated with curses, shocked crowds at Carnegie Hall. "She'd get to a certain part—'Kill them now or kill them later?'—and people, families who brought their children, you'd see them leave," says Schackman. "Kids were crying. Oh, they couldn't take it."

Stroud urged her to show her support through private donations to Martin Luther King's organization and others. "I had promised to get her over and get her things she wanted," says Stroud. "She wanted nice things—she wanted to move the house over and put in a swimming pool—and I said, Yeah, but you can't get it with 'Mississippi Goddam.' I said, If you would listen, if you would go out there and stroke the audience, we could get on these big TV shows for exposure, into Vegas in some of the big rooms."

And even as Simone reveled in her newfound sense of purpose, talking eloquently to reporters about her desire to "reflect the times" in her art, she grew bitter watching younger rivals like Aretha Franklin and Roberta Flack (who was imitating Simone's style) get appearances on late-night talk shows, soaking up the fame that she felt was her due.

Her erratic moods caused her to throw herself at Stroud's mercy one minute, rage against him the next. His prescriptions were limited. "Andy suggested pot every day for a while," she wrote in her diary. Elsewhere she wrote: "Andrew told me whenever I get depressed I should have sex again right then and say 'fuck it' to the depression."

Sex became her primary refuge. In her diary, she documented it obsessively, desperate for "the only thing that allows me to be an open and warm human being." She connected sex directly to her music. "Yesterday," she wrote in an undated entry, "I learned where the source of power is for my performances (the love songs are the best) so all my concentration is centered there, drawn out to a blunt statement about sex at the end."

But Stroud, a man with limited patience and zero interest in psychology, often lashed out in frustration at her unpredictable temperament. Simone wrote on August 6, 1964: "Andrew hit me last night (swollen lip) of course it was what I need after so many days of depression. I wish I had someplace to go (I wish I had some hope). All the motherfucker did was get me off him; it still leaves me with the same fucking problem—he actually thinks I *want* to be hit (he told me so). He believes like old-fashioned black men that I need beating up once in a while. The fool believes I like it—there are milder forms of discipline." (Stroud is hardly contrite: "I'm the type of guy, I don't take any shit off of anybody.")

Four days later, in another letter to Stroud, Simone explained that she had a compulsion toward violence herself, one ultimately driven by her own career, which seemed to sap her of life: "I must hurt someone—I can't help it—I'm also pushed too far. The value of a psychiatrist was he was paid to take my shit. . . . I didn't need him for the reasons I thought but work most of the time is like a deadly poison seeping into my brain, undoing all the progress I've made, causing me not to see the sun in the daytime, not to smile, not to want to get dressed, not to care about anything except death—and death to my childish mind is simply escaping into the unconscious."

During this period, Stroud checked Simone into Columbia Presbyterian Hospital for testing, trying to diagnose her depression. According to Stroud, "They had conducted every known test on the books at the time and had not been able to pinpoint anything." (In the late 1970s she would begin lithium treatment.)

In the fall of 1964, Simone recorded a dream, with images that suggest her underlying struggle: "I lost my way, looking for a flash light, next thing I know, there are animals—first a bear, then slightly familiar creatures like a puma, a skunk and the one which attacked me was like a miniature giraffe, but wild and heavier—it was tearing into my arms as I awakened."

That winter, she cracked the *Billboard* charts for the first time since 1959 with "Don't Let Me Be Misunderstood," written by professional songsmiths for her album.

I PUT A SPELL ON YOU

In January of 1965, Lorraine Hansberry died following a long battle with cancer. After the funeral, a numb Simone wrote a sparse entry in her diary: "She's gone from me and I'm sure it'll take like many years to accept this thing. It's so far out."

The next day, she and Stroud departed for a Caribbean cruise. Simone was despondent. "The rocking + rolling of the ship almost made me scream with pain," she wrote. "The thought of suicide returned briefly—I felt so hemmed in—didn't sleep at all—hated Andy + everyone—it occurred to me in my pain what Gerry [her psychiatrist in Philadelphia in the late 1950s] said years ago, 'I can't take disappointment.'"

She groped for answers: "I stole a book about psychic power which could be of tremendous use if I'd use it seriously," she wrote. "Perhaps I shall."

Her next single, recorded that same month and released in June 1965, would be a cover of Screamin' Jay Hawkins's "I Put a Spell on You."

The year 1965, says Stroud, marked an existential turning point for Simone, when she began regularly talking of suicide. "I can't beat the poverty, the inferiority complex, the sex *and* show business," she wrote from an unidentified dressing room. "It's like I came here whole and slowly through the years, I've wasted away to almost nothing—pretend you're happy when you're blue—pieces taken out of me hunk by hunk, slowly but surely—paying for whatever help I got with my blood—doing *anything* to be accepted (anything) and the tragedy of not being accepted after all—not accepting myself—I can't stand to look at myself in the mirror anymore—I can't stand the sight.

"But then," she concludes, "why haven't I killed myself?"

That spring, Simone had canceled a series of dates at the Village Gate to attend the civil rights march in Montgomery, Alabama, led by Martin Luther King Jr. On March 24, she had performed on a stage propped up by caskets donated by several local black-owned funeral homes, mingling with the likes of Mike Nichols and Elaine May, Dick Gregory, and Sammy Davis Jr. That evening, Simone met King for the first time. According to Al Schackman, Simone reached out her hand to King as he approached and loudly declared, "I'm *not* nonviolent!" King, momentarily taken aback, said gently, "Not to worry, sister." Simone softened, put out her hand and purred, "I'm so glad to meet you."

She was moved by the event, but Stroud wasn't, sensing Simone's commercial prospects dimming. Afterward, they went home to Mount Vernon and fought bitterly. In a fit of rage, Simone demanded sex from Stroud, as she often did, this time reveling in a new feeling of liberation from the "old fashioned black male." When Stroud rejected her advances, she wrote, "I lost complete control of myself and let loose with anger that had me screaming out the window, shrieking. I felt the freedom of anger—in complete confidence. I put on my diaphragm and told myself that I was going down to the house [from the guest house where she had retreated] and would kill him if he didn't appear—he appeared—we had a lovely time and fell asleep exhausted."

Even as she fought him, Simone constantly looked to Stroud for assurance. Some higher success was always out of reach. In 1964 and '65, she recorded the songs for *Let It All Out*, a commercial pop album that would emphasize romantic standards over protest music, including two songs written by Stroud himself. In the spring of 1965, Simone wrote, "Andy just informed me while I'm feeling sorry for myself in not having a hit record I should remember: the Supremes, the Impressions, Gale Garnett, even Peter Seeger—(these people make 1/2 what I do a night!), so even though I don't have hits, I command fees and respect that these other folks don't."

In July, Simone went on her first European tour, something she'd longed to do. It was a revelation. For the first time, Simone saw rock groups mimicking black music, including the Animals and the Rolling Stones. "All the music is negro," she wrote to her brother Sam Waymon on July 15. "We're bringing back an album of some kids who sound very negro. And one night the Animals (the rock + roll group that recorded my "Don't Let Me Be Misunderstood") took us to a dance hall that was just like all the old swinging negro halls where they danced . . . all the old dances that we used to do plus the new ones these kids do. . . . We're treated so beautifully here."

Simone was a sensation in Paris, too, where she was lauded by French singing star Jacques Brel for her interpretation of his hit "Ne Me Quitte Pas," which she had recorded the previous January. Afterward, Simone made a list of things she wanted to accomplish when she returned to the United States, penned on Air France letterhead. It fairly sums up Nina Simone in 1965: "Take French lessons, go swimming a lot, buy Langston Hughes books, get high, hire a girl once a week to take care of your clothes (sew, clean, organize closets), find a psychiatrist, a Spanish baby sitter, take dancing, find shoemaker, write Hazel Scott, find yellow pills, buy books [a photographer friend] told me about—stop abusing Andrew (think of surprises for him)."

NE ME QUITTE PAS

In 1966, a dam was about to burst in Nina Simone's marriage and in her art.

"Last night Andrew talked of my possible suicide," she wrote on January 20. "He let me know that he would not only *not* suffer, but, he would be relieved. I hate him—I have every intention of leaving him, if I live, and making him suffer in ways he hasn't ever dreamed of. I hate him."

That same month, Simone sent Stroud a Western Union telegram: "Everything is going to be fine. . . . 1966 is still our year. . . . I love you, Nina."

Simone couldn't square her constant yearning for personal and musical freedom with her need for stability and regular income. In an undated note from 1966 titled "Remember, Nina!" Simone urges herself to push into more explicitly black music, but only as far as white audiences will allow. "With every new turn of events in colored people's favor, you get a little looser—don't be afraid to go all the way 'colored' if they're ready—take your time starting—enjoy yourself! The white folks are condoning revenge now—remember 'Nevada Smith'?" (In the 1966 Steve McQueen western, the white son of a Native American avenges his father's death.)

That year, Simone recorded "Four Women," one of her few self-penned songs, a searing portrait of voiceless women struggling against poverty and victimization ("My skin is brown, my manner is tough / I'll kill the first mother I see"). Like much of her late-'60s material— such as "To Be Young, Gifted and Black," inspired by an unfinished Hansberry play—the song sought to define black consciousness, and gave her credibility with black youth. But Stroud, along with Philips record executives, continued to push Simone toward mainstream material, too. And, ironically, she recorded some of her most enduring ballads that year, like "Lilac Wine" and "Wild Is the Wind." In many ways, the intensity with which she imbued these songs was more telling of her inner life than her protest songs were.

> Like a leaf clings
> To a tree
> Oh my darling,
> Cling to me
> For we're creatures of the wind
> And wild is the wind
> So wild is the wind

By now, her reputation as a belligerent performer had eroded her standing among critics. Prominent activists like Harry Belafonte avoided her. As a review in *Life* magazine would later put it, "She still pollutes the atmosphere with a hostility that owes less to her color than to the rasping edge on her pride."

Stroud treated Simone like a volatile product to be managed. She battered him weekly with emotional meltdowns. He describes mornings when he would wake up and Simone would be sitting up, arms folded, glaring into the distance, coiled to fight him. She left little notes to Stroud using black Magic Marker: "One day, when I'm not so tired, I'll kill you."

By 1967, the year she sang "I Wish I Knew How It Would Feel to Be Free," Simone's activist persona was becoming more fierce and confident, but privately she was still filled with self-loathing. She complained bitterly about her image on her mid-'60s albums (a wide, toothy grin and a straightened, Kennedy-era bob: a photo negative of Doris Day) and kept a picture of herself in her wallet "to remind me of how I never want to look." In letters, she rails against "amateur" photographers sent by *Ebony* and *Look* who she felt made her ugly and caused her "shame." In December, in a note to herself, she mentions the launch of her and Stroud's new record company, called Ninandy, but she has no hope for the future.

"Everything I've had in terms of security (especially my music) seems to be slipping right between my fingers," she wrote. "I haven't been needed for a while. Nowhere in the press am I mentioned, voluntarily. Am I evolving again??? What is left for me now?"

For every battle Simone waged with her depression, however, a rawer, freer personality emerged: wearing African beads in her hair, she could now perform a sultry dance onstage and give impromptu lectures on black identity, casting herself as a messenger, the "high priestess of soul." Black people were a "lost race," she told an interviewer, according to Simone's recent biography, and her songs were meant to "provoke this feeling of who am I, where do I come from, you know? Do I really like me, and why do I like me?"

That year, while she was playing in Oakland, California, Stroud says he discovered Simone having an affair with the new dashiki-wearing guitarist in her band. Stroud confronted her, and they finally agreed to have an open marriage, their relationship strictly a business arrangement in which Stroud managed her career. "I knew all along that she was having these relationships with both men and women," claims Stroud, who also had several affairs.

In August 1969, Simone went on a monthlong vacation to Barbados. "It's nice to feel like a queen down here, be the most beautiful, and envied by all the women," she wrote to Stroud. "Money made these feelings possible—so Andrew, I thank you for teaching me this—though I'll probably forget it the moment I get back to HELL."

Hell, she stated plainly, was the United States. And not long after, upon leaving Stroud for good, she left America, too, the start of her years drifting around Africa, Europe, and the Caribbean, aided and undermined by a series of opportunistic handlers, sycophants, and wealthy patrons. Having finally gained her freedom, she was left alone to the merciless weather of her own moods, becoming a bizarre and sometimes embarrassing spectacle in concert—often riveting, occasionally miraculous, but also unhinged and frightening. She tried several comebacks, but none succeeded. Her musical output withered as she became a heavier drinker, periodically entering mental hospitals. By the time of her death, in 2003, Nina Simone had almost faded from American cultural memory, a cult figure living out her final years in the French Mediterranean.

The last page of her diary—undated, but likely from the late '60s— foreshadowed what was to come: "I learned that my pain (no matter how great) is a private matter (my hell is my own) and I must not tell it to any one else—there are no people who can help me." For Nina Simone, hell was not just a country, but a lifelong burden.

Darkness Invisible

Wendy Lesser

On the Sunday of Labor Day weekend, at a concert held at the Austrian Cultural Forum under the auspices of the Argento New Music Project, the adventurous and delightful JACK Quartet gave an unexpectedly dark performance. I mean this quite literally. The hundred or so people who had assembled to hear Georg Friedrich Haas's third string quartet sat in complete and total darkness for the entire concert. We were unable to see our hands before our faces, much less check our watches or glance at our companions or otherwise sense the presence in the room of anything but the strange, unsettling music that was emanating, strained note by strained note, from the four corners in which the musicians sat.

And we were thrilled to be there. For those of us who had followed the career of the JACK Quartet through recent performances in locales like (Le) Poisson Rouge and the Baryshnikov Arts Center, there was the certainty that these four young men—Christopher Otto and Ari Streisfeld on the violins, John Pickford Richards on the viola, and Kevin McFarland on the cello—would bring warmth and excitement to any piece of new music they chose to play. For others, there was the knowledge that Haas—an Austrian composer, born in 1953, who has already been much praised for his innovative work *in vain*—was capable of delivering something unusual and stirring, something that would combine music with a more overt kind of theatricality. And for all of us there was the pleasure of an extremely intimate concert that was both accessibly priced (requested donation: five dollars) and non-competitive (everyone who showed up got in, even those of us on the waiting list)—significant rarities in the hothouse world of New York music.

Once we had taken our seats, leaving vacant only the four black plastic chairs (one in each corner) that would eventually be occupied by the players, Argento's director, Michel Galante, got up to welcome us. He announced, among other things, that since we would be sitting in complete darkness for over an hour, he wanted to start by giving us a thirty-second sample of what this would feel like. He lowered the lights, and almost all survived it comfortably. (A single person left as soon as the lights came up.) But Galante urged us to keep our silenced cellphones handy in case anyone panicked in the darkness. "If you start to feel anxious during the concert," he said, "just say, 'Help!' and the people around you will pull out their cellphones and give you a little bit of light." This left me feeling torn for the duration of the concert: on the one hand, I wanted to experience the full score in uninterrupted silence; on the other, I was subversively eager to have the normal decorum of a concert hall broken by a sudden plea for help.

If you have never experienced complete darkness, you cannot really imagine what it is like. It's not just that you can't see at first, which is what happens when you wander into a darkened movie theater or go outside on a very dark night in the country. What happens in utter darkness is that your eyes never adapt at all. However long you sit there, the blackness remains impenetrable. And this in turn has other effects—psychological, physical, emotional—which can vary a great deal from person to person. The last time I experienced anything of this kind was in a Berlin restaurant called the *Unsicht Bar*. (You might ask why the Germans and the Austrians are particularly drawn to total darkness, but I think it's a question that probably answers itself.) Among our group of seven or eight diners at the restaurant, one or two obviously felt *very* uncomfortable, and made their discomfort audibly clear to the rest of us. I, on the contrary, found that not being able to see or be seen relaxed me. It was like being in a warm bath of nothingness, floating in one's own private world, and for the duration of that dinner, I thoroughly enjoyed the sensation.

That pleasant memory of the Unsicht Bar came back to me as I sat in the darkness of the Austrian Cultural Forum. In this case, though, there was not even the contact of other human voices or clattering cutlery or chomping teeth; the only detectable sounds came from the instruments. Haas's Quartet No. 3 is nobody's idea of a normal string quartet: it is more like a soundscape, or a series of aural inventions for strings. It is rarely unpleasant (though the noises are often harsh), but it never offers the sense of lift-off or propulsion that you get from more traditionally composed pieces. The music does not carry you along. Instead, it impinges on you as discrete sounds, elaborated by repetitions or variations of those sounds and punctuated by frequent brief silences. The piece is designed to be somewhat flexible: that is, the players—who of course are playing blind—are given some latitude in terms of how they follow the composer's instructions, and their performance can thus vary in length. (The JACK version lasts about seventy minutes.) And what you hear, in such a setting, will also depend partly on where you are sitting. Since I was directly in front of the violist, it seemed to me that he was the group's leader, while the cello seeped in more distantly from behind me and the violins emerged from two different locations off to my right. Had I been sitting elsewhere, I would no doubt have heard a different concert.

The quartet opens with a run of subdued, dully percussive, pizzicato-like notes, as if a small herd of mice were scurrying across the surface of a stringed instrument—a sound produced, I would guess, by fingers tapping their way quickly down the neck of the instrument. Later noises included the croak of a creaking door (the bow pressed hard against the string and pulled very slowly), the whisper of a rushing wind (horsehairs drawn across the very base of the strings, or perhaps even across the wooden part of the instrument), eerily high harmonics (the finger held so lightly on the bowed string that the note soars up to near-inaudibility), and brief episodes of the usual post-Bartók caterwauling and dissonance. Only at one point in the seventy-minute work did we get anything like a resolved chord, and that, it turned out, was an allusion to Gesualdo, the Renaissance composer whose Tenebrae setting apparently provided the quartet's obscure title ("In iij. Noct."), and whose influence was only audible—to me, at least—during those few brief moments of sustained harmony.

Sitting in the dark at a concert is a way of being at once alone and in the company of others. As I explored my unusual and cherished feeling of privacy (stretching about in ways I would never do in a lit concert hall, yawning widely, tilting my head way back or lackadaisically from side to side, and repeatedly holding my hands in front of my face to see if they had become visible yet), I thought of D. W. Winnicott's notion about how the child learns to be alone in the presence of its mother—that is, the baby gets to test out being solitary and accompanied at the same time. I imagined I was enjoying this childish sensation immensely, and yet on some level I must have felt a bit of fear or anxiety too, as I realized during one of my wild head-tilts, when I discovered that the room was not actually completely dark. There were two rows of very faint almost-lights barely visible in the ceiling, and another ghostly spot at the very back of the room—and this, strangely, filled me with the same kind of energetic hope that hostages in TV thrillers feel when they come upon a nail or some other sharp protrusion against which they can slowly fray away their binding ropes. But try as I might, I could not free myself from the darkness: I could never manage to see a thing, not even my pale hands waved directly in front of my face. Once, in a moment of casual listening such as one might do at a regular concert, I closed my eyes, and the shock when I opened them and perceived *no difference at all* was severe.

Seventy minutes might seem long, objectively, but you lose track of time when you are in the dark. As it happens, I had just that afternoon gone to an Ida Lupino movie at MoMA that lasted exactly seventy-six minutes, so I thought I had a very good sense of what that length of time felt like. But the movie and the concert seemed to occupy completely different time scales. The film (*Hard, Fast, and Beautiful*, from 1951—well worth seeing, by the way) was never boring, but it seemed to go on for a very long time. The Haas quartet had its tedious moments, but overall it seemed to go by very quickly: if I had not been told its actual length, I would have guessed that we had only been sitting in the concert hall for half an hour or less.

For most of its duration, the music seemed to be going nowhere in particular, but towards the end I could sense it coming to a conclusion. The pace and the volume both picked up significantly, after which—quite suddenly—the whole thing dropped to the pizzicato-like mouse-runs we had heard at the beginning. And then, finally, there was complete silence. I'd estimate that this lasted a minute or more (but again, it is hard to gauge time in the dark). Then the lights came up, and the squinting, blinking audience vigorously applauded the squinting, blinking, grinning performers. Was that last minute of silence a part of the score, or was it just us, failing to realize the piece was over? Hard to say.

As I listened to these four immensely talented players perform the Haas Quartet No. 3, I found myself wondering what it would be like to listen in complete darkness to the performance of a quartet I know well: Beethoven's op. 131, for instance. Would the familiarity of the music shield me, at least in part, from the strangeness of the setting? Or would the wrenching emotional quality of Beethoven's music intensify the sense of physical darkness? And what about a piece of new, as-yet-unheard music, but one that had more tonal melody than Haas's work—a new chamber work by Jörg Widmann, say, or David Bruce, or another of the younger composers less wedded than Haas to the rigors of the avant-garde? How would *that* come across in total darkness, with the musicians spread about the room? Suddenly I longed to hear everything in this way; total darkness began to seem the ideal environment for listening to just about anything. And yet, given the difficulties of setting up and enacting a performance like this, it's likely that I'll never in my life have another experience of this kind. In fact, I feel quite lucky to have had it even once.

OTHER NOTABLE
MUSIC WRITING OF 2010

Stacey Anderson, "The Jazz Evangelism of Woody Allen," *Village Voice*, July 1, 2010

Noah Arjomand, "Rap in the Capital: Hip-Hop Tehran-Style," PBS Frontline, April 22, 2010

Jake Austen, "The Woman on the Right," *Chicago Reader*, February 11, 2010

Zach Baron, "Flux=Rad," *Slate*, March 18, 2010

Mike Barthel, "Scissor Sisters 'Night Work.' Yay for Sex and Drugs and Pleasure," The Awl, June 28, 2010

Angus Batey, "The Hip-Hop Heritage Society," *The Guardian*, October 7, 2010

Adrien Begrand, "They Did It Their Way," *Decibel*, October 2010

Trish Bendix, "The 'If I Were a Boy' Trend in Music," After Ellen, November 16, 2010

J. Bennett, "A Serious Man," *Decibel*, August 2010

Gavin Bertram, "Part Past Part Fiction," *Real Groove*, 2010

Mark Binelli, "How Jay-Z Became King of America," *Rolling Stone*, June 24, 2010

Larry Blumenfeld, "How Treme Can Get It Right," *Village Voice*, March 30, 2010

Jonathan Bradley, "Just Being Miley," *American Review*, April 21, 2010

Norman Brannon, "So, hey Nicki Minaj. It's real talk time," Nervous Acid, November 4, 2010

Frank Bruni, "An Ageless Diva of a Certain Age," *The New York Times*, November 21, 2010

Brett Campbell, "Gonzalo Ruiz, Oboist, Restoring Bach," *Wall Street Journal*, July 15, 2010

Jon Caramanica, "Seeping Out of Houston, Slowly," *The New York Times*, November 4, 2010

Rodney Carmichael, "The Making of OutKast's *Aquemini*," *Creative Loafing*, June 24, 2010

Conor Christofferson, "About a Grandson," *Seattle Weekly*, August 18, 2010

John Cline, "Henry Flynt," *Oxford American*, The 2010 Music Issue

Ta-Nehisi Coates, "Travelling Music," *The Atlantic*, February 19, 2010

John Colapinto, "New Note," *The New Yorker*, March 15, 2010

Alex V. Cook, "The Ozzy Osbourne T-shirt," *OffBeat*, November 2010

Sergeant D, "The Final Word on Metal Drumming," Metal Sucks, December 3, 2010

Jane Dark, "Vomiting Up Tequila & Glitter: Pop 2010," *Lana Turner*, December 2010

Dessa Darling, "Dessa Reflects on Her Artistic Journey," *City Pages*, August 18, 2010

Andy Davis, "The Globalisation of Ooga Booga," Mahala, May 6, 2010

Jonathan Dee, "New Orleans Gender-Bending Rap," *The New York Times*, July 22, 2010

David Dennis, "Curren$y: The New High Life," *OffBeat*, September 2010

Rachel Devitt, "Justin Bieber Cracks Up," *Village Voice*, August 18, 2010

Barry Divola, "Hopelessly Devoted," *Sydney Morning Herald*, July 8, 2010

Camille Dodero, "Live from Insane Clown Posse's Gathering of the Juggalos," *Village Voice*, September 8, 2010

Sady Doyle, "Rivers Cuomo Messes You Up Forever," The Awl, April 27, 2010

Baz Dreisinger, "Reggae's Civil War," *Village Voice*, March 2, 2010

Andrew Earles, "Jay Reatard Remembered," *Spin*, January 28, 2010

Chuck Eddy, Frank Kogan, Michaelangelo Matos, Katherine St. Asaph, John Seroff, Al Shipley, and Martin Skidmore, "Far East Movement ft. Cataracs & Dev—Like a G6," The Singles Jukebox, September 28, 2010

Gavin Edwards, "Dr. Luke's Awesomely Trashy Pop Sound Is Ruling the Airwaves," *Rolling Stone*, April 29, 2010

Josh Eells, "The Semi-Charmed Life of Vampire Weekend," *Rolling Stone*, February 4, 2010

Jeremy Eichler, "There Is Magic in the Music," *Boston Globe*, July 11, 2010

Tom Ewing, "Shiny Shiny: A Future History of the CD Revival," Pitchfork Media, March 5, 2010

Jonathan L. Fischer, "Our Year in Moombahton," *Washington City Paper*, December 24, 2010

Sidik Fofana, "Refugee for Prez," Corner Boy Jazz, November 7, 2010

Mick Foley, "The Wrestler and the Cornflake Girl," *Slate*, September 28, 2010

Tad Friend, "Sleeping With Weapons," *The New Yorker*, August 16, 2010

Yoav Fromer, "Message," *Tablet*, November 23, 2010

Jeanne Fury, "This Is Why They're Hot," *Decibel*, November 2010

Leor Galil, "Everything's Coming Up Kittens," *Chicago Reader*, October 14, 2010

Luis-Manuel Garcia, "Showdown in Spreepark," Resident Advisor, November 26, 2010

Gus Garcia-Roberts, "Scott Storch Raked in Hip-Hop Millions and Then Snorted His Way to Ruin," *Miami New Times*, August 22, 2010

Tavi Gevinson, "Love," Style Rookie, November 7, 2010

Rachel Kaadzi Ghansah, "He Shall Overcome," *New York Observer*, November 30, 2010

Sarah Godfrey, "Private School Go-Go Goes Public," TBD.com, August 12, 2010

Thomas Golianopoulos, "Jay Electronica: Man or Myth?," *Spin*, July 2010

Peter Gordon, "Teenage Days With Captain Beefheart," Nedslist/The Daily Swarm, December 20, 2010

Joe Gross, "In Praise of the Vuvuzela," *Austin American-Statesman*, June 29, 2010

Matthew Guerrieri, "Complexity Wars," New Music Box, September 8, 2010

Jack Halberstam, "What's Paglia Got To Do With It?," Bully Bloggers, September 14, 2010

Shirley Halperin, "Who Destroyed Epic Records?," *Hollywood Observer*, November 18, 2010

Steve Haruch, "Women Account for Less Than 5 Percent of Producers and Engineers," *Nashville Scene*, June 3, 2010

Eric Harvey, "This Is Not a Photograph," Pitchfork Media, September 13, 2010

Dave Heaton, "A Mexico State of Mind," PopMatters, November 9, 2010

Virginia Heffernan, "Sound Logic," *The New York Times*, February 19, 2010

David Hepworth, "When the Last Recording Studio Goes, What Will Go With It?," The Word, March 13, 2010

Monica Herrera, "The Year That Went Pop," *Billboard*, December 10, 2010

Kenny Herzog, "The Latin Implosion," *Wax Poetics*, May/June 2010

Geoffrey Himes, "Hillbilly Heaven," *Baltimore City Paper*, May 26, 2010

Marc Hogan, "What's the Matter with Sweden?," Pitchfork Media, March 29, 2010

Hua Hsu, "The Passing of a Record Store," *The Atlantic*, September 7, 2010

Steven Hyden, "Part 5: 1994: Kurt Cobain is dead! Long live Soundgarden!," *Onion AV Club*, November 30, 2010

Ethan Iverson, "Interview with Gunther Schuller," Do the Math, September 19, 2010

Vijay Iyer, "Thelonious Monk: Ode to a Sphere," *JazzTimes*, January/February 2010

Maura Johnston, "Dirty Projectors, Solange Knowles, and the Perils of Music-Racism," *Village Voice*, January 19, 2010

Maura Johnston and Christopher R. Weingarten, "The 20 Worst Songs of 2010, #1: Train 'Hey, Soul Sister'," *Village Voice*, December 22, 2010

Rich Juzwiak, "A Collage for a Collage," Fourfour, July 15, 2010

Aryan Kaganof, "Aryan Kaganof Interviews Johnny Mbizo Dyani," Kagablog, April 7, 2010

David Kastin, "Fred Ho and the Evolution of Afro-Asian New American Multicultural Music," *Popular Music and Society*, April 7, 2010

Lenny Kaye, "Dennis Wilson: Like the River to the Sea," eMusic, 2010

Frank Kogan, "Ke$ha Day 2," Koganbot, March 4, 2010

Dan Kois, "Tickets Out," *The New Yorker*, September 20, 2010

Toshitaka Kondo, "Making Minaj," *Complex*, October/November 2010

Chris Kornelis, "Marco Collins Picks Up the Pieces," *Seattle Weekly*, December 29, 2010

Molly Lambert, "In Which John Mayer Is a Douchebag for Possibly the Last Time," *This Recording*, February 11, 2010

David Lowery, Selections from 300 Songs, 300 Songs, 2010

Fiona Maddocks, "Bayreuth Festival 2010," *Observer*, August 1, 2010

Sharanya Manivannan, "In Song and In Silence," Venus Flytrap, June 12, 2010

Greil Marcus, "Skip James on Art," *Oxford American*, The 2010 Music Issue

Chris Martins, "Flying Lotus Rising," *LA Weekly*, May 13, 2010

Michaelangelo Matos, "Three Singles Featuring 3Oh!3," *The Stranger*, July 13, 2010

Erik Maza, "Cuban Punk Rockers Gorki and Gil Used Music to Take on Castro," *Miami New Times*, June 24, 2010

Ben Meadows-Ingram, "Last Man Standing," *Vibe*, May 2010

Anne Midgette, "Is Anybody Listening? American Opera Faces Crossroads as Audiences for Performing Arts Slide," *Washington Post*, June 27, 2010

Barbara Mitchell, "DECEMBER BOYS GOT IT BAD," *Blurt*, March 24, 2010

Larry Mizell, Jr., "Taste That Crown," *The Stranger*, January 5, 2010

Trent Moorman, "A Q&A with Bon Jovi's Pyrotechnic Specialist," *Billboard*, July 6, 2010

Evie Nagy, "DEVO: How to Get Ahead With Advertising," *Billboard*, July 11, 2010

Sean Nelson, "It Might Get Loud Pitch Meeting," Tweet series @seantroversy, 2010

Tavia Nyong'o, "Lady Gaga's Lesbian Phallus," Bully Bloggers, March 16, 2010

Jennifer Odell, "Christian Scott Shows His Teeth," *Downbeat*, April 2010

Ben Patashnik, "A Day to Remember: The New Sound of Sacrifice Rock," *Rock Sound*, November 2010

David Peisner, "When the Bottom Fell Out," *Spin*, July 2010

Matthew Perpetua, "At the End of the World with Gauntlet Hair," The Awl, December 28, 2010

Chris Randle, "Curtis Jackson and the Jeweled Skull," *Social Text*, October 1, 2010

Gillian Reagan, "On Rap and Rape and Dudes in a Room," Shield Your Eyes, November 11, 2010

Eugene Robinson, "Lena Horne: A Glamorous Revolutionary," *Washington Post*, May 11, 2010

Lisa Robinson, "Lady Gaga's Cultural Revolution," *Vanity Fair*, September 2010

John Roderick, "Chucked Profit: Benefit Shows Can Be Bad Business," *Seattle Weekly*, November 23, 2010

Jody Rosen, "Joanna Newsom, the Changling," *The New York Times*, March 7, 2010

Katrina Stuart Santiago, "The Charice Challenge," *GMA News*, September 20, 2010

Scott Saul, "Off Minor," *Boston Review*, September/October 2010

Rebecca Schmid, "To Teach the World . . . ," *BBC Music Magazine*, August 2010

Solvej Schou, "Hanging at Lemmy's Virtual Castle in ROCKTropia: Watch Out for the Demon Spawn," *Los Angeles Times*, May 10, 2010

Shea Serrano, "Out of the Box," *Houston Press*, June 24, 2010

Ben Sisario, "Looking to a Sneaker for a Band's Big Break," *The New York Times*, October 6, 2010

RJ Smith, "Debasement Tapes," *Spin*, November 2010

Deborah Solomon, "Straight Outta Wesleyan," *The New York Times*, December 5, 2010

Sam Stephenson, "Dorrie Glenn Woodson," *The Paris Review*, December 22, 2010

Kevin Stewart-Panko, "Death on Two Legs," *Decibel*, June 2010

Lisa Taddeo, "The Ke$ha-Loving, Command-Defying Army Auteur," *New York Magazine*, August 1, 2010

Stephen Titmus, "Boy's Own: A History," Resident Advisor, January 12, 2010

Aidin Vaziri, "Big Stage Exposes Justin Bieber's Limitations," *San Francisco Bay Guardian*, July 19, 2010

Gabe Vodicka, "Why the Caged King Sings," *Creative Loafing*, December 13, 2010

Ray Waddell, "Jamey Johnson: The In Outlaw," *Billboard*, September 25, 2010

Jesse Walker, "2010: The Year John Cage Broke," Reason.com, December 30, 2010

Theon Weber, "The Iceberg Songs of Taylor Swift," *Village Voice*, November 3, 2010

Christopher Weingarten, "The Life and Death of Alan Carton, 23, the RIAA-Defying Creator of @diditleak," *Village Voice*, January 22, 2010

Jeff Weiss, "The Madlib Mystique," *LA Weekly*, June 24, 2010

Carl Wilson, "Busby Madoff Dreams: 'Fuck You' and the Gold Diggers of 2010," Back to the World, August 26, 2010

Zachary Woolfe and Seth Colter Walls, "Renée Fleming's 'Dark Hope': June Cleaver Does Muse," The Awl, June 16, 2010

Bill Wyman, "Please Allow Me to Correct a Few Things," *Slate*, November 5, 2010

Rob Young, "Cloud of Knowing," *The Guardian*, June 12, 2010

LIST OF CONTRIBUTORS

Nitsuh Abebe is the pop music critic at *New York Magazine* and a monthly columnist at Pitchfork. (You can also find him at agrammar.tumblr.com.)

Marcia Adair is a freelance writer living in Canada. She can be found at TheOmniscientMussel.com.

Jonathan Bogart has been writing about music on the Internet since 2004. He blogs at jonathanbogart.tumblr.com, writes about the *Billboard* Latin chart at bilboslaptop.blogspot.com, and discusses the history of twentieth-century music at justonesongmore.tumblr.com. He lives in Arizona, where he listens to the radio in his car.

Franklin Bruno's scholarly and critical writing has appeared in *Journal of Aesthetics and Art Criticism*, *Popular Music and Society*, *The Nation*, and *The Believer*. His book on Elvis Costello's *Armed Forces* was published in Continuum Books' 33 1/3 series in 2006. As a solo artist and member of Nothing Painted Blue and the Human Hearts, his current band, he has released fifteen albums of original songs since the early 1990s. A native of Southern California's Inland Empire, he lives and writes in Jackson Heights, Queens.

Jason Cherkis got his start in the early '90s writing overly poetic rock criticism for *Option* magazine and the *LA Weekly*. He went on to work for more than a decade as a cops reporter/rock critic for the *Washington City Paper* where he amassed a large collection of vintage vinyl and criminal rap sheets. He is currently obsessed with the new Alan Lomax–types still traveling the world in search of great lost songs. He works as a reporter for Huffington Post.

Nate Chinen writes about music for *The New York Times*. He's also a columnist for *JazzTimes* and coauthor of *Myself Among Others*, the autobiography of impresario George Wein. For each of the last six years, he has received the Helen Dance–Robert Palmer Award for Excellence in Newspaper, Magazine or Online Feature or Review.

Jace Clayton is a writer and musician based in Brooklyn, who performs internationally as DJ Rupture. He's currently at work on a book to be published by Farrar, Straus and Giroux.

Drew Daniel lives in Baltimore and teaches in the department of English at Johns Hopkins University. He is the author of *20 Jazz Funk Greats* (Continuum) and *The Melancholy Assemblage: Affect and Epistemology in the English Renaissance* (Fordham, forthcoming). He is one-half of the electronic group Matmos, and all of The Soft Pink Truth.

Justin Davidson has been the classical music and architecture critic at *New York Magazine* since 2007. Before that, he spent twelve years as classical music critic at *Newsday*, where he also wrote about architecture and was a regular commentator on cultural issues. He won a Pulitzer Prize for criticism in 2002.

Jeremy Denk is a classical pianist, and as if that wasn't nerdy enough, he is also a blogger about being a classical pianist. He performs his wide-ranging repertoire around the world, working with eminent orchestras, conductors, and multifarious collaborators. He has so far released two solo discs: one devoted to American iconoclast Charles Ives's two mammoth piano sonatas, another to J.S. Bach's Partitas. A native of New Mexico, he attended Oberlin as a double major (piano and chemistry), then hit up Indiana University and Juilliard, but credits his wonderful English professor at Oberlin, David Walker, for gently suggesting he should mean what he writes.

Chet Flippo is Editorial Director of CMT and CMT.com. Before joining CMT, Flippo was Country Music Editor for Sonicnet.com and *Billboard*'s Nashville Bureau Chief. He was *Rolling Stone*'s Senior Editor for a number of years. He is the author of books on Hank Williams, Paul McCartney,

Graceland, the Rolling Stones, and David Bowie. He has also published an anthology, *Everybody Was Kung-Fu Dancing*. Flippo has written articles for *The New York Times*, *TV Guide*, *Texas Monthly*, *Q Magazine*, *Oxford American*, and other publications. He has also written TV scripts for VH1, CBS, and CMT.

Sasha Frere-Jones joined *The New Yorker* as a staff writer and pop-music critic in 2004. Prior to that, he was a critic for the *Village Voice*, beginning in 1995. He has also written for *Spin*, *The New York Times*, the *New York Post*, *The Wire*, and *Pretty Decorating*. He is a member of the bands Calvinist and Piñata. In 1991, Frere-Jones formed the band Ui, which toured America and Europe and released five albums. Frere-Jones maintains a website at sashafrerejones.tumblr.com.

Caryn Ganz is the editor of the Yahoo! blog The Amplifier. She's previously worked as an editor at RollingStone.com, *Spin*, and MTV News, and co-wrote the book *Fool the World: The Oral History of a Band Called Pixies*. She lives on the Lower East Side, where encyclopedic knowledge of Nicki Minaj's mixtapes has come in handy.

Dan Geist is a senior editor and arts critic at Tehran Bureau. He has written on cinema, television, popular music, and other subjects for Inter Press Service, the *Wall Street Journal*, and Knight Ridder. He has also been an actor, stage manager, and music video production manager.

Nancy Griffin has written extensively about the entertainment industry for publications including *Vanity Fair*, *The New Yorker*, *The New York Times*, *Esquire*, *Premiere*, and *GQ*. She is coauthor with Kim Masters of the 1995 best seller *Hit and Run: How Jon Peters and Peter Guber Took Sony for a Ride in Hollywood*. She lives in Venice, California.

Vanessa Grigoriadis is a contributing editor to *New York Magazine*, *Rolling Stone*, and *Vanity Fair*. She is a winner of the National Magazine Award in profile writing.

Joe Hagan is a contributing editor at *New York* and *Vanity Fair* magazines. His music writing, on subjects ranging from Buck Owens (the country pioneer's last interview) to doom metal (the calming effects of), has appeared in *The New York Times*, *Rolling Stone*, and *The Believer*. He lives in Tivoli, New York.

David Hajdu is the music critic for *The New Republic* and a professor at the Columbia University Graduate School of Journalism. He is the author of three books on music, all of which won the Deems Taylor Award for music writing, and all of which were finalists for the National Book Critics Circle Award.

Jessica Hopper is a feminist culture critic in Chicago. Her work regularly appears in the *Chicago Reader*, the *Village Voice*, and the *Chicago Tribune*. She is the author of *The Girls' Guide to Rocking*.

Amy Klein is a writer, musician, and feminist. While working as a guitarist in the punk band Titus Andronicus, she began posting her tour diary entries on the website amyandronicus.tumblr.com. Her blog attracted a loyal following of thousands and led to the birth of a new feminist arts movement known as the Permanent Wave.

Wendy Lesser is the editor of *The Threepenny Review*, which she founded in 1980; she is also the author of nine books, including a novel called *The Pagoda in the Garden* and eight nonfiction books, among which are *Pictures at an Execution*, *The Amateur*, and (most recently) *Music for Silenced Voices: Shostakovich and His Fifteen Quartets*. She divides her year between Berkeley and New York.

Morad Mansouri is a writer, a drum-player, and an organizer in Iran's twin underground labor/protest (Green) movements. He was born in 1983 in Kashan, Iran. He describes himself as a Liberal Anarcho-Marxist. He writes under various pseudonyms. His writings penned under his own name have appeared in Iranian media and earned him two national prizes. He is a member of IranArte collective.

Evelyn McDonnell is Assistant Professor of Journalism and New Media at Loyola Marymount University. She's the author of *Mamarama*, *Army of She*, and *Rent* and co-editor of *Rock She Wrote* and *Stars Don't Stand Still in the Sky*. She has been the editorial director of MOLI.com, pop culture writer at the *Miami Herald*, and senior editor at the *Village Voice*. Her articles have appeared in the *Los Angeles Times*, *The New York Times*, and *Spin*. She's currently writing a book about the Runaways.

Chris Norris is a New York–based writer on popular and unpopular culture whose work appears in *The New York Times Magazine*, *Rolling Stone*,

Film Comment, and elsewhere. He is coauthor of the bestselling hip-hop Künstlerroman, *The Tao of Wu,* with Wu Tang Clan founder RZA, whose description of him as "student of philosophy and a very smart guy" is, as usual, nothing to fuck with.

Geoffrey O'Brien is a poet and critic whose books include *Dream Time: Chapters from the Sixties* (1988), *The Phantom Empire* (1993), *The Browser's Ecstasy* (2000), *Castaways of the Image Planet* (2002), *Sonata for Jukebox: An Autobiography of My Ears* (2004), and *The Fall of the House of Walworth* (2010). His poetry has been collected most recently in *Early Autumn* (2010). He is editor-in-chief of The Library of America.

Ann Powers is a critic at NPR Music. She was the chief pop critic at the *Los Angeles Times* from 2006 to 2011. Special thanks to Sean Meredith for conversation that informed the piece included in this volume.

Chris Richards is the pop music critic at the *Washington Post,* where he covers White House concerts, DIY house shows, go-go, and Gaga.

Kelefa Sanneh is a staff writer at *The New Yorker.*

Philip Sherburne has been writing about music in print and online since the late '90s, with a focus on electronic music (for dancing and otherwise). A native of Portland, Oregon, he lived in San Francisco before moving overseas in 2005—first to Barcelona and then Berlin, where he currently resides. When not writing, he also DJs and produces his own electronic music (for dancing and otherwise).

Dave Tompkins's vocoder book, *How to Wreck a Nice Beach,* has been called a "mega-pill of mule-choking insights." Amazon selected it as entertainment book of the year. One irate Amazon customer griped that it made him do a faceplant on the carpet, revealing that he'd been sniffing the book while on foot. Or maybe just tripping. Tompkins will be presenting at the 2011 National Cryptology Symposium. An expanded paperback will be out in November. In the muletime, he is researching the Bass properties of seashells and a U-boat attack off the coast of Florida.

Michael Turbé has been plumbing the depths of the New York metal scene for seventeen years. He founded Sunyata: Mindful of Metal several years ago as an alternative to spamming friends and family with impassioned album recommendations. Under the pen name Atanamar, Michael chronicles his concert experiences and scribbles ebullient reviews of the albums that inspire him. His writing also appears on Metal Injection.

Lauren Wilcox Puchowski grew up in Durham, North Carolina, and lives in Jersey City, New Jersey, with her husband and two children. She has written for the *Washington Post Magazine*, the *Smithsonian*, and the *Paris Review*, among others. She wrote about the soul singer Esther Phillips and rockabilly singer Dale Hawkins for the *Oxford American* magazine, and keeps an illustrated blog about Jersey City at jcstringer.tumblr.com. Other work is at laurenwilcox.com.

James Wood was born in 1965 and educated at Cambridge University. He is a staff writer for *The New Yorker* and the author of four books: two collections of essays; a novel, *The Book Against God*; and, most recently, a book about fiction, *How Fiction Works* (2008), which has been translated into eight languages.

CREDITS

"Jetlagged Manifesto" by Jeremy Denk. Published May 25, 2010, on Think Denk (http://jeremydenk.net/blog/). Copyright © 2010 Jeremy Denk.

"NASHVILLE SKYLINE: Searching for the Heart of Country," by Chet Flippo. First published by CMT.com, November 4, 2010. Copyright © 2010 Chet Flippo.

"The Long War" by Sasha Frere-Jones. First published in *The New Yorker*, March 22, 2010. Copyright © 2010 Sasha Frere-Jones.

"The Curious Case of Nicki Minaj" by Caryn Ganz. First published in *Out*, October 10, 2010. Copyright © 2010 Caryn Ganz. Reprinted with the acknowledgment of HERE.

"The 'Thriller' Diaries" by Nancy Griffin. First published in *Vanity Fair*, July 2010. Copyright © 2010 Nancy Griffin. Reprinted with the acknowledgment of *Vanity Fair*.

"Growing Up Gaga" by Vanessa Grigoriadis. First published in *New York Magazine*, March 28, 2010. Copyright © 2010 Vanessa Grigoriadis and *New York Magazine*.

"I Wish I Knew How It Would Feel to Be Free" by Joe Hagan. First published in *The Believer*, July 2010. Copyright © 2010 Joe Hagan.

"Giant Steps: The Survival of a Great Jazz Pianist" by David Hajdu. First published in *The New York Times*, January 31, 2010. Copyright © *The New York Times*. Reprinted with permission.

"Making Pop for Capitalist Pigs" by Jessica Hopper. Copyright © 2010 Jessica Hopper.

"Tour Diary Day Four: Rock and Roll is Dead" by Amy Klein. First published in Amy Andronicus, August 28, 2010. Copyright © 2010 Amy Klein.

"Darkness Invisible" by Wendy Lesser. First published in *The Threepenny Review*, Winter 2011. Copyright © 2010 Wendy Lesser.

"The Underground Rises" by Morad Mansouri, with assistance from Dan Geist. First published on the FRONTLINE/Tehran Bureau website, October 1, 2010. Copyright © 2010 WGBH Educational Foundation. Reprinted with permission.

"Wild Thing" by Evelyn McDonnell. First published in *LA Weekly*, March 19–25, 2010. Copyright © 2010 Evelyn McDonnell.

"The Black Eyed Peas—*Will.i.am* and the Science of Global Pop Domination" by Chris Norris. First published in *Rolling Stone*, April 29, 2010. Copyright © 2010 *Rolling Stone*.

"The Grandest Duke" by Geoffrey O'Brien. First published in the *New York Review of Books*, October 28, 2010. Copyright © 2010 *New York Review of Books*. Reprinted with permission.